Schools and the Culturally Diverse Exceptional Student:

Promising Practices and Future Directions

Edited by **Alba A. Ortiz** **Bruce A. Ramirez**

A Product of the ERIC Clearinghouse on Handicapped and Gifted Children
Published by The Council for Exceptional Children

Library of Congress Cataloging-in-Publication Data

Schools and the culturally diverse exceptional student: promising practices and future directions / edited by Alba A. Ortiz, Bruce A. Ramirez.

"A product of the ERIC Clearinghouse on Handicapped and Gifted Children."
Includes bibliograpies.
1. Special education–United States–Congresses. 2. Children of minorities–Education–United States–Congresses. 3. Intercultural education–United States–Congresses. I. Ortiz, Alba A. II. Ramirez, Bruce A. III. Council for Exceptional Children. IV. ERIC Clearinghouse on Handicapped and Gifted Children.
LC3981.S364 1988
371.9'0973–dc19
88–3622 CIP
ISBN 0–86586–182–X

A product of the ERIC Clearinghouse on Handicapped and Gifted Children.

Published in 1988 by The Council for Exceptional Children, 1920 Association Drive, Reston, Virginia 22091–1589.

Third Printing 1992.

Stock No. P326

This publication was prepared with funding from the U.S. Department of Education, Office of Educational Research and Improvement, contract No. 400–84–0010. Contractors undertaking such projects under government sponsorship are encouraged to express freely their judgment in professional and technical matters. Prior to publication the manuscript was submitted to The Council for Exceptional Children for critical review and determination of professional competence. This publication has met such standards. Points of view, however, do not necessarily represent the official view or opinions of either The Council for Exceptional Children or the Department of Education.

Printed in the United States of America.

Cover design by Angeline V. Culfogienis.

Contents

Preface

The 1986 Ethnic and Multicultural Symposia sponsored by The Council for Exceptional Children in Dallas, Texas, featured a broad spectrum of presentations on educational opportunities for Black, Hispanic, Asian, and American Indian exceptional children and youth. The symposia and this collection of the key papers presented are a continuation of the Council's efforts to further the field's knowledge base with respect to culturally and linguistically diverse handicapped and gifted and talented children and youth.

Schools and the Culturally Diverse Exceptional Student: Promising Practices and Future Directions presents state-of-the-art information on the education of culturally and linguistically diverse exceptional students. While the volume addresses many timely and important topics and issues, it should not be viewed as a comprehensive treatment since not all aspects of service delivery are included.

Chapter 1 provides a provocative portrait of our changing society in terms of ethnicity, age, socioeconomic status, birth rate, and school completion. In relating current and emerging demographic characteristics to special education policy, organization, training, research, and scholarship, James Yates reminds us that the special education profession is not immune from such forces. Rather, special educators must be aware of these trends and prepare to respond to the changing ethnic nature of our society and schools.

In Chapter 2, Alba Ortiz and Shernaz Garcia set forth a process to minimize inappropriate referrals of Hispanic students to special education. The prereferral procedure described encompasses eight sequential steps to identify the sources of a student's learning problem and improve performance. Through careful consideration of teacher, student, curriculum and instruction, related factors, and alternative programs, educators can determine that cultural, linguistic, and other student characteristics have been accommodated prior to recommending a referral to special education.

Alejandro Benavides in Chapter 3 reports on the development and use of a screening instrument for use with language minority students. Completion of the prereferral instrument requires information about the student's previous educational experiences, including native and second language proficiency, achievement, behavior, and previous assessments. A case example is provided to illustrate the instrument's use in determining whether an individual student evaluation is warranted and the language(s) to be used in conducting such an assessment.

In Chapter 4, Alba Ortiz and Eleoussa Polyzoi examine assessment procedures for limited-English-proficient (LEP) handicapped students. The discussion includes a report on a longitudinal study to identify techniques that effectively distinguish between LEP students who are handicapped and those exhibiting characteristics of second language acquisition. The complexities of assessing the language skill of LEP students are reviewed as are research issues related to the diagnosis of speech and language handicaps in bilingual children.

In Chapter 5, Vicki Jax reviews the language demands of schools and difficulties with conventional language proficiency measures in predicting the academic achievement of language minority children. It is suggested that language assessment include the assessment of syntactic competencies as well as discourse abilities. She discusses the potential of story construction in determining the relationship between language proficiency and academic performance.

Chapter 6 reports the results of a series of studies on the identification and placement of LEP Hispanic students conducted by the Handicapped Minority Research Institute on Language Proficiency at the University of Texas at Austin. Alba Ortiz and James Yates review research findings related to the referral, assessment, and placement of LEP students in programs for the learning disabled, mentally retarded, and speech and/or language handicapped. Policy and practice implications related to special education and regular education are discussed.

In Chapter 7, George Sugai emphasizes the need for schools to recognize and understand the impact of culture on student academic and social success. Classroom-based assessment and evaluation strategies for use with culturally diverse, behaviorally disordered students are reviewed and discussed. An interventionist approach to assessment and evaluation is suggested to reduce biases and improve educational decision making.

Black, Hispanic, and American Indian children and youth continue to be noticeably underrepresented in gifted and talented programs. In Chapter 8, Donnelly Gregory, Waveline Starnes, and Arlene Blaylock discuss the early identification and nurturing of Black and Hispanic students. The impact of the Program of Assessment, Diagnosis, and Instruction (PADI) is discussed in terms of improved achievement and entry into gifted and talented programs.

As a group, Asians are extremely diversified in terms of origin, culture, immigration and settlement history, and acculturation. In Chapter 9, Esther Leung sets forth a practical frame of reference for understanding and appreciating the similarities and differences among Asian Americans. These characteristics are related to improved special education identification, programming, and family involvement.

Parent involvement continues to be a major consideration in the education of culturally and linguistically diverse exceptional children and youth. In Chapter 10, LaDelle Olion delineates cultural, social, and economic considerations unique to Black families. Improved communication, greater utilization of resources within the Black community, outreach and partnership programs, and support for the development of advocacy programs are suggested as ways to enhance the involvement of Black parents.

Chapter 11 reports the findings of school-based research in California to identify effective bilingual special education programs and instructional practices. Jana Echevarria-Ratleff and Victoria Graf review the selection of the bilingual special education model sites and offer suggestions for replicating promising bilingual special education programs and instructional features.

Ron Phillips and Ford Cranwell (Chapter 12) provide an instructive discussion of Native Band-Operated schools in Manitoba, Canada, and their special education program needs. The model for community-based special education program development and ensuing discussion of future funding and policy directions are timely in view of the movement throughout North America of greater Native involvement and control of Indian education.

The number of educators from various multicultural groups is alarmingly small and in some instances the supply has been decreasing. In Chapter 13, Ruben Gentry and Shih-sung Wen describe the findings of their study of Black special education teachers and the factors influential in their selection and continued participation in the profession. Implications for special education teacher recruitment and retention on a state-wide basis are discussed.

In Chapter 14, Bruce Ramirez and Marilyn Johnson provide an overview of educational opportunities for American Indian handicapped and gifted and talented students in the United States. Suggestions for improved service delivery and needed research are discussed in light of service delivery advances over the past decade and newly enacted federal early intervention, preschool, and vocational rehabilitation legislation.

Together these varied selections make a valuable contribution to our understanding of the educational needs of culturally and linguistically diverse exceptional children and youth and some of the practices, programs, and policy advances that hold promise for improving their educational experiences.

CHAPTER 1

Demography As It Affects Special Education

James R. Yates

One of the most powerful forces affecting education in general, and special education specifically, is demography. While changes in demography are exceedingly important to educators, it is almost totally beyond the control of educators to alter or change the directions of demography. Therefore, educators must familiarize themselves with demographic characteristics in order to formulate appropriate responses by the educational enterprise.

DEMOGRAPHIC VARIABLES

Age

This country's population continues to grow older. The median age has increased to approximately 32 years for White citizens, and there are more than 30,000 people in the United States who are over 100 years of age. Every week, 210 Americans celebrate their 100th birthday. We have more than 2.2 million people over 85 years of age; significantly, more than half of them voted in the 1980 presidential election. Between 1980 and the year 2000, the number of 85-year-olds in this country will have increased 123% (Longino, 1986). By the year 2000, 75% of all heads of household will be over 45 years of age (Exter, 1986). Obviously, this is a powerful and increasingly politically active group of citizens. One need only look at the effect of having a majority of voters that *DO NOT* have children in school to understand the effects of this large older population upon resources and programs of schools.

Ethnicity

Not only is the U.S. population becoming older, but it is becoming less White. The numbers of Black, brown, and Asian citizens are dramatically increasing, with Hispanics representing the fastest growing population in this country (*Austin American Statesman*, 1986). The Census Bureau reported that as of March, 1985, the Hispanic population in the United States had increased some 16% in a little over 5 years, compared to the national population increase of 3.3%. Hispanics now represent 16.9 million people in the United States, an increase of approximately 2.3 million since the 1980 census. Reich (1986) projects that, by the year 2080, the Hispanic population in the United States, now representing 7% of the population, will have increased to 19%. Currently there are approximately 247 Black mayors in the United States, and almost 6,000 Black elected officials. In 1986, there were 3,202 elected Hispanic officials (Lim, 1986)—an amazing statistic since 65% of the Hispanic population are too young to vote, and some 14% are legally ineligible to vote. The political power and influence of minorities is undeniable in a nation which, by the year 2000, will have 260 million people, one of every three of whom will be either Black, Hispanic, or Asian-American.

Language Minorities

A dramatic and clearly defined increase in the number of language minorities has occurred in this country (Omark & Erickson, 1983). In 1980, there were 14 or 15 major language groups with almost 2,400,000 students between the ages of 5 and 14, and this number of language minority students is projected to increase by approximately one-third by the year 2000. By far, the largest language minority group is Spanish-speaking, with more than two-thirds of the entire language minority population being represented by Spanish speakers. The number of Spanish speakers in this country is projected to increase some 48% between 1980 and the year 2000, numbering more than 22 million persons by the year 2000 (Macias, 1985).

Youth

Not only is the population growing older and becoming less White, but the odds are significantly greater that its youth will be members of ethnic minority groups. Taken together as a group, it is a more frequent phenomenon for ethnic minorities to comprise the majority of public school students. For example, in the state of Texas, 51% of kindergarten students are Hispanic, with the majority of elementary age students being members of minority groups. Before one hastens to associate these demographic shifts with a specific geographic area such as the Southwest, one must remember that Chicago represents the third largest Hispanic population center in the United States (La Familia en Marcha, 1984). It should also be noted that even today more than 50% of the population of the United States resides east of the Mississippi River. Large city school populations are overwhelmingly minority: Miami, 71%; Philadelphia, 73%; Baltimore, 80%; and so forth (McNett, 1983).

These shifts in the ethnic membership of public school populations are not a temporary bubble in the population stream, but rather the emerging future. As mentioned previously, the typical White person in this country is 32 years of age. The American Black is typically 25; the American Hispanic is 22 years of age. It is a rather simple task to determine who will have the most children within the next 15 years. The White population is basically leveling off in terms of women of child-bearing age, while the population of Hispanic women of child-bearing age is increasing dramatically. In addition, Hispanic women have the highest fertility rate of American women, 107 per 1,000 (Schwartz, 1986). A new baby boom will occur, but this time it will be Hispanic (Hodgkinson, 1985a).

Environmental Factors

Major changes have also taken place in terms of the social environment for children born in this country. For every 100 children born today, 12 are born out of wedlock, 40 are born to parents who divorce before the child is 18, 5 are born to parents who separate, 2 are born to parents one of whom will die before the child reaches 18, and 41 reach age 18 having been raised in a "normal" family environment.

Of children born out of wedlock, 50% are born to teenage mothers. Almost unbelievably, very young mothers—13 and 14 years of age—exist. In fact, every day in America, 40 teenage girls give birth to their third child. In 1979 dollars, each child born to a teenager eventually costs taxpayers $18,710 (Burt, 1986). Teenage mothers tend to give birth to children who are premature, of low birth weight, with a significantly higher incidence of major health problems, and in turn, with dramatically increased likelihood of having major handicaps. This group of high risk children is entering the educational system in rapidly increasing numbers.

Socioeconomic status remains a consistent correlate of school learning and learning problems. The Congressional Budget Office (1984) notes that approximately 22% of children under 17 years of age live in poverty and that this number is increasing. Given the corresponding increase in the number of minority children of school age, the known disparity in income levels for minorities and Whites, and continued differentiation and representation of minorities in professional and other high-income-earning activities, it can be conclusively projected that the number of poor children in school will dramatically increase in both real and percentage representation, between now and the year 2000.

Dropouts

It is difficult to obtain reliable data relative to school dropouts. Schools and other agencies have little motivation to collect such data, because these data provide indirect, if not direct, evidence of the failure of the system to serve segments of its population. Once a youngster disappears, she or he is of little interest to the organization. However, the best data appear to indicate that approximately 14% of White students, 25% of Black students, and more than 40% of Hispanic students drop out. Overall, more than 50% of minority students in large cities drop out (Boyer, 1983). Most drop-out statistics are based on cohorts of 9th and 10th graders; however, a recent Texas study of census data indicated that 30% of students drop out prior to the 9th grade (Cardenas & Roblado, 1987). There are fairly significant regional variations in these figures, with some states, such as Minnesota, maintaining better than 86% of their students, while other states, such as Mississippi, maintain barely over 60% of their students. It has been established (Singh, 1986) that school dropouts have the highest rate of children born out of wedlock.

In summary, demographic information indicates that this country's population is growing older and less White. Its children are less secure financially. Public school students are increasingly likely to be minority, and to come from homes where a language other than English is spoken.

IMPLICATIONS FOR SPECIAL EDUCATION

There is a clear difference between the emerging demographic characteristics of this country and the demography of special education as a discipline and in its professional organizations. Special education and its leadership are, at this time, most likely to be White, monolingual, and English-speaking, with special education research, training, and professional development activities generally focused upon areas unrelated to the emerging demographic characteristics of the student population in this country. Issues such as ethnicity, minority status, bilingual education, second language acquisition, nonbiased assessment, socioeconomic status, and so forth are generally perceived by the special education profession as unrelated to special education as a discipline. The configurations of special education and its professional organizations are not greatly incompatible with the past, but are quite discrepant with the emerging future.

Demographic variables suggest the possibility that there will be an expansion of groups eligible for special education services. Some examples of this emerging population would be victims of child abuse, juvenile delinquents, increased numbers of children situationally handicapped due to low socioeconomic status, children handicapped through effects of chemical abuse by their parents, children handicapped by sexually transmitted diseases such as acquired immune deficiency syndrome (AIDS) and herpes, and children both younger and older than the traditional age categories currently served by special education. This expanded group of individuals with problems which inhibit their normal progression in the educational system may cause the system to respond in its historical fashion of "dumping" all children who don't fit the institutional norm into special education. These effects may result in special education continuing the current trend of serving larger and larger numbers of mildly handicapped students.

Other variables such as the cost of special education and the general reduction of resources available in education may, however, precipitate a reaction formation to this expanded population for special education services. Such a reaction formation may cause the pendulum to swing back toward services for the more severely handicapped through a more careful delineation of eligibility criteria, primarily through policy and procedure structuring. This would result in only the defined handicapped individual receiving the unique specialized services of special education.

A number of courses of action appear rather obvious; however, they represent significant and difficult changes to be made within the discipline and the profession. For example, institutions of higher education, as well as others who provide training to special educators, must initiate training programs such as bilingual special education. Such programs exist today in relatively small numbers and with small training capacity. Training programs for regular educators, as well as special education, must begin to include content associated with second language acquisition, English-as-a-second-language instruction, bilingual education, cultural and linguistic uniqueness of student populations, and so forth. If they do not, there is less likelihood that appropriate student referral to special education will occur (Garcia & Yates, 1986).

There are other less obvious incompatibilities within the special education discipline and profession. For example, the name "The Council for Exceptional Children" displays some evidence of incompatibility with the demography. That is, in the future, special education will be faced with an increase in the amount of activity and services, research, and so forth, devoted to and related to adults and older citizens. Therefore, the word "Children," as part of the title of the major special education professional organization, becomes less appropriate as the U.S. population grows older.

As it becomes more acceptable for the older handicapped individual to receive special education services, special education professional organizations may need to reach out and interface with other nontraditional service agencies for special education, specifically organizations serving senior citizens. This outreach effort will, of course, create complex linkages and demand for appropriate "boundary spanners" to link the organizations. The identification and development of such boundary spanners will, in itself, call for unique demands on the special education profession.

Currently, parent and advocacy groups are no better prepared or configured than special education for the emerging changes and shifts in demography. There are fewer Whites of child-bearing age, and as the population becomes more culturally and linguistically diverse, special education parent organizations and advocacy groups must begin to make systemic adjustments in order to remain visible, viable, and influential. Just as special education has historically been powerful in the formulation of legislation and utilization of the judicial system to accomplish aims and goals for the handicapped, it must now, as a discipline and profession, recognize the growing political power of the Hispanic, the Black, the culturally and linguistically different populations in this country.

Recruitment efforts within special education at the level of preservice, continuing education, and practice must focus on bringing larger numbers of language and ethnic-minority individuals into the profession in order to provide appropriate practitioner/researcher/trainer knowledge, role models, and sufficient manpower to address the clearly changing demography of special education futures.

These efforts to recruit appropriate individuals to serve the emerging ethnic- and language-minority population may call for specific review of areas such as certification or licensing requirements of special educators. In the future it may be appropriate, given the percentage of the population represented by ethnic and language minorities, for all teachers, including special education teachers, to demonstrate competence in bilingual education instructional procedures or, at a minumum, English-as-a-second-language instructional techniques.

Since the majority of educators are, in fact, Anglo, monolingual speakers of English, and the composition of the teaching force will not change as rapidly as the ethnic and language composition of the students to be served, there are clear implications for continuing education or inservice training. Specifically, the population of special educators who are currently mostly White must be provided with appropriate training to produce understanding of the educational and learning implications of cultural, language, ethnicity, and learning style differences in the emerging student population. One need only review the range of typical training agendas provided special educators to recognize that topics ordinarily considered as appropriate in training are, in fact, dramatically different from what is being suggested to prepare the special educator to serve the emerging student population.

In summary, the political, organizational, training, research, and scholarly activities within special education as a discipline and a profession must be alerted and adapted to the powerful and long-term demographic changes occurring in this country.

REFERENCES

Boyer, E. (1983). *High school*. New York: Harper & Row.

Burt, M. R. (1986). Estimating the public cost of teenage child-bearing. *Family Planning Perspectives, 18*(5), 221–226.

Cardenas, J. A., & Del Refugio-Roblado, M. (1987, February). Attrition rates as indicators of school drop-outs. *IDRA Newsletter*, 1–4.

Congressional Budget Office. (1984). *Poverty among children*. Washington, DC: Author.

Exter, T. (1986, October). The Census Bureau's household projections. *American Demographics*, 44–47.

Fiesta Educativa. (1984). *La familia en marcha: Final report*. Chicago: Author.

Garcia, S. B., & Yates, J. R. (1986). Policy issues associated with serving bilingual exceptional children. In A. Willig & H. Greenberg (Eds.), *Bilingualism and learning disabilities: Policy and practice for teachers and administrators* (pp. 113–134). New York: American Library Publishing Company, Inc.

Hispanic population found to be growing rapidly. (1986, January 29). *Austin American Statesman*, A–11.

Hodgkinson, H. L. (1985a). *All in the system: Demographics of education—Kindergarten through graduate school*. Washington, DC: Institute for Educational Leadership.

Hodgkinson, H. L. (1985b). Teaching tomorrow's students. In S. Roueche (Ed.), *Celebrating teaching excellence* (pp. 29–42). Austin, TX: The University of Texas.

Lim, G. (1986, September 18). Ranks of Hispanics in government showed two percent rise in new study. *Austin American Statesman*, A–12.

Longino, Jr., C. F. (1986, November). A state-by-state look at the oldest Americans. *American Demographics*, 38–42.

Macias, R. F. (1985). National language profile of the Mexican origin population in the United States. In W. Connor (Ed.), *Mexican Americans in comparative perspective* (pp. 285–308). Washington, DC: The Urban Institute Press.

McNett, I. (1983). *Demographic imperatives for educational policy*. Washington, DC: American Council on Education.

Omark, D. R., & Erickson, J. G. (1983). *The bilingual exceptional child*. San Diego, CA: College Hill Press.

Reich, K. (1986, September 26). Hispanic population likely to double by 2020. *Austin American Statesman*, A–4.

Schwartz, J. (1986, November). Back to work. *American Demographics*, 56–57.

Singh, S. (1986). Adolescent pregnancy in the United States: Interstate analysis. *Family Planning Perspectives, 18*(5), 210–220.

NOTE: The author wishes to express appreciation and to acknowledge Harold L. "Bud" Hodgkinson for many of the conceptualizations and examples he has cited in various publications and speeches relative to demography and its effect upon the future state of the country and its educational system.

CHAPTER 2

A Prereferral Process for Preventing Inappropriate Referrals of Hispanic Students to Special Education

Alba A. Ortiz
Shernaz B. Garcia

Schools frequently fail Hispanics. According to Brown, Rosen, Hill, and Olivas (1980), the school drop-out rate for Mexican Americans is 66 percent. Evidence that Hispanics are undereducated is also found in standardized achievement test scores which show that these students traditionally score 2 to 3 years below grade level in critical skill areas such as reading, math, and science. Add to this a serious overrepresentation of Hispanics in programs for the learning disabled (Ortiz & Yates, 1983) and one would have to conclude that Hispanics have met with limited educational success. When such a dramatic proportion of the school population is unsuccessful, it is not appropriate to raise questions concerning pathology of individual Hispanic students. Rather, specific questions must be raised about the efficacy of the organizational system responsible for their education.

Regular educators seem to have difficulty distinguishing Hispanic students who have learning problems which can be addressed by adapting the regular education program from those who should be referred for comprehensive assessments because of suspected handicapping conditions. One explanation for this is that when students' cultural and linguistic characteristics are perceived as *deficiencies* rather than as *differences*, there is a tendency to blame the student for lack of success, rather than to question the effectiveness of the curriculum or instruction. According to Cummins (1984), when children experience failure:

> The orientation of the teacher and assessment specialist (or "teacher-consultant") should be first to examine critically the instruction offered to the child to assess the extent to which it is compatible with the way people acquire language and other cognitive skills. Essentially, this involves asking whether language use in the classroom is integrated with activities that the child is intrinsically motivated to carry out. (p. 268)

In a similar vein, Heller, Holtzman, and Messick (1982) argue that the major issues related to the disproportionate placement of minority children in special education are the *quality* of instruction provided in the mainstream and the *validity* of referral and assessment processes. Thus every district and every campus should have a clearly identifiable prereferral process in place to facilitate problem solving when students experience school-related difficulties. An effective prereferral process can help distinguish achievement difficulties associated with a lack of accommodation of individual differences in regular classrooms from problems that stem from a handicapping condition. The purpose of this paper is to suggest a process which incorporates considerations related to the education of multicultural populations in general and of Hispanics, in particular.

LEARNING PROBLEMS ENCOUNTERED IN CLASSROOMS

Reasons for academic failure can be broadly classified into one of three types of learning problems (Adelman, 1970). The first type of learning problem occurs when students are in classroom environments which do not accommodate their individual differences or learning styles. For example, limited-English-proficient (LEP) students who need native language or bilingual instruction, but who are taught solely in English, can be expected to experience such academic difficulties. A second type of learning problem involves children who have mild to moderate achievement difficulties but, because these are not the result of handicapping conditions, are able to make satisfactory progress when instruction is adapted to accommodate their needs. This would be the case when a child did not learn to read because of excessive absences but overcame this difficulty after instruction was provided specific to skills he or she was lacking. Students experiencing these first two types of problems are at risk of being special education's "false positives" (Tucker, 1981). In these instances, rather than placing students in special education, teachers and other support personnel should receive training and assistance to more effectively accommodate students' needs and, thus, to increase the likelihood of school success. The third type of learning problem is that encountered by students who have major disorders that interfere with the teaching-learning process. These students require special education instruction to help them achieve their maximum potential.

Examination of characteristics of limited-English-proficient Hispanic students in programs for the learning disabled and the speech and language handicapped (Cummins, 1984; Ortiz et al., 1985; Ortiz, Garcia, Wheeler, & Maldonado-Colon, 1986) suggests that neither the data gathered as part of the referral and evaluation process, nor the decisions made using these data, reflect professionals' understanding of issues related to limited English proficiency, second language acquisition, or cultural and other differences which mediate students' learning. These findings support a growing body of literature indicating that many students served in special education are, in reality, "curriculum casualties" (Hargis, cited in Gickling & Thompson, 1985); that is, they experience difficulties which are "pedagogically induced" (Cummins, 1984). According to Hargis:

> These children, who are in fact the curriculum casualties or curriculum handicapped, would not have acquired their various labels had the curriculum been adjusted to fit their individual needs, rather than having tried to force the children to achieve in the artificial but clerically simpler sequence of grades, calendar and materials that comprise the curricula. (cited in Gickling & Thompson, 1985, p. 209)

MAKING CURRICULUM AND INSTRUCTION RESPONSIVE TO STUDENT DIVERSITY

The education of linguistically and culturally different students is the responsibility of regular educators. The prereferral process described in the following sections assumes that school districts endorse a philosophy of cultural pluralism and multicultural education, and that educators understand the influence of students' linguistic and cultural characteristics on learning and academic success. However, since teachers often have difficulty adjusting curriculum and instruction for students from cultural backgrounds different from their own, they should be assisted in developing skills that will enable them to teach from a multicultural perspective as well as teach a culturally diverse student population (Gollnick & Chinn, 1986). A major goal of such a philosophy is to alter the educational environment so that all students will develop competencies in multiple cultures and be afforded equal educational opportunity

(Bennett, 1986). The following principles summarize the major goals of multicultural and pluralistic educational programs (Gollnick & Chinn, 1986):

1. The educational program must use teaching approaches and materials that are sensitive and relevant to students' sociocultural backgrounds and experiences,
2. Learning styles of teachers and students and teaching styles of teachers need to be understood and used to develop effective instructional strategies,
3. Students' involvement in the learning process should be increased through an analysis and modification of oral and nonverbal communication patterns between teachers and students,
4. Educational programs must begin at the students' functioning level,
5. Multicultural content should be integrated at all levels of the curriculum rather than giving superficial, fragmented attention to these issues,
6. Educational programs must "deal with the social and historical realities of American society and help students gain a better understanding of the causes of oppression and inequality, including racism and sexism" (Suzuki, 1980, cited in Gollnick & Chinn, 1986, p. 271),
7. Resources from the local community should be incorporated into the educational program and activities.

CULTURAL AND LINGUISTIC CONSIDERATIONS IN THE PREREFERRAL PROCESS

This paper attempts to build upon existing prereferral efforts (Graden, Casey, & Christenson, 1985; Heller, Holtzman, & Messick, 1982; Tucker, 1981) by raising a series of questions specific to multicultural populations which must be addressed before a referral to special education is appropriate (see Figure 1).

Step 1: Is the student experiencing academic difficulty?

Because of the range in student backgrounds and abilities typically found in regular classrooms, it is to be expected that some students will experience academic difficulty. When this occurs, prereferral interventions aimed at identifying the sources of the problem and improving the student's performance in the mainstream should be attempted, *before* referral to special education is considered.

Step 2: Is the curriculum known to be effective for Hispanic students?

Because of the inadequacy of currently available curricula, districts are likely to find that they must continuously be involved in adapting and supplementing existing curricula, and in developing and/or validating new materials tailored for the multicultural populations they serve. For example, bilingual education and English-as-a-second-language programs were developed in recognition that limited-English-proficient students could not master the regular curriculum without a program of study to help them become competent in English. Native language curricula were incorporated as an integral part of bilingual instruction to ensure that LEP students did not fall behind Anglo peers on grade level subjects or skills while they learned English as a second language.

A beginning point in addressing the effectiveness of curricula is to examine achievement patterns in a district or on an individual campus. Representation of students at the high, middle, and low levels of standardized achievement scores should be proportional with the ethnic composition of the educational unit being studied. If Hispanic students historically make the lowest achievement scores, and constitute the majority of underachievers, indications are that either the curriculum is ineffective for these students or that it has been poorly implemented. If student failure can be attributed to the use of inappropriate curricula,

FIGURE 1

Preventing Inappropriate Placements of Hispanic Students in Special Education: A Prereferral Process

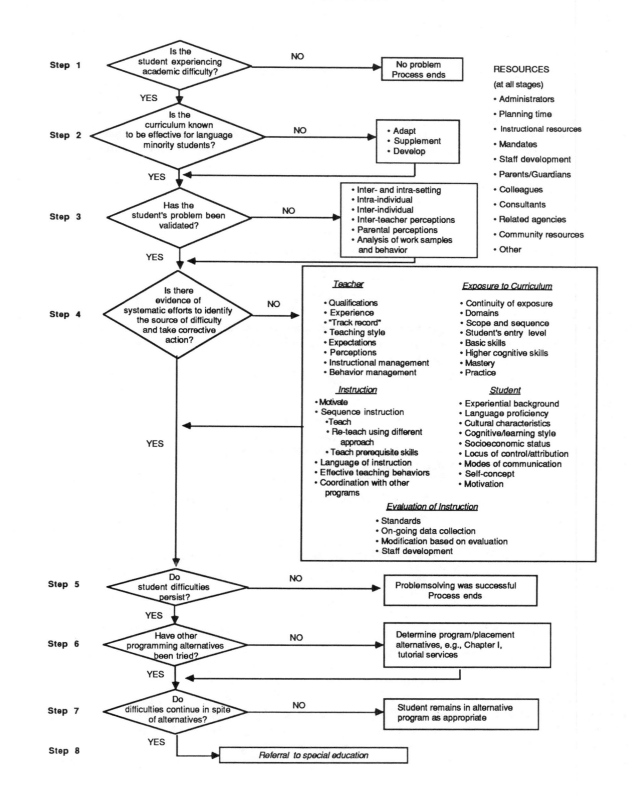

then referrals to special education are unwarranted. Efforts, instead, should focus on modifying or creating more effective instructional programs.

Step 3: Is there evidence that the child did not learn what was taught?

Identification of a student "problem" typically involves a judgment that the behavior is deviant from the norm. Several factors must be considered before this judgment can be validated, including observation and data collection in the following areas (Tucker, 1981):

1. *Inter- and intra-setting comparisons* must be made to measure the extent to which the perceived problem is manifested across different occasions and settings. For instance, is the difficulty evident in small group, large group and/or individual assignments?
2. *Inter-individual comparisons* must also be made to assess whether the perceived problem behaviors differ from those of other students in the class. Cultural, linguistic, socioeconomic, and other relevant characteristics of the comparison group must be similar to those of the target student.
3. *Inter-teacher perceptions* are useful in identifying any teacher- or setting-specific problems that may exist, as is the case when similar problems are not noted by the student's other teachers.
4. *Parental perceptions* of their child's behavior are critical in determining the extent to which these are real problems. If parents confirm the school's perception, it is more likely that a true problem exists. When cross-cultural comparisons do not support such a conclusion, alternatives must be explored, including modifying the school environment or teaching the student the desired behaviors, without labeling "deviant" that which is culturally appropriate.
5. *Student work samples* can assist the teacher and other personnel involved in the prereferral phase in determining the specific nature of the perceived problem. Analysis of student products allows the teacher to define the problem in precise measurable terms, rather than with broad, general descriptors such as "below grade level in math," or "cannot read well." Work samples can also help develop hypotheses about the source of the difficulty; for example, is the student experiencing difficulty with division because he or she cannot multiply? Work samples are particularly important for students in bilingual education programs in that they serve to verify, or question, results obtained from standardized achievement tests which do not usually include representative samples of Hispanics and which do not measure Spanish language skills or achievement.

Step 4: Is there evidence of systematic efforts to identify the source of difficulty and take corrective action?

Once the problem has been validated, the fourth stage in the prereferral process requires that resolutions be approached from various perspectives, to include teacher-, student-, curriculum-, and instruction-related factors. Thus, in some instances, corrective actions include professional development and training for teachers; in other cases, the student may have to be taught prerequisite skills; in still other situations, a redirection of curricula and evaluation of instructional programs may be required. Since failure itself is a multifaceted phenomenon, it is likely that the solution, too, will involve more than one aspect of the child's school experience.

Teacher Characteristics

Many teachers, even today, are products of preservice training programs which focus predominantly on the education of White, middle class, English-monolingual students. As a result, teachers may not possess the knowledge, skills, and experience to be effective with the increasing number of students from diverse cultural, linguistic, and socioeconomic back-grounds. When teacher and student characteristics vary along any or all of these dimensions, the potential for conflict and failure increases considerably. Such differences are often manifested as conflicts which could be *substantive* (e.g., disagreement over educational goals), *procedural* (e.g., mismatch of teaching and learning styles) or *interpersonal* (e.g., culturally relevant behaviors interpreted as behavior "problems") (Gay, 1981). All three conditions affect the teaching-learning process and a student's ability to profit from instruction. Given the high rates of failure among Hispanic students, it becomes essential to question the effectiveness of instruction, including the teacher's qualifications, experience, and teaching history, during the prereferral stages.

Teaching Style. Teachers are predisposed to teach in ways that correspond to their own learning styles (Ramirez & Castaneda, 1974). This poses few difficulties for students whose learning styles correspond to the teacher's teaching style, but can be devastating for those whose styles are incompatible with the instructional approaches being used. Teachers should be aware of their own learning and teaching styles and the extent to which their personal preferences dominate, not only management of behavior and instruction, but their expectations for students as well. Teachers can maximize learning by using a variety of techniques when they deliver instruction, thus giving *all* students the opportunity to utilize their own modality preferences or cognitive styles. This can be achieved by the use of multisensory teaching aids, learning centers where students can learn material in a variety of ways, diversified grouping patterns, variations in reinforcement systems, and so forth. Additionally, students can be taught to use alternative learning styles, thus increasing their chances of being successful, regardless of task conditions.

Teacher Expectations and Perceptions. In trying to determine the source of difficulty, the teacher's expectations should be evaluated, to ensure that they are neither too high nor too low, since student frustration and failure can occur under either condition. Teachers sometimes judge students' competence on the basis of race, sex, socioeconomic, linguistic, and cultural differences, rather than on actual abilities (Bergen & Smith, 1966; Jackson & Cosca, 1974; Rist, 1970; Ysseldyke, Algozzine, Richey, & Graden, 1982). Research on teacher expectations (Good & Brophy, 1973) further suggests that teachers interact differentially with students for whom they hold low expectations. For example, they wait less time for students to respond, offer fewer and poorer opportunities to learn, focus on student behavior and discipline rather than academic work, reinforce inappropriate behaviors, seat low expectation students further away, and call on them less frequently. Differential behaviors have also been noted in the treatment of boys and girls. Teachers who hold traditional sex role stereotypes may do a task for girls but give boys extended directions to complete the activity, interpret girls' silence as ignorance versus interpreting boys' silence as evidence of thought and reflection, and provide girls with less feedback, positive or negative, than boys (Sadker & Sadker, 1982). As the quality of instruction is diminished over time, for specific groups of students this alone could explain differences in achievement levels.

Exposure to the Curriculum

The central questions to be answered in determining whether a child has had sufficient exposure to the curriculum are whether he or she has been taught the subject or skill and/or whether this instruction has been interrupted. Students experience discontinuity of instruction for a variety of reasons, including having to stay home to take care of younger brothers and sisters in family emergencies, fatigue because they work late hours to help support the family, or simply because they are experiencing so many school-related problems that not attending is a way of relieving the pain of failure. These interruptions of schooling can negatively affect academic achievement and, if not addressed promptly can have cumulative effects devastating to future success. Unless teachers provide ways for underachieving students to catch up with peers, learning problems are more likely to be associated with the lack of opportunity to learn, rather than with handicapping conditions. Filling in instructional gaps requires that teachers understand skill domains (e.g., that

11

reading requires that children have an adequate language foundation and that they master both word recognition and comprehension skills), so they can assess each child's entry level skills and sequence instruction accordingly.

Basic Skills. Because special education referrals are usually concerned with mastery of basic skills, the prereferral process should document the extent and nature of prior instruction in these areas. Of particular interest is the language in which skills were initially taught. It is not uncommon for Hispanic students to be referred to special education on the basis of low English skills, even though their first schooling experiences were in bilingual education programs in which basic skills were taught in Spanish. For these students, a referral would be inappropriate until data such as the following are analyzed: (a) the child's English and Spanish language proficiency, (b) informal assessment results describing level of basic skills functioning in Spanish and English, (c) information about when the transition to English language instruction occurred, and (d) whether the child was functioning adequately in Spanish at the time of the transition. These data can help determine whether the child's problems are pedagogically induced, as might be the case, for example, if English language instruction were begun before the child had adequately mastered basic skills in Spanish or before she or he had acquired appropriate levels of English language proficiency.

Mastery and Practice. Sufficient time must be allocated for students to achieve subject or skill mastery and for skills practice. Students are sometimes engaged in independent practice activities before they have demonstrated adequate understanding of the task and, thus, incorrect patterns or behaviors are reinforced as they work on their own. According to Rosenshine (1983), ensuring adequate exposure to the curriculum requires that a child demonstrate mastery at a level of 95%–100% accuracy. Berliner (1984) stresses that, especially for academically less able and for younger students, almost errorless performance results in higher achievement. He suggests that teachers check students' understanding during lesson presentations and that pupils first participate in guided or controlled practice, during which teachers monitor performance to be sure that students are working with a high level of accuracy. Only then should students be involved in independent, unsupervised activities. At the prereferral stages, data are gathered to describe adequacy of lesson presentations and whether the student has had sufficient time to master and practice skills. Evidence that the child received appropriate instruction, but did not profit from it, can later be used to justify a referral for a comprehensive assessment.

Higher Cognitive Skills. Cazden (1984) criticizes school effectiveness research because it places too much emphasis on development of skills which are easily quantifiable (e.g., math activities in which answers can be judged as right or wrong) and virtually ignores teaching involving more complex, abstract concepts and development of critical thinking skills, the outcomes of which are oftentimes difficult to measure. Cummins (1984) concurs, indicating that the predominant instructional model, in regular and special education, is based on task analyses which structure learning in such small, sequential steps that the student may be able to complete each step but be unable to reconstruct the whole task because it has been stripped of meaning. Task analysis is antithetical, not only to higher order skill development, but, in the case of limited-English-proficient students, to the acquisition of English-as-a-second-language skills. Cummins recommends, instead, a reciprocal interaction model in which the teacher serves as a facilitator of learning, focuses on higher order cognitive skills, and integrates language use and development into all aspects of curriculum content. Such a model produces more effective learners and may decrease the need for specialized intervention outside the mainstream. The prereferral process should describe the instructional model being used by the teacher to determine whether the approach, in and of itself, is maintaining low functioning levels and reinforcing marginal, semi-dependent behavior (Harth, 1982).

Instruction

Before referring a student, teachers should carefully document adaptations of instruction and programs which have been attempted to improve performance in the mainstream. Adelman (1970) suggests that instruction be carefully sequenced as follows: (a) teach basic skills, subjects, or concepts; (b) reteach skills or content using significantly different strategies or approaches for the benefit of students who fail to meet expected performance levels after initial instruction; and (c) refocus instruction on the teaching of prerequisite skills for students who continue to experience difficulty even after approaches and materials have been modified.

Documentation of this teaching sequence is very helpful if the child fails to make adequate progress and is subsequently referred to special education. Referral committees will be able to judge whether the adaptations attempted are appropriate given the student's background characteristics. It is possible, for example, that a child will fail to learn to read, even after a teacher attempts several different reading approaches, because the child is being instructed in English but is not English proficient. In this case, the interventions would be judged inappropriate and other instructional alternatives would need to be recommended. Ultimately, if the child qualifies for special education services, information about prior instruction is invaluable to the development of individualized educational programs because the types of interventions which work, and those which have met with limited success, are already clearly delineated.

Language of Instruction. Instruction should be consistent with what is known about language acquisition and about the interrelationship between first and second language development. The research literature (Cummins, 1984; Krashen, 1982) indicates that the native language provides the foundation for acquiring English-as-a-second-language skills. Therefore, strong promotion of native language conceptual skills will be more effective in providing a basis for English literacy (Cummins, 1984). Conversely, a premature shift to English-only instruction not only interferes with a natural developmental sequence, but also interferes with intellectual and cognitive development. Teachers should mediate instruction using both the first and the second language, and integrate English development with subject matter instruction. Along with this, teachers should also respond to, and use, cultural referents during instruction, observing the values and norms of the home culture even as the norms of the majority culture are being taught (Tikunoff, 1985). Above all, teachers must communicate high expectations for students and a sense of efficacy in terms of their own ability to teach linguistically diverse students.

Student Characteristics

The complexity of providing appropriate instructional opportunities is immediately apparent when one considers the diversity of characteristics among Hispanic students. Student variables are discussed last to underscore that inadequacies of the instructional environment should be ruled out *before* attention is focused on assessing student characteristics to determine reasons for school failure. Otherwise, because referrals to special education frequently lead to comprehensive assessments which, given a lack of appropriate instruments and procedures, yield questionable results, the child may become the victim of an inadequate schooling system.

Language Proficiency. There is wide diversity in the language characteristics of Hispanic students, diversity which at one extreme is descriptive of individuals reared in communities where the primary language is Spanish and at the other extreme characteristic of Hispanics reared in environments where the primary language is English. Determining the point on the language continuum which is most characteristic of students' first and second language skills is important to choosing the language of instruction (Ortiz, 1984). The first step in the instructional process should be determination of the child's language proficiency, or level of skill in each language. Language evaluations should provide data which describe the child's interpersonal communication skills and should emphasize analysis of English pragmatic skills, rather than structural accuracy (e.g., correctness of phonology, syntax, grammar). The emphasis on pragmatic skills is important because the child, precisely because he or she is in the process of acquiring English as a second language, will make numerous errors in the surface forms of English. Teachers may inaccurately conclude that these errors suggest a possible language disability rather than that they verify the student's LEP status.

Critical to distinguishing learning disabilities from linguistic differences is the assessment of a child's academic language proficiency (Cummins, 1984). In addition to evaluating interpersonal communication skills, assessments should also measure the literacy-related aspects of language. Procedures which capture whether a child understands teacher-talk (e.g., tests of dictation or story retelling) and whether she or he can handle the language found in texts (e.g., cloze procedures or comprehension checks which tap evaluation or inferential skills) are recommended. Unless these skills are measured, teachers may attribute low achievement to learning disabilities when they may, in fact, be related to lack of academic language proficiency.

Culture. Understanding cultural characteristics is an important aspect of distinguishing differences from handicapping conditions. While some behaviors do not conform to the desired or expected behaviors of the majority society, they may, nonetheless, be normal given a student's ethnic or cultural group. Such behaviors are best characterized as differences rather than handicapping conditions. Educators must learn as much as possible about diversity within cultures, and about the contemporary culture of students, so they can create learning environments and curricula which are uniquely compatible with student characteristics, with expectations and desires of parents, and with school and community norms.

Socioeconomic Status. Development of children from poverty environments may differ from that of middle class students. When children's experiences do not match those expected by teachers and schools, teachers may attribute school problems to "deficient" environments and may lower their expectations for student success (Ortiz & Yates, 1984). Unfortunately, teachers sometimes fail to recognize that economic differences affect cognitive and learning styles, causing children to respond deferentially to instruction. For example, children from lower socioeconomic backgrounds may have difficulty processing information or profiting from instruction presented from a framework of independence and intrinsic motivation. They fail to perceive their own effort as an important cause of success or failure. These students will not be successful unless they are taught using strategies compatible with their own cognitive orientations and/or until they are taught "learning to learn" strategies (e.g., setting goals, planning for goal attainment, sequencing behavior, intrinsic motivation, etc.).

The student characteristics discussed in the preceding sections serve only to suggest the range of student variables which must be considered in planning instruction. A comprehensive description of background and experiences is required to make instruction uniquely appropriate to the student. The prereferral process should verify that the teacher has been able to tailor instruction to the needs of the student in question.

Evaluation of Instruction

Obviously, any instructional program must involve a continuous monitoring system to determine whether goals and objectives are being met. One type of evaluation is teacher driven and requires that teachers continuously check student progress through daily quizzes, 6-week exams, or informal observations, for example, and that they provide feedback to students about academic progress. It does not help to return a student's spelling test or math assignment with answers marked wrong but with no indication as to why responses were incorrect and, thus, no suggestion as to how performance can be improved. Simply marking answers as right or wrong does not clue the teacher about how to modify instruction or plan subsequent lessons for students experiencing difficulty. A data-based approach involving simple, informal observation and analysis of student work samples is more effective in increasing student achievement (Zigmond & Miller, 1986). For limited-English-proficient Hispanic students, data must describe the child's functioning levels in English and Spanish.

Another level of evaluation is provided by instructional supervisors, most typically school principals, and pinpoints staff development needs if a teacher experiences problems, for example, teaching a particular subject or skill or a specific group of students. In districts which serve minority populations, staff development is often necessary because institutions of higher education do not adequately prepare educators to serve multicultural populations. Supervisors can assist teachers in developing professional growth plans and selecting appropriate inservice activities.

The discussions in the preceding sections are not exhaustive but are simply designed to highlight that learning problems occur for a variety of reasons, including that teachers do not have the necessary skills to teach multicultural populations, the student does not receive instruction, instruction is not consistent with entry level skills or is inappropriately sequenced, and/or there is no system for evaluating and modifying instruction as needed. Consequently, there will be instances when intervention will be focused on teachers and programs, rather than on students.

Step 5: Do student difficulties persist?

If, after evidence is provided that systematic efforts were made to identify the source of difficulty and to take corrective action, student difficulties persist, the next step in the process is to explore other programming alternatives within the mainstream.

Step 6: Have other programming alternatives been tried?

A linguistically different student may have been inaccurately classified as English proficient and may be experiencing difficulty because he or she needs a bilingual education or English-as-a-second-language program. In other instances, it may be possible for students to be served through compensatory education programs which provide remedial instruction. Unless alternatives such as these are readily available, referral to special education will continue to be a trigger response when teachers are unable to improve students' achievement. There is an assumption, of course, that teachers understand the purpose of alternative programs and that they are familiar with eligibility criteria for placement (i.e., which students are served by which program). Otherwise, misplacements in special education can continue to occur despite the availability of options such as Chapter 1, migrant education, bilingual education programs, etc. (Garcia, 1984).

Step 7: Do difficulties continue in spite of alternatives?

If mainstream alternatives prove to be of no avail, then a referral to special education is appropriate. The evidence most critical to determining eligibility will accompany the referral, that is, verification that: (a) the school's curriculum is appropriate; (b) the child's problems are documented across settings and personnel, not only in school, but also at home; (c) difficulties are present both in the native language and in English; (d) the child has been taught but has not made satisfactory progress; (e) the teacher has the qualifications and experience to effectively teach the student; and (f) instruction has been continuous, appropriately sequenced, and has included teaching of skills prerequisite to success. A child who does not learn after this type of systematic, quality intervention is a good candidate for special education. The referral indicates that a decision has been reached that the child cannot be served by regular education programs and that she or he is likely to be handicapped. A comprehensive assessment is requested to determine the nature of the handicapping condition.

FACTORS INFLUENCING IMPLEMENTATION

Prereferral intervention should be a formal process, governed by a clearly recognizable set of procedures, which is accepted and followed by all personnel on a district- or campus-wide basis, and which is under the jurisdiction of regular education. Prereferral procedures may already be in place in some districts; in others, a major system overhaul will be required.

Special Education

Prereferral intervention cannot work unless special educators reaffirm that their responsibility is to serve *handicapped* individuals, not students whose problems are induced by ineffective teachers or programs. While this may seem a somewhat harsh stance, there is insufficient evidence to suggest that special education is any more effective than regular education in serving linguistically different students (see, for example, the discussion of special education reevaluation outcomes in Chapter 6 by Ortiz & Yates). Rather than placing Hispanic students in more restrictive environments, it seems more appropriate to improve the quality of regular education.

Allocation of Resources

Access to, or creation of, alternative mainstream programs for underachieving students is an important component of prereferral, as is coordination of staff and services across programs to ensure that the goals and objectives being addressed by all those serving the student are compatible. Flexible scheduling and release time for teachers and others to meet and discuss student problems and to generate potential solutions is necessary. Scheduling is also an important consideration if changes in students' daily routines are required, for example, when remedial program services are recommended. These considerations suggest the need for strong support from administrators to ensure that the necessary resources are available for successful implementation of the process.

Staff Development

An important goal of staff development is to build more effective linkages with parents and the community. Parents must be provided information, assistance, and counsel to help them understand the instructional services provided their children and the various proceedings and deliberations which occur when a change in placement is considered for a child. Parental involvement is critical to addressing the question of differences versus disabilities, and especially in determining whether the child meets the norms and expectations of his/her cultural or reference group and, thus, whether behavior is normal or deviant. If adequate services are not available through the local education agency, then community resources need to be explored.

Some faculty and administrators may be resistant to training as many of the issues to be addressed through staff development are socially, politically, or professionally sensitive. For example, the prereferral process raises the question of whether regular education is effectively serving Hispanic students and suggests that dramatic changes in service delivery are required. These changes involve developing knowledge among professionals that, heretofore, may not have been within their expertise.

It is surprising that some professionals, who are not themselves bilingual, fail to see that they share responsibility for ensuring that bilingual populations are effectively served in public schools. Developing this sense of responsibility, and the skills to fulfill it, is particularly important for the success of those students who are bilingual but who are English proficient and therefore served in regular education programs where instruction is presented entirely in English. Unless regular educators understand second language acquisition, they will fail to provide the necessary language development support these students need to be academically successful. That the primary focus of the prereferral process is initially on evaluating regular educators' competence in serving linguistically and culturally different students can serve as a powerful motivator for participating in programs designed to increase the ability of regular educators to serve multicultural populations.

Cost Effectiveness

There are major benefits to be gained from the successful implementation of a prereferral process. Serving students in the mainstream is more cost effective than placement in special education, particularly if the student is underachieving, but not handicapped. More importantly, perhaps, are the long-term benefits for students themselves, who will have a greater chance of achieving their social, political, and economic potential because they are provided an appropriate education. Unless drop-out rates among Hispanic students are decreased and academic achievement of these students is improved, the loss of earning power and the concomitant drain on society's resources will continue to be astronomical. Development of prereferral interventions, in which the major goal is to improve the effectiveness of regular education for Hispanic students, seems a very cost-effective investment in the future.

SUMMARY

Because institutions of higher education often fail to prepare instructional personnel to teach language minority students, Hispanic students are prone to school failure, as evidenced by high drop-out rates, poor performance on standardized tests of achievement, and overrepresentation in programs for the learning disabled. It is important that school districts have in place procedures which document that linguistic, cultural, and other unique student characteristics have been accommodated, before a referral to special education is accepted. Only in this way can members of ethnic and multicultural populations have the same opportunity for academic success as their Anglo peers and can the number of inappropriate special education referrals be minimized.

REFERENCES

Adelman, H. (1970). An interactive view of causality. *Academic Therapy, 6,* 43–52.

Bennett, C. I. (1986). *Comprehensive multicultural education: Theory and practice.* Boston: Allyn and Bacon.

Bergen, J., & Smith, J. O. (1966). Effects of socioeconomic status and sex on prospective teachers' judgments. *Mental Retardation, 4,* 13–15.

Berliner, D. C. (1984). The half-full glass: A review of research on teaching. In P. L. Hosford (Ed.), *Using what we know about teaching* (pp. 511–577). Alexandria, VA: Association for Supervision and Curriculum Development.

Brown, G. H., Rosen, N. L., Hill, S. T., & Olivas M. A. (1980). *The condition of education for Hispanic Americans.* Washington, DC: National Center for Educational Statistics.

Cazden, C. (1984). *Effective instructional practices in bilingual education.* Washington, DC: National Institute of Education.

Cummins, J. (1984). *Bilingualism and special education: Issues in assessment and pedagogy.* Clevedon, Avon, England: Multilingual Matters Ltd.

Garcia, S. B. (1984). *Effects of student characteristics, school programs and organization on decision-making for the placement of Hispanic students in classes for the learning disabled.* Unpublished doctoral dissertation, The University of Texas at Austin.

Gay, G. (1981). Interactions in the culturally pluralistic classroom. In J. A. Banks (Ed.), *Education in the 80's: Multiethnic education.* Washington, DC: National Education Association.

Gickling, E. E., & Thompson, V. P. (1985). A personal view of curriculum-based assessment. *Exceptional Children, 52,* 205–218.

Gollnick, D. M., & Chinn, P. C. (1986). *Multicultural education in a pluralistic society* (2nd ed.). Columbus, OH: Merrill.

Good, T. L., & Brophy, J. E. (1973). *Looking in classrooms*. New York: Harper & Row.

Graden, J. L., Casey, A., & Christenson, S. L. (1985). Implementing a prereferral intervention system: Part I. The model. *Exceptional Children, 51*, 377–387.

Harth, R. (1982). The Feuerstein perspective on the modification of cognitive performance. *Focus on Exceptional Children, 15*(3), 1–12.

Heller, K. A., Holtzman, W. H., & Messick, S. (Eds.) (1982). *Placing children in special education: A strategy for equity*. Washington, DC: National Academy Press.

Jackson, G., & Cosca, C. (1974). The inequality of educational opportunity in the Southwest: An observational study of ethnically mixed classrooms. *American Educational Research Journal, 11*, 219–229.

Krashen, S. (1982). *Principles and practice in second language acquisition*. New York: Pergammon Press.

Ortiz, A. A. (1984). Choosing the language of instruction for exceptional bilingual children. *TEACHING Exceptional Children, 16*, 208–212.

Ortiz, A. A., Garcia, S. B., Holtzman, Jr., W. H., Polyzoi, E., Snell, Jr., W. E., Wilkinson, C. Y., & Willig, A. C. (1985). *Characteristics of limited English proficient Hispanic students in programs for the learning disabled: Implications for policy, practice, and research*. Austin, TX: The University of Texas, Handicapped Minority Research Institute on Language Proficiency.

Ortiz, A. A., Garcia, S. B., Wheeler, D., & Maldonado-Colon, E. (1986). *Characteristics of limited English proficient students served in programs for the speech and language handicapped: Implications for policy, practice, and research*. Austin, TX: The University of Texas, Handicapped Minority Research Institute on Language Proficiency.

Ortiz, A. A., & Maldonado-Colon, E. (1986). Recognizing learning disabilities in bilingual children: How to lessen inappropriate referrals of language minority students to special education. *Journal of Reading, Writing, and Learning Disabilities International, 1*(1), 47–56.

Ortiz, A. A., & Yates, J. R. (1983). Incidence among Hispanic exceptionals: Implications for manpower planning. *Journal of the National Association for Bilingual Education, 7*(3), 41–53.

Ortiz, A. A., & Yates, J. R. (1984). Linguistically and culturally diverse handicapped students. In R. S. Podemski, B. M. Price, T. E. C. Smith, & G. E. Marsh II (Eds.), *Comprehensive administration of special education* (pp.114–141). Rockville, MD: Aspen.

Ramirez, M., & Castaneda, A. (1974). *Cultural democracy, biocognitive development, and education*. New York: Academic Press.

Rist, R. (1970). Student social class and teacher expectations: The self-fulfilling prophecy in ghetto education. *Harvard Educational Review, 40*, 411–450.

Rosenshine, B. V. (1983). Teaching functions in instructional programs. *Elementary School Journal, 83*, 335–352.

Sadker, M., & Sadker, D., (1982). Between teacher and student: Overcoming sex bias in classroom interaction. In M. Sadker & D. Sadker (Eds.), *Sex equity handbook for schools*. New York: Longman.

Tikunoff, W. J. (1985). *Applying significant bilingual instructional features in the classroom*. Rosslyn, VA: National Clearinghouse for Bilingual Education.

Tucker, J. (1981). *Sequential stages of the appraisal process: A training manual*. Minneapolis, MN: National School Psychology Inservice Training Network.

Ysseldyke, J., Algozzine, B., Richey, L., & Graden, J. (1982). Declaring students eligible for learning disability services: Why bother with the data? *Learning Disability Quarterly, 5*, 37–44.

Zigmond, N., & Miller, S. (1986). Assessment for instructional planning. *Exceptional Children, 52*, 501–509.

CHAPTER 3

High Risk Predictors and Prereferral Screening for Language Minority Students

Alejandro Benavides

Studies indicate that a disproportionate number of racial and language minority students are assigned to certain special education classes. The problem is closely associated with the screening, referral, psychoeducational assessment, and labeling of children to determine their eligibility for special education. Studies suggest that placement in special education is often related to socioeconomic, linguistic, and cultural factors rather than psychoeducational factors.

This chapter reviews the literature on the assessment of language minority students, their placement in special education, and prereferral screening. The Prereferral Screening Instrument (Benavides, 1985) is also presented and demonstrated. The Instrument was designed to determine whether students suspected of needing special education should be referred for a case-study evaluation and whether it should be a bilingual case study.

DISPROPORTIONATE REPRESENTATION

Disproportionate representation of racial and language minorities refers to the recurrent finding that based upon their representation in the general school population, there are either many more, or fewer, minority students in special education classes than would be expected. This phenomenon is neither a new discovery nor an isolated practice (Maheady, Algozzine, & Ysseldyke, 1984). Discrimination in the special education evaluation and placement process is a matter of serious concern to courts and to professional federal and state agencies. A National Academy of Sciences Panel was formed to study the problem (Heller, Holtzman, & Merrick, 1982).

There are conflicting reports on the disproportionate placement of minorities in special education. Data from states where the Hispanic population is more than 10% indicate that on a straight percentage basis, limited-English-proficient (LEP) children continue to be overrepresented in classes for the mentally handicapped and underrepresented in classes for the learning disabled (LD) and gifted (Brown, Rosen, & Hill, 1980; Figueroa, Sandoval, & Merino, 1984; Melesky, 1985). Finn (1982) used complex indices of over- and underrepresentation for a study which found evidence of disproportionate representation of minorities in special education programs. A study of the patterns of service incidence in Texas by Ortiz and Yates (1983) indicates that Hispanics were overrepresented in LD programs, but underrepresented in all other categories of exceptionality.

Garcia (1985) reports that the trend in service incidence for handicapped Hispanics over the past 10 years highlights two major phenomena: (a) the rise in LD enrollments has been accompanied by a parallel decline in placements in programs for the mildly mentally retarded (this observation was based on a study by Tucker, 1980); (b) approximately 80% of all handicapped Hispanics are served in two language-related categories: LD and speech handicapped (this was based on a study by Ortiz & Yates, 1983). Jones, Sacks, & Bennett (1985) used simultaneous comparisons to identify disproportionate racial representation in special education. Their research found Hispanic children overrepresented in classes for speech correction and educable mentally handicapped students in many of the local education agencies (LEAs) studies. However, in other LEAs, Hispanic children were underrepresented in classes for emotionally disturbed, neurologically impaired speech correction, perceptually impaired, and mentally handicapped.

Two studies from the U.S. General Accounting Office (USGAO, 1981a, 1981b) reported a major concern over the disproportionate number of minority children served in certain special education programs. One of these studies (1981a) showed that in 1978, 50% of the Asian American students in special education were classified as speech impaired. Almost half of the American Indian students in special education were in LD classes. Another study reported that in the Chicago Public Schools, Hispanic students, with 4.73% enrollment in special education programs, were "substantially underrepresented in special education overall" (Designs for Change, 1982, p. 16). The report, *Caught in the Web*, indicated that often Hispanics with learning difficulties remained in the bilingual education program without being referred; however, the "standard bilingual programs were not designed to deal with handicapped children" (p. 16). Factors such as insufficient staff and services, and the discouragement of referral for a special education evaluation, were blamed for the "...limited access to special education for Hispanic students..." (p. 16).

The true cause of disproportionate representation in special education is unknown (Maher & Bennett, 1984; USGAO, 1981a). According to Heller, Holtzman, and Messick (1982), the cause does not appear to be a single factor or source, but rather a combination and interaction of variables.

LIMITED-ENGLISH-PROFICIENT STUDENTS: ASSESSMENT

Longitudinal data and studies suggest that language minority children are often placed in special classes because of their limited proficiency in English and not as a result of being handicapped as defined by The Education for All Handicapped Children Act, P.L. 94–142 (Cummins, 1984; ISBE, 1984; USGAO, 1981a, 1981b). LEP students are individuals who have not acquired English language proficiency skills comparable to their English-monolingual peers. Federal and state regulations require that LEP students be evaluated in their native language, combination of languages, and language use patterns (ISBE, 1978; ISBE, 1985; The Education for All Handicapped Children Act, P.L. 94–142, 1975).

An example of discriminatory linguistic practices on the psychological evaluation is the case of *Diana v. California State Board of Education* (1970). The suit was filed on behalf of nine Mexican American students, ages 8–13, placed in classes for educable mentally handicapped students. The *Diana* plaintiffs charged that the testing procedures were prejudicial because the tests placed heavy emphasis on English verbal skills; the test questions were culturally biased; and tests were standardized on White, native-born Americans (Weintraub & Abeson, 1977). The *Diana* out-of-court settlement stipulated that LEP children be tested in English and in their own language.

In spite of P.L. 94–142 requirements and the *Diana* decision, research evidence suggests that LEP students are currently being misclassified due to the inability of educational personnel to recognize characteristics of second language acquisition, the influence of limited English proficiency on academic achievement, and the failure to provide bilingual case study evaluations (Ortiz, 1986).

A study from the Handicapped Minority Research Institute on Language Proficiency (Ortiz, 1986) revealed that assessment procedures used by districts for LEP students are essentially the same as those used for English monolingual students. Ortiz reported that though the most frequently cited reason for referral of LEP students was poor academic progress in general, "It is possible that more than half of all referrals were, in reality, related to students' limited English proficiency" (p. 1). Additionally, although all subjects were classified as LEP, language status was given little attention by assessment personnel or by placement committees. Ortiz reported that only 25% of students' folders contained evidence of current language testing. Moreover, very few students were tested in Spanish or bilingually.

Another study by Ortiz (1987), on communication disorders among LEP Hispanic students, indicates that data found in the students' eligibility folders were insufficient to determine whether the students were in the process of normal second language acquisition, or whether their speech and language behavior were symptomatic of a speech or language disorder.

Besides the numerous areas of concerns cited in the forementioned studies, of particular concern to the author is the issue of using the student's "language dominance" versus "language use patterns" to determine whether to conduct a bilingual case-study evaluation. P.L. 94–142 requires that state and local educational agencies ensure that test and evaluation materials be provided and administered in the child's native language, and, among other things, the child be assessed in all areas related to the suspected disability. New York, like many other states, uses the student's dominant language to determine the language to be used for assessment (The University of New York, 1982). An Illinois statute (ISBE, 1985) requires that a student's language-use patterns and English proficiency be determined before initiating a case study evaluation.

Language-use pattern is defined as (a) the language(s) spoken in the child's home and language(s) used most comfortably and frequently by the child and (b) the language or combination of languages which the child uses to conceptualize and communicate those conceptualizations. When the student's language-use patterns involve two or more languages, a child must be evaluated in each of his or her languages. The state education agency stresses that this total process is of particular importance to a student with a primary language other than English in order to ensure that assessment and test selection and administration are nondiscriminatory in nature. It is the author's opinion that using the concept of dominant language to determine which language to use for assessments discriminates against students from a nonEnglish background whose language-use patterns include two or more languages. Besides the reality of the instrument and/or procedure used to determine dominance, it is discriminatory to deny the student an equal opportunity to be evaluated in all areas of cognitive development and ability. Students whose language-use patterns include a language other than English should have a bilingual evaluation.

SCREENING AND REFERRAL

In order to qualify for federal special education funds, states must ensure that all handicapped children in need of special education and related services be identified and evaluated regardless of the severity of their disability (P.L. 94–142, 1975). The mandate to identify children for special education services led to the implementation of screening programs in schools across the country (Gracey, Azzara, & Reinherz, 1984).

A national survey by Gracey et al. (1984) reported that 33 states mandate some form of screening in the preschool or early school years. The authors indicated that in states where screening is required, information is collected from parents, teachers, other school personnel, and/or other adults (e.g., a nurse). The primary focus of the survey is the areas assessed. These are grouped into the following four domains:

1. Physical: motor, sensory, current health, health history, immunizations, dental.
2. Language: speech, language, bilingualism.
3. Cognitive: cognitive skills, learning, aptitude.
4. Behavioral: behavior, social and emotional functioning.

The authors reported that 22 states require screening in more than one domain; however, 11 states require comprehensive screening for all four domains. The only requirement in one state was to screen for "bilingualism."

Gracey et al. (1984) indicate that there is an ongoing amibiguity about the nature and function of screening. According to the authors, "This is reflected in a confusion of terms; in some cases, screening, assessment, evaluation, and identification are used interchangeably; in others, each has a distinct meaning" (p. 102). The authors define screening as a process of identifying, from among all children in a population, those possibly in need of special services. Based on the screening results, certain children are evaluated to determine whether a disability in fact exists and, if so, its nature and extent.

Graden, Casey, and Christenson (1985) state that current practices in special education can be characterized as inconsistent and problematic at each phase of the assessment and decision-making process. The problems cited are (a) the referral, (b) testing for identification/ classification, (c) decision making for an eligibility determination, and (d) program planning. White and Calhoun (1987) report that "the referral stage has been criticized for lacking sufficient safeguards for prevention of inappropriate referral and for introducing biasing effects that undermine appropriate program and placement decisions" (p. 460).

Ample research reports that the referral is the most important point in the special education placement process. A 5-year longitudinal study on LD students conducted by Ysseldyke et al. (1983) indicates that students are referred in increasing numbers, often inappropriately. Their study indicated that once referred, students are almost automatically tested, often with technically inadequate tests. Once tested, the majority of the students are placed in special education. A national study by Algozzine, Christenson, and Ysseldyke (1982) suggests that once a student is referred, there is a 92% probability the student will be tested. Additionally, 73% of those tested were subsequently placed in special education. Ysseldyke et al. (1983) reported that placement was often based on inconsistent and inherently problematic LD definitions and LD criteria. Another study (Ysseldyke & Algozzine, 1981) found that 51% of the decision makers pronounced "normal" students with average performance on achievement and intellectual measures as eligible for special placement.

A study by Foster, Ysseldyke, Casey, and Thurlow (1984) found that 72% of the students referred were placed in special education and most were placed in the category for which they were referred. It was also reported that referral rates varied with school district guidelines, perceived competence of the person who received the referral, kind of referral form, amount of paperwork, and teacher attitude and theoretical beliefs. The authors added that sociopolitical climate, external agency influences, federal and state guidelines, and parental pressure also influence the referral rates.

A longitudinal Canadian study (Cummins, 1984) of the reasons students from minority language backgrounds were referred for a psychological evaluation reported the following categories and percentages of referrals:

1. Academic (78%)
2. Behavior (12%)
3. Companionship (7%)
4. Home (1%)

The study concluded that there was a slightly greater likelihood for immigrant students to be referred for language and attendance (68% and 63% of referrals in these categories involved nonCanadian born students), whereas these students were less likely to be referred for special learning difficulties (41%) and speech or perceptual difficulties.

PREREFERRAL

Prereferral screening is a growing trend (Evans, 1976; Graden, Casey, & Bonstrom, 1985; Graden et al., 1985). Research suggests that prereferral screening reduces bias and idiosyncratic opinions and provides more relevant information. Prereferral screening is also reported as reducing erroneous classification during the referral-placement process.

Graden et al. (1985) developed and implemented a prereferral intervention system model which demonstrated many positive features. Their prereferral intervention system is based on an ecological model which views students' problems in the context of the classroom, teacher, instructional variables, and student variables. The authors report that prereferral intervention is in keeping with the least restrictive doctrine established by P.L. 94–142.

Archer and Edwards (1982) identified numerous student characteristics which are considered high-risk predictors. The authors suggest that the use of such high-risk predictors is helpful in the development of diagnostic and screening devices that identify children at risk of requiring special education. Some progress has already been made in that endeavor. For example, Ferguson, Davis, Evans, and Williams (1970) translated eight of the *Plowden Report's* criteria for the identification of educational priority areas into specific quantifiable measures. Additionally, data was gathered on the frequency of occurrence in schools serving various types of communities. Evans (1976) collected information thought to be associated with "educationally disadvantaged" students at risk. The data was gathered from a number of children at the time of their school entry. Two years later, this information was related to school achievement in an attempt to isolate valid predictors for such achievement. From their data, a screening profile was constructed.

Benavides (1983) identified and prioritized high-risk predictors which should be assessed prior to the referral of an LEP student for a case-study evaluation. The study found that educational high-risk predictors ranked higher than did the home-background high-risk predictors. The student's native language proficiency and amount of education were equally ranked as the highest priority. These were followed by academic history, English language proficiency, self-esteem, and physical and health problems.

All these efforts are of a preliminary nature and there is general agreement that much more is required. Of particular interest is the need to develop a simple prereferral screening instrument that provides essential information. Instruments that require home interviews and extensive psychometric assessments are useful; however, due to time constraints and other limitations, the use of such instruments is often impractical. Numerous sources stress the need for a simple and easily administered prereferral instrument that minimizes unwarranted referrals, costly evaluations, and inappropriate placement in special education.

In 1984, with assistance from the Illinois Bilingual Resource Center and the Illinois State Board of Education, a two-day prereferral symposium was conducted. Professionals from four large school districts (Waukegan, Evanston, Elgin, and Rockford) were invited to assist in the development of a prereferral screening instrument. The participants were bilingual and English monolingual special education teachers and administrators, principals, school psychologists, social workers, and other related services personnel serving LEP students. Based on the prototype prereferral instrument (Benavides, 1983) the participants recommended revisions of the instrument. In 1985 the instrument was further modified by the Chicago Public School Task Force. The Task Force formed to develop a procedure by which schools could determine whether a referred student was in need of a case-study evaluation and the language(s) to be used for administering the evaluations. The *Prereferral Screening Instrument* (PSI) is illustrated in Figure 1.

THE PREREFERRAL SCREENING INSTRUMENT

The PSI is divided into four sections:

1. *General Background*: Provides relevant general information about the student and reason(s) for referral.
2. *Educational Information*: Provides information on the history of school experiences, programs, and services.

FIGURE 1

Prereferral Screening Instrument (PSI)

I. GENERAL BACKGROUND

```
Student Name_____ID#_____Date_____
Birthdate_____Age_____Sex: F__ M__ School_____District_____
Birthplace: Father_____Mother_____Student_____
Language/s Other Than English_____Current Grade Placement_____
Current Education Program/s_____
Teacher's evaluation of student's language proficiency level: I, II,III,IV,V (circle one)
Bilingual Instructional Category_____Reasons/s for referral_____
_____

Have parents been notified  Yes___  No___      Translator required  Yes_____    No_____
Language/s students speaks with parents/guardian_____sibling_____friends_____
Language/s parent/guardian speaks to student_____
Migrant Student Record Transfer System  I.D. No._____
```

II. EDUCATIONAL BACKGROUND

```
SCHOOL EXPERIENCE:
. Country Outside U.S.
Age started school_____Terminated_____Restarted_____
Circle each grade completed outside the U.S.
       PreK   K   1   2   3   4   5   6   7   8   9   10   11   12
Retained: Yes__No__Grade/s_____Social Promotion/s Yes__No__Grade/s_____
Attendance:Good___Poor___Circle number of school/s attended  1   2   3   4   5   6   7   8

. United States
Age started school_____Terminated_____Restarted_____
Circle each grade completed in the U.S.   On the line below each grade
    write the number of days absent or NIA   (No Information Available)
       PreK   K   1   2   3   4   5   6   7   8   9   10   11   12
Days absent: ___  ___  ___  ___  ___  ___  ___  ___  ___  ___  ___  ___  ___  ___
Circle number of school/s attended:  1    2    3    4    5    6    7    8
Retained Yes__No__Grade/s_____ Social Promotion Grade/s Yes___No__Grade/s_____
```

HISTORY OF PROGRAM/S and services student has received. Use one line per program

Grade Placement (PreK-12)	General Program	Bilingual Program (Type)	ESL Only	Special Education Category	Pre-school Headstart	Other	Amount of time in program months/years

```
Completed by_____  Date_____
```

Continued

24

FIGURE 1 (Continued)

Prereferral Screening Instrument (PSI)

III. ACHIEVEMENT-BEHAVIORAL PROFILE

Rate the student on the following skills, comparing him/her with other students in his/her present classroom grade placement by marking a point on the rating scale for each skill. To compute the *Average Rating* for each of the areas below, divide the sum from each section (A, B, C, D, E) by the number of items in that section. To compute the *Total Profile*, divide the sums from the *Average Rating* by five.

RATING SCALE

Achievement - Behavioral Areas	Very Poor 1	Poor 2	Below Average 3	Average 4	Above Average 5	Very Good 6	Excellent 7	Progress Being Made Circle Yes or No
A. PSYCHOMOTOR SKILLS								
1. Gross Motor								Yes No
2. Fine Motor								Yes No
B. ACADEMIC SKILLS ENGLISH (L2)								
1. Oral Language								
a. Comprehension								Yes No
b. Expression								Yes No
2. Reading								Yes No
3. Written Language								Yes No
4. Mathematics								Yes No
a. Computation								Yes No
b. Problemsolving								Yes No
c. Concepts								Yes No
C. LANGUAGE OTHER THAN ENGLISH (L1) *								
1. Oral Language								
a. Comprehension								Yes No
b. Expression								Yes No
2. Reading								Yes No
3. Written Language								Yes No
4. Mathematics								
a. Computation								Yes No
b. Problemsolving								Yes No
c. Concepts								Yes No
D. SOCIAL EMOTIONAL								
1. Self-concept								Yes No
2. Peer Interactions								Yes No
3. Adult Interactions								Yes No
E. ADAPTIVE BEHAVIOR								
1. Works Independently								Yes No
2. Cooperates in Group								Yes No
3. Seeks Assistance Appropriately								Yes No
4. Uses Organizational Skills								Yes No
5. Stays on Task								Yes No
6. Shows Ability to Change Tasks								Yes No
7. Accepts Responsibility at School								Yes No
8. Follow School Rules								Yes No

Note: Section C (Language Other Than English) must be completed by a teacher bilingually endorsed in the students native language.

AVERAGE RATING: A. Psychomotor Skills_____ B. Academic Skills: L1_____ C. L2_____
D. Social-Emotional_____ E. Adaptive Behavior_____ Total Profile_____

(Name_____ ID #_____ Date_____)

IV. PREVIOUS TESTS: List assessments for any of the areas above (language proficiency, educational assessment, speech and language, etc.).

Date_____Test & language/s_____
Results_____
Date_____Test & language/s_____
Results_____
Date_____Test & language/s_____
Results_____

OTHER COMMENTS
_____
_____

Case-study evaluation recommended: Yes__No__   Bilingual evaluation recommended: Yes__No__
FORM COMPLETED BY_____TITLE_____DATE_____

3. *Achievement-Behavioral Profile*: Provides a visual profile of the student's psychomotor level, native and second language proficiency, academic skills, social-emotional condition, and adaptive behavior.

4. *Previous Tests and/or Screening*: Provides information on the assessments and tests administered, dates, and results.

It should be noted that because of the PSI's supplemental nature and space limitations, the medical and social-work information are not included on the instrument shown in Figure 1. This, however, is remedied by using the district's existing form and/or format to report the said information. It is essential for local education agencies to ensure that all the information gathered and used to complete the PSI be linguistically and culturally appropriate as required by state and federal statute.

The PSI was designed to create visual patterns which can facilitate the identification of information and high-risk variables which may account for or contribute to the reason/s for concern. Additionally, the PSI indicates whether bilingual evaluations are required. The PSI is completed prior to actually referring the student. It is essential to realize that once a student is referred, the 60-day time-limit clock begins ticking. Completion of the PSI does not require the administration of any assessments or evaluations. It does require that the assessment of the student's language(s) proficiency and all other relevant prereferral information be current. With the exception of information obtained from the parents or guardian, all the information required to complete the PSI is in the student's school records. The Migrant Student Record Transfer System ID number was included to facilitate obtaining information on migrant students.

COMPLETING THE PSI

To complete the PSI, start by completing the *General Background* section. It is advisable to obtain the student's "Language Use Patterns" information from the parents or guardian.

Next complete the section entitled *Educational Information*. First, complete the section related to the student's "School Experience." Use the student's records for this section. For migrant students, the MSRTS ID number is essential to obtain their records. If no information is available, write NIA for "no information available."

Complete the section entitled "History of Program/s" by listing all the programs and services the student received in each grade. Noting the amount of time (months/years) students received the programs/services is important. By circling the grades completed in the native country and the United States, and filling in information requested, the student's school experience is easier to visualize and interpret. Once all the programs/services are filled in, any academic or remedial voids are easily identified.

Complete the *Achievement-Behavioral Profile* section. The ratings of the student's skills should be based on teacher judgment and observation. As much as possible, the rating should be based on documented information. The student's skills are rated on a Lickert-type scale (very poor = 1 to excellent = 7). Once the rating scale points are established, the points are connected with a line. After the "Progress Being Made" column is completed, the PSI provides a visual profile of student strengths, behavior, limitations which may inhibit learning, language(s) proficiency (expressive, receptive, written, reading), and math. Simple calculations provided on the PSI for the ratings values from the various skills areas provide an "average" on each area and the student's total profile. Students with achievement and behavioral areas rated as 1 (very poor) or 2 (poor) should be considered as high risk for requiring a case study. However, the rating scale cutoff points are not the sole criteria for recommending a case study. All the information on the PSI must be considered before making a recommendation.

The completed PSI organizes information in such a way that the causes for concern often become apparent once the profile is completed. Though the PSI was originally developed for language minority students, it is designed to be used with all children. The intervention strategies to be used are also often easier to identify. The PSI is completed at the school by staff most familiar with the student and the person initiating the prereferral screening request. In implementing the PSI it is recommended that the school use a system such as the Teacher Assistance Team (TAT) model (Chalfant, 1980). The TAT team reviews the PSI and makes recommendations on the student's need and disposition of the PSI case. The TAT system resembles a multidisciplinary staffing conference; however, for those students not recommended for a case study evaluation, the TAT then assists the student's teacher with the problems which caused the request for prereferral screening.

INTERPRETATION OF THE PSI

To operationalize the PSI, a sample case was developed and is illustrated in Figure 2. Prior to discussing and interpreting the sample PSI case (Figure 2), carefully review the case. Should the student be recommended for a bilingual case-study evaluation? Would you refer for a case-study evaluation and would it be bilingual? Why?

In the sample case, notice that although the student is not currently in a bilingual program and speaks English, the language use pattern includes English and Spanish, hence, any required evaluation would need to be bilingual. Traditionally, students described in this sample case are not provided with appropriate bilingual evaluations because the schools mistakenly believe that they do not require bilingual evaluations because the student "speaks English" and/or is "English dominant."

In the Education Background Section observe the student's academic history. The student's education was all in the United States and uninterpreted as is often the case with migrant students. Observe that although the student was not in a bilingual program in kindergarten, bilingual pull-out (resource-room) service was provided for a year and 4 months in first and second grades. Hence, we "assume" the student was given an appropriate transitional bilingual education program and was exited from the program because he was English proficient. Also observe that the student repeated fifth grade. Also notice the increase of school absenteeism, especially after repeating fifth grade. As you review the PSI, high-risk items (e.g., absenteeism, repeating) begin to spring up like little red flags. It is these flags which give a good indication of whether or not to refer.

In the Academic and Behavioral Section, the pattern formed by the rating scale format provides an immediate "visual profile" of the student. Skills rating to the left side of rating scale as shown on the sample indicate below average skills. A review of the low score average (2.75) at the bottom of the scale will also give you a good indication that this case is high-risk. The student's skill in English is higher than in Spanish (2.8 vs 1.4). This information is also relevant for the IEP recommendation on language usage for instruction and amount of time. It is important to remember that not all students who receive a bilingual case-study evaluation will require bilingual instructional services. The purpose for using a bilingual approach for an evaluation is different from that of a transitional bilingual education program. Simply put, one is required to assure a nondiscriminatory evaluation, and the other is for classroom instruction.

All indications are that this case should definitely be referred for a bilingual Case Study Evaluation. Had the student not received bilingual services and skills in the native language had been skewed to the above or above-average side of the rating scale, we would question whether the problem was a result in second acquisition and inappropriate exit criteria and not because of a handicapping condition. If there are any indicators of a handicapping condition, they will appear both in English and the native language. A discrepancy in this guideline generally means an inappropriate referral for a Case Study Evaluation. However, it is essential to remember that although it may be an inappropriate referral, the student was referred because of perceived problems. In such cases, it is the TAT's responsibility to identify the problem and make appropriate recommendations. To return the student to the referring teacher without recommendations and follow-up resources is to put the student's educational progress at risk.

FIGURE 2

Prereferral Screening Instrument (PSI) Sample Case

I. GENERAL BACKGROUND

Student Name __B_____ ID#_____ Date_____
Birthdate_____ Age _13_ Sex: F __ M _✓_ School_____ District_____
Birthplace: Father _Puerto Rico_____ Mother _Chicago___ Student _Chicago___
Language/s Other Than English _Spanish___ Current Grade Placement __7th__
Current Education Program/s _General Program_____
Teacher's evaluation of student's language proficiency level: I, II,III,IV,V (circle one)
Bilingual Instructional Category_____ Reasons/s for referral _Poor academic_
progress; attention, behavior, and reading problems
Have parents been notified ? Yes___ No _✓_ Translator required Yes___ No _✓_
Language/s students speaks with parents/guardian_Eng/Span_sibling _Eng._ friends_Eng/Span_
Language/s parent/guardian speaks to student _Eng/Span_____
Migrant Student Record Transfer System I.D. No._____

II. EDUCATIONAL BACKGROUND

SCHOOL EXPERIENCE:
. Country Outside U.S.
Age started school___5_____ Terminated_____ Restarted_____
Circle each grade completed outside the U.S.
    PreK K 1 2 3 4 5 6 7 8 9 10 11 12
Retained: Yes__No__Grade/s_____ Social Promotion/s Yes__No__Grade/s_____
Attendance:Good__ Poor__ Circle number of school/s attended 1 2 3 4 5 6 7 8

. United States
Age started school_____ Terminated_____ Restarted_____
Circle each grade completed in the U.S. On the line below each grade
    write the number of days absent or NIA (No Information Available)
    PreK (K) (1) (2) (3) (4) (5)R (6) (7) 8 9 10 11 12
Days absent: ___ _2_ _4_ _5_ _10_ _22_ _30_ _36_ _32_ ___ ___ ___ ___
Circle number of school/s attended: 1 2 3 (4) 5 6 7 8
Retained Yes_✓_No__Grade/s _5th_ Social Promotion Grade/s Yes__ No_✓_Grade/s__

HISTORY OF PROGRAM/S and services student has received. Use one line per program

Grade Placement (PreK-12)	General Program	Bilingual Program (Type)	ESL Only	Special Education Category	Pre-school Headstart	Other	Amount of time in program months/years
K	✓						1 yr
1	✓						1 yr
1		Pull-Out					4 mos
2	✓						1 yr
2		Pull-Out					1 yr
3	✓						1 yr
4	✓						1 yr
5	✓						1 yr
5 Retained	✓						
6	✓					Social Worker	1 yr
7	✓						6 mos

Completed by_____ Date_____

Continued

FIGURE 2 (Continued)

Prereferral Screening Instrument (PSI) Sample Case

III. ACHIEVEMENT-BEHAVIORAL PROFILE

Rate the student on the following skills, comparing him/her with other students in his/her present classroom grade placement by marking a point on the rating scale for each skill. To compute the *Average Rating* for each of the areas below, divide the sum from each section (A, B, C, D, E) by the number of items in that section. To compute the *Total Profile*, divide the sums from the *Average Rating* by five.

RATING SCALE

Achievement - Behavioral Areas	Very Poor 1	Poor 2	Below Average 3	Average 4	Above Average 5	Very Good 6	Excellent 7	Progress Being Made Circle Yes or No
A. PSYCHOMOTOR SKILLS								
1. Gross Motor					●			(Yes) No
2. Fine Motor						●		(Yes) No
B. ACADEMIC SKILLS ENGLISH (L2)								
1. Oral Language								
a. Comprehension		●						Yes No
b. Expression			●					Yes No
2. Reading		●						Yes No
3. Written Language		●						Yes No
4. Mathematics								Yes No
a. Computation			●					Yes No
b. Problemsolving		●						Yes No
c. Concepts		●						Yes No
C. LANGUAGE OTHER THAN ENGLISH (L1) *								
1. Oral Language								
a. Comprehension		●						Yes No
b. Expression		●						Yes No
2. Reading	●							Yes No
3. Written Language	●							Yes No
4. Mathematics								
a. Computation			●					Yes No
b. Problemsolving		●						Yes No
c. Concepts	●							Yes No
D. SOCIAL EMOTIONAL								
1. Self-concept			●					Yes No
2. Peer Interactions		●						Yes No
3. Adult Interactions		●						Yes No
E. ADAPTIVE BEHAVIOR								
1. Works Independently			●					Yes No
2. Cooperates in Group		●						Yes No
3. Seeks Assistance Appropriately		●						Yes No
4. Uses Organizational Skills		●						Yes No
5. Stays on Task		●						Yes No
6. Shows Ability to Change Tasks			●					Yes No
7. Accepts Responsibility at School			●					Yes No
8. Follow School Rules		●						Yes No

Note: Section C (Language Other Than English) must be completed by a teacher bilingually endorsed in the students native language.

AVERAGE RATING: A. Psychomotor Skills _5.5_   B. Academic Skills: L1 _1.42_   C. L2 _2.28_
D. Social-Emotional _2.3_   E. Adaptive Behavior _2.25_   Total Profile _2.75_

IV. PREVIOUS TESTS:

List assessments for any of the areas above (language proficiency, educational assessment, speech and language, etc.).

Date_____ Test & language/s _Lang. Asses. Scales (LAS) Eng 4 + Span 2_
Results_____
Date_____ Test & language/s _____
Results_____
Date_____ Test & language/s _____
Results_____

OTHER COMMENTS

_____
_____

Case-study evaluation recommended: Yes__ No__   Bilingual evaluation recommended: Yes__ No__
FORM COMPLETED BY_____ TITLE_____ DATE_____

29

SUMMARY

Using a prereferral system is the least restrictive means of gathering data about student performance without the traditional and costly case study evaluation. Student information can be continuously gathered by using various intervention strategies intended to ameliorate the areas of concern. Should the intervention prove unsuccessful, the case study evaluation team and multidisciplinary staffing conference participants will have relevant data on which to base their recommendations.

Prereferral screening and intervention addresses concerns about the costly and often stigmatizing placement into special education. Resources, traditionally used to evaluate and place students in special education, are redirected towards assisting teachers in the general classroom. Inappropriate referrals and placement in special education will be minimized. Additionally, the potential cost-saving factor of reduced referrals, evaluations, and placement in special education should be an incentive for LEAs. In considering the findings of Ysseldyke and Algozzine (1981), the 51% of "normal" students who were made eligible for special education translates into a huge waste of money. More important even than money is the human factor of students in need of help. Making sure they receive appropriate services must continue to be our major goal.

REFERENCES

Algozzine, B., Christenson, S., & Ysseldyke, J. E. (1982). Probabilities associated with the referral to placement process. *Teaching Education and Special Education, 5*(3), 19–23.

Archer, P., & Edwards, J. R. (1982). Predicting school achievement from data on pupils obtained from teachers: Towards a screening device for disadvantaged. *Journal of Education Psychology, 74,* 761–770.

Benavides, A. (1983). *Prereferral assessment of high-risk predictors for limited English proficient students.* Unpublished research study. Southern Illinois University at Carbondale.

Benavides, A. (1985). High-risk predictors and prereferral screening for language minority students. In M. B. Kaskin (Ed.), *Best practices in special education assessment* (pp.56–83). Forest Park South, IL: Governor's State University.

Brown G. H., Rosen, H. L., & Hill, T. S. (1980). *The condition of education for Hispanic America.* Washington, DC: National Center for Education Statistics, U.S. Government Printing Office.

Chalfant, J. C. (1980). *A teacher assistance model: Inservice training for teachers and administrators.* Final Report: Grant No. G007801745. Washington, DC: U.S. Department of Education, Bureau of Education for the Handicapped.

Cummins, J. (1980). The entry and exit fallacy in bilingual education. *NABE Journal,* 4, 25–60.

Cummins, J. (1981). The role of primary language development in promoting educational success for language minority students. In California State Department of Education (Ed.), *Schooling and language minority students: A theoretical framework.* Los Angeles: Evaluation, Dissemination and Assessment Center.

Cummins, J. (1984). *Bilingualism and special education: Issues in assessment and pedagogy.* Clevedon, England: Multilingual Matters Ltd.

Designs for Change. (1982). *Caught in the web. Misplaced children in Chicago's classes for the mentally retarded.* Chicago: Author.

Diana v. California State Board of Education (1970). C–70–37 RFP (District Court of Northern California).

The Education for All Handicapped Children Act, P.L. 94–142. (1975). Reston, VA: The Council for Exceptional Children.

Evans, R. (1976). The prediction of educational handicapped: A longitudinal study. *Educational Research, 19*(1), 56–68.

Ferguson, N., Davis, T., Evans, R., & Williams, P., (1970). The Plowden Reports. Recommendations for identifying children in need of extra help. *Educational Research, 13,* 210–213.

Finn, J. D. (1982). Patterns in special education placement as revealed by the OCR surveys. In K. A. Heller, W. H. Holtzman, & S. Messick (Eds.), *Placing children in special education: A strategy for equity.* Washington, DC: National Academy Press.

Foster, G. G., Ysseldyke, J. E., Casey, A., & Thurlow, M. L. (1984). The congruence between reasons for referral and placement outcome. *Journal of Psychoeducational Assessment, 2*, 209–217.

Garcia, S. B. (1985). Characteristics of limited English proficient Hispanic students served in programs for the learning disabled: Implications for policy, practice, and research (Part I). *Bilingual Special Education Newsletter, IV*(1), pps. 3–6. Austin: The University of Texas.

Gracey, C. A., Azzara, C. V., & Reinherz, H., (1984). Screening revisited: A survey of U.S. requirements. *The Journal of Special Education, 18*(2), 101–107.

Graden, J. L., Casey, A., & Bonstrom, O. (1985). Implementing a prereferral intervention system: Part II. The data. *Exceptional Children, 51*, 487–496.

Graden, J. L., Casey, A., & Christenson, S. L. (1985). Implementing a prereferral intervention system: Part I. The model. *Exceptional Children, 51*, 377–387.

Heller, K. A., Holtzman, W. H., & Messick, S. (1982). *Placing children in special education: A strategy for equity.* Washington, DC: National Academy Press.

ISBE. (1978). *Illinois rules and regulations for transitional bilingual education.* Springfield, IL: Illinois State Board of Education.

ISBE. (1984). *Focus on reform: State action to improve schooling in Illinois.* Springfield, IL: Illinois State Board of Education.

ISBE. (1985). Procedural safeguards, case study evaluation and placement of limited English and non-English speaking students in special education. Department of Specialized Educational Services. *Administrative Bulletin*, DSES Bulletin #14, Dec. 30. Springfield, IL: Ill. St. Board of Education.

Jones, D, H., Sacks, J., & Bennett, R. E. (1985). A screening method for identifying racial overrepresentation in special education placement. *Ed. Evaluation and Policy Analysis, 7*(1), 19–34.

Maheady, L., Algozzine, B., & Ysseldyke, J. E. (1984). Minority overrepresentation in special education: A functional assessment perspective. *Special Services in the Schools, 1*(2), 5–19.

Maher, C. A., & Bennett, R. E. (1984). *Planning and evaluating special education services.* Englewood Cliffs, NJ: Prentice-Hall.

Melesky, T. J. (1985). Identifying and providing for the Hispanic gifted child. *NABE Journal, 9*(3), 43–56.

Ortiz, A. A. (1986). Characteristics of limited English proficient Hispanic students served in programs of the learning disabled: Implications for policy and practice (Part II). *Bilingual Special Education Newsletter, IV*(1), pps. 3–5. Austin: The University of Texas.

Ortiz, A. A. (1987). Communication disorders among limited English proficient Hispanic students. *Bilingual Special Education Newsletter, V*(1), pps. 3–5, 7–8. Austin: The University of Texas.

Ortiz, A. A., & Yates, J. R. (1983). *Incidence of exceptionality among Hispanics: Implications for manpower planning.* Journal of the National Association of Bilingual Education, 7(3), 41–53.

Tucker, J. A. (1980). Ethnic proportion in classes for the learning disabled: Issue in nonbiased assessment. *Journal of Special Education, 14*, 93–105.

The University of New York. (1982). *IEP performance levels and individual needs.* Albany, NY: The State Department of Education.

USGAO. (1981a). *Disparities still exist in who gets special education. Report to the Chairmen, Subcommittee on Selected Education, Committee on Education and Labor, House of Representatives of the United States.* Washington, DC: U.S. General Accounting Office.

USGAO. (1981b). *Unanswered questions on educating handicapped children in local public schools. Report to the Congress of the United States.* Washington, DC: U.S. General Accounting Office.

Weintraub, F. J., & Abeson, A. (1977). New education policies for the handicapped: The quiet revolution. In R. E. Schmid, J. Moneypenny, & R. Johnson (Eds.), *Contemporary issues in special education* (pp. 40–49). New York: McGraw-Hill Book Co.

White, R., & Calhoun, M. L. (1987). From referral to placement: Teachers' perception of their responsibilities. *Exceptional Children, 53*, 460–468.

Ysseldyke, J. E., & Algozzine, B. (1981). Diagnostic classification decisions as a function of referral information. *Journal of Special Education, 15*, 429–435.

Ysseldyke, J. E., Thurlow, M., Graden J., Wesson, C., Algozzine, B., & Dino, S. (1983). Generalizations from five years of research on assessment and decision-making. The University of Minnesota Institute. *Exceptional Education Quarterly, 4*, 75–93.

CHAPTER 4

Language Assessment of Hispanic Learning Disabled and Speech and Language Handicapped Students: Research in Progress

Alba A. Ortiz
Eleoussa Polyzoi

Current research (Holtzman, Ortiz, & Wilkinson, 1986; Ortiz et al. 1985; Ortiz, Garcia, Wheeler, & Maldonado-Colon, 1986) suggests that accurately identifying handicapping conditions among limited-English-proficient students is difficult. Available assessment procedures and existing procedural safeguards do not appear to provide diagnosticians and speech and language therapists adequate information to distinguish characteristics of second language learners from those of handicapped students. This lack of appropriate assessment data, particularly regarding students' native language and English language proficiency, may lead to inaccurate placement of limited-English-proficient children in special education.

This article examines issues involved in the *assessment of language skills* of culturally and linguistically different students who are referred for special education, and it explores the use of pragmatic criteria for distinguishing a "true" handicapping condition from a language difference among limited-English-proficient (LEP) students. The discussion of issues dealing with the special education referral of LEP students suspected of having learning disabilities or speech and language disorders is followed by a brief description of an ongoing 3–year longitudinal study which attempts to address some of these issues through empirical means. This study, conducted by the Handicapped Minority Research Institute on Language Proficiency at The University of Texas at Austin, focuses on language assessment procedures which can be used to evaluate LEP Hispanic students suspected of being either communication disordered or learning disabled. The major purpose of this research is to identify the best techniques, or combination of techniques, which effectively distinguish between LEP students who are truly handicapped and those who are merely exhibiting characteristics of normal second language acquisition. Of specific interest is whether the use of pragmatic criteria is a better alternative than the use of standardized language assessment instruments for distinguishing normal from abnormal language acquisition among language minority students.

INCIDENCE OF HANDICAPPING CONDITIONS AMONG HISPANICS

Patterns of representation of minority children in special education programs have received increasing attention in the literature (Dew, 1984; Manni, Winikur, & Keller, 1980; Mercer, 1976; Ortiz & Yates, 1983; Tucker, 1980). Examination of placement trends has raised concerns regarding the accuracy of the diagnostic process in placing language minorities in special education and the effectiveness of intervention programs selected to provide these students with appropriate educational opportunities.

In 1978, 74% of Hispanic students in special education were in programs for the learning disabled (44%) or the speech/language impaired (30%) (U.S. GAO, 1981). In Texas, Ortiz and Yates (1983) found that representation of Hispanics in speech and language therapy was below national estimates of prevalence (2.4% as opposed to 3.2%) but that there was a serious overrepresentation of Hispanic students in LD programs. Ortiz and Yates indicated that while procedural safeguards were found in policy, legislation, and judicial decisions, there was a lack of guidelines to effectively implement these safeguards and a lack of bilingual assessment personnel and appropriate instruments and procedures to ensure accurate identification of handicapping conditions.

While both national and state incidence figures of handicapping conditions for ethnic/racial groups are available, the prevalence of exceptionality among limited-English-proficient students is more difficult to determine. No national prevalence studies are currently available for this population. Similarly, state education agencies and local school districts typically do not report special education enrollments by students' language proficiency level. However, since the number of language minority students is dramatically increasing, with Hispanics constituting the largest segment of this population, educators need to understand better the interaction of language proficiency and handicapping conditions (Ortiz & Yates, 1983).

ISSUES RELATED TO LANGUAGE ASSESSMENT

Language minority children are frequently referred to special education on the basis of behaviors which do not fit the expectations of educators and are placed, not because they are handicapped, but because placement committees erroneously interpret linguistic, cultural, economic, or other background characteristics as deviant (Ortiz & Yates, 1983; 1984). For example, the literature documents characteristics of second language learners and suggests that the processes involved in learning a second language are very similar to those involved in native language acquisition (Celce-Murcia, 1978; Dulay, Burt, & Krashen, 1982; Krashen, 1982; Oller, 1983). There is also evidence to suggest that many of the characteristics of children normally acquiring a second language are similar to behaviors considered symptomatic of language or learning disabilities (Damico, Oller, & Storey, 1983; Mattes & Omark, 1984; Ortiz & Maldonando-Colon, 1986). Behaviors such as poor comprehension, limited vocabulary, or grammatical and syntactical errors may signify handicapping conditions for some students but, for others, reflect a lack of English proficiency.

It is possible, then, that special education referrals result from teachers' lack of understanding of how children acquire English as a second language. Teachers' perceptions that children are handicapped are confirmed when speech pathologists and diagnosticians rely on assessment procedures that focus on students' mastery of surface structures of language (e.g., tests of phonology, syntax, grammar, etc.), rather than on their ability to understand and communicate meaning (e.g., pragmatic criteria). While one could argue that Hispanic students profit from the individualized instruction provided by specially trained teachers and therapists, the placement of normal, as opposed to handicapped, students in special education decreases the effectiveness of appraisal and instructional personnel available to serve the truly handicapped.

Native Language Assessment

Analysis of speech and language characteristics is problematic when the child is limited-English-proficient. It is difficult to determine, for example, whether the child distorts or omits certain features of English syntax because of an articulation disorder or whether the error is developmental in nature and indicates that the student is in the process of normal second language acquisition (Damico, Oller, & Storey, 1983). Since speech and language disorders affect common language processes which underlie different surface structures of the languages spoken by the child (Cummins, 1982; 1984), it is not possible for a bilingual child to have a language disorder in one language and not in the other (Juarez, 1983; Ortiz, 1984). This suggests that diagnostic criteria must include evidence that the disorder occurs in the native language, not only in English.

In a similar vein, a learning disability occurs because of some type of abnormal cognitive process or deficit; if this deficit is demonstrated in English, it must also be evident in the native language. For LD students, it is important to assess literacy-related aspects of language proficiency in addition to the assessment of interpersonal communication skills. It is critical, for example, to determine whether the LEP student has adequate language proficiency to profit from academic instruction delivered solely in English. Cummins (1984) suggests that many LEP students are placed in special education because educators fail to distinguish between basic interpersonal communication skills and academic language proficiency. On the surface, the child appears to speak effectively with his/her peers but has not developed sufficient levels of academic language proficiency to achieve success in a monolingual English classroom.

Traditional Language Assessment Approaches

According to Damico (1985), the tests most frequently used by special education appraisal personnel to identify speech and language disorders or handicapping conditions are not sensitive to functional aspects of language because of their emphasis on correctness of linguistic structures. He summarizes the major problems with traditionally used tests of discrete language skills (e.g., measures of vocabulary or phonology) as follows:

1. Traditional assessment instruments are based on the assumption that language can be separated into various components (i.e., phonology, morphology, syntax, grammar, and vocabulary) and that these components can be isolated and assessed independently.

2. Traditional approaches tend to give more weight to syntax because mastery of syntactical structures is considered to be the best indicator of increasing linguistic proficiency (Dulay, Hernandez-Chavez, & Burt, 1978). The influence of variables such as speaker, intent, and context are virtually ignored.

3. The popularity of discrete point tests may be that they produce scores to describe language performance, a characteristic particularly attractive to assessment personnel charged with demonstrating that children meet eligibility criteria for special education placement. Comparing performance against cut-off scores for eligibility simplifies decision-making processes. However, high error rates on discrete point tests may inaccurately be attributed to a handicapping condition and may result in the placement of second language learners in special education programs.

4. A key characteristic of traditional assessment instruments is that they are norm referenced. An individual child's performance can be compared to that of a particular chronological age or peer group. This creates some problems, however, for older students because the majority of available assessment instruments are normed on younger children. For older students, norms reflect acquired knowledge or academic abilities rather than oral language skills. Consequently, students are more likely to be classified as learning disabled and interventions developed without adequate understanding of more basic language needs.

5. Norm referenced tests offer the advantage of standardized testing procedures which allow comparison of an individual's performance with peers over time, in various testing situations, and with different examiners. In the case of language testing, however, standardized procedures can introduce a tremendous amount of artificiality in communication (Leonard, Prutting, Perozzi, & Berkley, cited in Damico, 1985). This probably explains the discrepancies which are common when skills measured by instruments and those observed in spontaneous conversation are compared.

The most serious criticism of traditional language assessment instruments is that they do not accurately represent spontaneous communication. Because language consists of some aspect of *content* or meaning that is coded or represented by linguistic *form* for some purpose or *use* in a particular environment (Bloom & Lahey, 1978), the initial focus in language assessment should be on how these three components *interact*. Focusing on this interaction results in linguistic description rather than on quantification of correct or incorrect responses and is, consequently, more descriptive of a child's performance in natural communication.

ASSESSMENT OF PRAGMATIC SKILLS

There has been a recent shift in the area of language assessment to a greater emphasis on evaluation of pragmatic skills. Damico (1985) recommends the use of procedures which allow analysis of language data holistically and which sample communication interactions rather than responses on tests of mastery of surface structures of the language. He developed a procedure, Clinical Discourse Analysis, which incorporates clinical observation and analysis of data obtained from conversation samples to identify behavior patterns that interfere with interpersonal communication. He uses pragmatic criteria which include, for example, linguistic nonfluencies, nonspecific vocabulary, poor topic maintenance, and inappropriate responses.

Damico and Oller (1980) conducted a study which indicated that pragmatic criteria were effective in aiding teachers to accurately identify language disordered students. Teachers using these criteria referred significantly more children for testing, but the accuracy of their referrals was significantly greater, as indicated by the number of children ultimately judged by speech pathologists to be eligible for speech and language therapy. In a second study, Damico, Oller, and Storey (1983) used the same behaviors (pragmatic and discrete point) as predictors of language-based academic problems in Spanish-English bilingual children. The results again indicated that the inclusion of pragmatic and discrete-point behaviors together resulted in a more effective index of language/learning difficulties as measured by academic and social progress over one academic year.

A LONGITUDINAL STUDY OF LANGUAGE ASSESSMENT OF HANDICAPPED LEP HISPANIC STUDENTS

In October 1983, the Department of Special Education, College of Education, at The University of Texas at Austin established a Handicapped Minority Research Institute on Language Proficiency (HMRI) to conduct research specific to exceptional limited-English-proficient (LEP) and bilingual students (English/Spanish). The Institute, funded for a 5–year period by the United State Department of Education, Office of Special Education and Rehabilitative Services, is exploring the interaction of language proficiency and handicapping conditions, with a focus on Hispanic students who are learning disabled, and/or communication disordered.

The Handicapped Minority Research Institute is currently conducting a 3–year longitudinal study of oral language assessment for Hispanic LEP kindergarten students who have been classified as either speech and language handicapped (SLH) or learning disabled (LD). The primary focus of this research is to explore the relationship among various measures of English and Spanish oral language proficiency (global, pragmatic, and discrete) to special education placement decisions made by educators for SLH and LD limited-English-proficient students. Of secondary interest is the relationship of each of these measures to student achievement in the English and Spanish languages.

Subjects

The study involves a sample of 120 handicapped and nonhandicapped Hispanic LEP kindergarten students, with 30 in each of four categories: (a) speech and language handicapped, (b) learning disabled, (c) nonhandicapped achievers, and (d) nonhandicapped underachievers. Sites for data collection include two Texas school districts with bilingual and special education programs, with concentrations of Hispanic students (over 50%), and with relatively large student enrollment (33,000 for one school district; over 50,000 for the other school district). Identification of speech and language handicapped students and learning disabled students was based on each district's assessment and placement of LEP students in their respective classification. Identification of "achieving" and "underachieving" students was based on teachers' sorting of their LEP students according to those who had/had not mastered 80% of their instructional objectives, or the state-mandated "essential elements" for kindergarten. Teachers were directed to make their judgements based on students' mastery of language arts, mathematics, science, and social studies objectives in English and/or Spanish.

Instrumentation

Language assessment procedures used include the pragmatic and surface structure analyses of elicited English and Spanish conversation samples; measures of overall English and Spanish language proficiency using the Language Assessment Scales (LAS) (De Avila & Duncan, 1981); and various measures of discrete surface structures such as phonology, vocabulary, and grammar, which are **commonly used by local school districts** to assess students referred to special education. Academic achievement, as measured by the Woodcock-Johnson Psycho-Educational Battery (English) and the Bateria Woodcock Psico-Educativa en Espanol (Spanish), was also assessed.

Language Samples. Two 30–minute language samples (one in English and one in Spanish) were elicited by trained bilingual interviewers in natural conversations with each child. Two separate 15–minute conversations constituted the sample for each language. Tapes of these conversations were transcribed and subsequently segmented into utterances, using procedures adapted from Barrie-Blackey, Musselwhite and Rogister (1978). Approximately 180 utterances in each language were then analyzed using the pragmatic criteria outlined by Damico, Oller, and Storey, 1983 (see Figure 1). A second set of analyses was also conducted on these same samples to determine the child's mastery of certain morpho/syntactic surface structures. The Developmental Sentence Score (DSS) classification system developed by Lee (1974) was used for analysis of the English samples and the Developmental Assessment of Spanish Grammar (DASG), an adapted DSS classification system developed by Toronto (1976), was used for the Spanish samples. These instruments provide procedures to analyze complete, simple to complex sentences utilizing a sample of 50 utterances. The DSS was normed on 200 English-speaking children in the Illinois area, between the ages of 2–0 and 6–11 years. The DASG was standardized on 128 Mexican-American and Puerto Rican Spanish-speaking children between the ages of 3–0 and 6–11 years in Chicago.

Language Assessment Scales (LAS). Fall and Spring LAS (English and Spanish) test scores were obtained for each student from school records. The LAS (DeAvila & Duncan, 1981) is an individually administered, standardized, global oral proficiency measure composed of five subtests: minimal pairs, lexical, phonemes, sentence comprehension, and oral production. Parallel forms of the test in English and Spanish allow for the comparison of students' proficiency in the two languages, both at the discrete level (auditory discrimination, articulation, vocabulary production, and sentence comprehension) and the integrative level (story retelling). In addition, the subtest raw scores are weighted and then added to produce a total score and overall level of proficiency in each language.

Test of Language Development-Primary (TOLD-P). The Test of Language Development-Primary (Newcomer & Hammill, 1982), is an individually administered English test, designed

FIGURE 1

Pragmatic Criteria (Damico, Oller, & Storey, 1983) Used in the Analysis of the HMRI Language Samples

1. *Revisions:* Is the child's speech constantly disrupted by numerous false starts or self-interruptions?
    Example:
    E[a]: "How big is your little brother?"
    C[b]: "He's about half...he comes...he's here on me." (points to shoulder)

2. *Linguistic Nonfluencies:* Is the child's speech characterized by a disproportionately high number of repetitions, pauses, or hesitations?
    Example:
    C: "Sh...She...She comes...She comes at dinner time."

3. *Delays Before Responding:* Is the child's speech characterized by pauses of inordinate length?
    Example:
    E: "And what did you do then?"
    C: "...(pauses approximately 3 seconds) We played tag."

4. *Nonspecific Vocabulary:* Does the child make frequent use of expressions such as "it," "thing," "stuff," "this/that," etc., when the listener has no way of knowing what is being referred to?
    Example:
    E: "So, did you help them move?"
    C: "Yeah...but they were mad cuz I drop it."
    E: "Oh? What did you drop?"
    C: "That thing of Rosa's."

5. *Inappropriate Responses:* Does the child have trouble attending to the examiner's prompts or probes and continue to respond inappropriately?
    Example:
    E: "How do you like school?"
    C: "I don't know him yet."

6. *Poor Topic Maintenance:* Does the child tend to keep changing the topic without providing transitional clues to the examiner?
    Example:
    C: "I went to bed at 6:30."
    E: "That early? You must have had a hard day."
    C: "Yeah."
    E: "What made it such a hard day?"
    C: "The raking. Our teacher said, whoever wins in checkers—I won—goes to McDonalds."

7. *Need for Repetition:* Does the child constantly ask the examiner to repeat questions or information due to a lack of comprehension?
    Example:
    E: "What did the boy do then?"
    C: "..."
    E: "What did the little boy do?"
    C: "Wh...What?"
    E: "What did the little boy do after he saw the bunny rabbit?"

[a]E = Examiner
[b]C = Child

for children aged 4–0 to 8–11 years. The TOLD-P consists of five principal and two supplemental subtests, each of which taps a different component of children's receptive and expressive language abilities. Included are subtests which measure the child's understanding and meaningful use of spoken words, knowledge of differing aspects of grammar, and ability to say words correctly and to distinguish between words that sound the same or different. Results of TOLD-P subtests reveal strengths, weaknesses, and irregularities in specific areas of language development. The TOLD-P was standardized on 1,836 children from 19 states including Texas and one Canadian province.

Test of Auditory Comprehension of Language (TACL): English/Spanish. The Test for Auditory Comprehension of Language (TACL) (Carrow-Woolfolk, 1973) is an individually administered test appropriate for children aged 3–0 to 9–11 years. This test instrument permits the assessment of oral language comprehension without requiring language expression from the child. It measures auditory comprehension of word classes and relations, grammatical morphemes, and elaborated sentence constructions. Although the TACL-R was nationally standardized on 1,003 subjects representing the U.S. population according to age, sex, race, and geographic region, the older version was standardized on only 159 children, aged 2–10 through 7–9 years. A Spanish translation of the TACL exists, but no norms are available. The older version of the TACL (versus TACL-R) was used in the current study because of the availability of a Spanish version of this test. No Spanish version of the TACL-R exists.

Peabody Picture Vocabulary Test-Revised (PPVT-R)/Test de Vocabulario en Imagenes Peabody (TVIP). The Peabody Picture Vocabulary Test-Revised (Dunn & Dunn, 1981) is an individually administered measure of receptive vocabulary designed for children aged 2 1/2 years to adult. When presented with four possible pictorial responses, the child points to the picture that best describes the verbal stimulus. Versions of the test in both English and Spanish are available. Standardization for the PPVT-R was based on a nationally representative sample of children and adolescents, aged 2 1/2 through 18 years, and a sample of adults, aged 19 through 40 years. The Spanish version of the test (TVIP; Dunn, Padilla, Lugo, & Dunn, 1986) was standardized *separately* in Mexico and Puerto Rico. In Mexico, 1,219 preschool, elementary, and high school children, aged 2–6 to 5–11 years, were tested. In Puerto Rico, 1,462 children aged 2–6 to 17–11 years, selected from public and private schools, homes, and nursery schools were tested. Both Mexican and Puerto Rican groups were stratified by age and sex.

Woodcock-Johnson Psycho-Educational Battery/Bateria Woodcock Psico-Educativa En Espanol (Achievement subtests only). The Woodcock-Johnson Psycho-Educational Battery (Woodcock & Johnson, 1977) is an individually administered test designed for children aged 4 years to adult. Achievement subtests used in the current study measure skills needed in the areas of reading, mathematics, and written language. The Woodcock-Johnson was standardized using a national sample of 3,935 K–12 children, but the technical manual provides norms for ages 3 to 63 years. The Bateria Psico-Educativa En Espanol (Woodcock, 1982) is the Spanish version of the Woodcock-Johnson test and was normed in Costa Rica, Mexico, Peru, Puerto Rico, and Spain. The Bateria Woodcock en Espanol is designed for children ages 3–0 to 9–11 years.

Special Education Assessment Data. Special Education records for each SLH and LD student involved in the study provided relevant information regarding the background of these students. Data included referral information; test results from the comprehensive psycho-educational assessment and/or the speech and language evaluation; and Admission, Review, and Dismissal (ARD) Committee placement decisions.

Students' Instructional Schedules. Information regarding the extent of bilingual education instruction offered to each child was also gathered. The homeroom teacher of each student was asked to complete a one-page form indicating the language (English, Spanish, or mixed) and number of minutes per week of instruction given to each student in Language Arts, Mathematics, Science, and Social Studies.

Status of Year 1 of the Research Study

Data for the first year of the study have been collected and coded, and are currently being analyzed. Correlational analysis will be conducted to establish the degree of interrelatedness between the various oral language measures employed. Multiple discriminate function analyses will establish the power of each oral language proficiency indicator to predict whether LEP subjects are (a) handicapped (SLH or LD) versus nonhandicapped (achievers or underachievers) and (b) achievers versus underachievers versus SLH versus LD. Because of the low incidence of limited-English-proficient students labeled as learning disabled in kindergarten (see also Ortiz et al., 1985), there were no LD subjects in Year 1 of the study. However, grade 1 LEP LD students were included in Year 2. The following are findings to date.

The within-group division of males and females indicated a greater proportion of males for all groups, particularly for language handicapped students. This finding is consistent with literature which indicates that there are more males than females in special education programs. In addition, the majority of the language handicapped students in the sample had been referred in early childhood with the mean age at referral of 5 years and 1 and 1/2 months. Since language handicapped students' problems are manifested in oral communication, abnormal behaviors may be more readily distinguishable than achievement-related problems, the criteria upon which learning disabilities are based.

Instructional Schedules. The students' instructional schedules, as reported by their teachers, indicate that most students receive some instruction in Spanish (either Spanish-only or a combination of English and Spanish) as opposed to English-only instruction. This pattern holds for all groups and across all subject areas. For example, in language arts, 80.7% of achievers, 91.3% of underachievers, and 81.8% of language handicapped students receive mixed instruction and/or Spanish-only instruction. However, in examining the language of instruction received by subjects when only ONE language is used, it is evident that Spanish is used more frequently in language arts, while English is used more frequently in math, science, and social studies. This finding is surprising in that these are LEP students and subjects such as science and social studies have heavy verbal loads. The emphasis given to English and/or mixed language instruction for these kindergarten students raises questions about the implementation of bilingual education programs.

Reasons for Referral. The reasons most frequently cited for referring language handicapped students were: Articulation/language (27.3%), speech (18.2%), articulation (13.6%), stuttering (9.1%), and unintelligible speech (9.1%). In 66.7% of the cases, therapists diagnosed the problem as being articulation and language; in 16.7% of the cases, therapists diagnosed the problem as being articulation, voice, and language. Students were equally spread (5.6%) among the remaining categories: Language-only; articulation/fluency/language; and language/ fluency. Severity of the problem was more often judged to be moderate-severe or severe (66.6%), than mild-moderate or moderate (33.3%). The above data show that while the majority of the students may have been referred for either articulation and/or language, recommended services were more often language-related. This finding confirms the results of other research conducted by the HMRI (Ortiz, Garcia, Wheeler, & Maldonado-Colon, 1986). It may be that once the child is administered a comprehensive individual assessment, students referred for articulation problems are also found to be in need of language services. However, since it is common practice to administer an English language development test as part of the assessment process and since language minority students typically perform poorly on these tests, it also may be that the subjects in this study are identified as having a language disorder when in fact they are exhibiting normal characteristics of second language acquisition.

LAS Results. A visual inspection of LAS scores shows that all groups improved in their overall proficiency levels from fall 1985 testing to spring 1986 testing in both English and Spanish.

In the fall, students' Spanish proficiency levels were higher than their English levels. This linguistic advantage was maintained when the students were retested in the spring. In both fall and spring, achievers consistently scored higher than underachievers, who scored higher than or equal to language handicapped students. This was the case for both English and Spanish. Similar patterns were observed within the two districts.

In fall 1985, achievers' language proficiency scores tended to cluster at low levels in English and low to moderate levels in Spanish. Spring 1986 tests showed movement toward moderate proficiency levels for English and moderate-to-high proficiency levels for Spanish. Under-achievers, on the other hand, showed low ability in both languages in the fall testing. Nine months later, their English proficiency was still at a low level while their Spanish had improved moderately. Finally, language handicapped children's scores clustered at the lowest levels for both languages in the autumn. Their scores, however, *remained* at this same low level in the spring. These patterns are similar across the two school districts.

Pragmatic Criteria. Students displayed poorer communication skills (as measured by Damico's pragmatic criteria) as well as syntactical skills (as measured by DSS/DASG) in the English than in the Spanish conversation samples. This is not unexpected since English is the children's weaker language. Damico's (1985) criteria do not seem to distinguish between those LEP kindergarten children who are language handicapped and those who are normal in either English or Spanish, suggesting that these criteria may not be appropriate for kindergarten students.

Syntactical Analysis. The English syntactical criteria (as measured by DSS) did not distinguish among groups; however, achievers and underachievers exhibited a higher percentage of syntactically correct utterances in Spanish than language handicapped subjects. Language handicapped students' low syntactical scores in both English and Spanish may reflect the presence of a language disorder. A true language disability among students who are LEP is typically displayed through poor mastery of skills not only in English, but in their native language as well. In contrast, the fact that achievers, underachievers, and language handicapped students did not differ on their DSS scores may be attributed to their common lack of English proficiency.

Analyses completed to date suggest that an individual subject's language proficiency level, as measured by the LAS, is unrelated to the child's communication skills as measured by Damico's pragmatic criteria, and unrelated to his or her syntactical skills as measured by the DSS and the DASG. This suggests that different skills are being tapped by each of these measures.

Expected Outcomes/Anticipated Contributions

The expected outcomes from this research include (a) empirically supported recommendations to practitioners as to the best oral language measure, or combination of measures, to use in the diagnosis and placement of LEP students referred to special education; (b) the importance of assessing *relative* (English/Spanish) oral language proficiency for exceptional language minority students; (c) the relationship of various oral language assessment measures in English and Spanish to students' academic achievement; and (d) the rate of gain/loss of various aspects of LEP students' oral language in English and Spanish over time.

Issues in the Assessment and Analysis of Natural Language Samples

The need for further research on the use of clinical discourse analysis and pragmatic ratings of students' speech samples in the diagnosis of speech and language handicaps in bilingual children is already evident.

Elicitation Procedures. The procedures recommended by Damico (1985) require that the examiner be able to effectively engage the student in conversation. Achieving this type of interaction was found to be difficult with the kindergarten subjects involved in the first year of the HMRI study. It is possible that the interviewers were not familiar to the subjects and that insufficient time was given to establishing rapport. The elicitation process, however, was difficult even when the examiner had had prior contacts with the students, as when the interviewer had conducted other assessments before attempting language sampling, or when the interviewer was the individual regularly assigned to the campus to do LAS testing. This suggests that age of the subjects may have contributed to the difficulty in engagement. These students averaged 6 years, 4 months (with a range of 5 years, 7 months to 6 years, 7 months) at the time of testing; Damico's pragmatic criteria were developed with much older subjects, ranging from 6 years, 7 months to 22 years, 3 months (Damico, 1985).

Alternative procedures for obtaining language samples should be explored, including, for example, using teachers or parents as interviewers or using pictures or manipulatives to elicit language production. The latter, however, may not constitute a natural "conversation," suggesting that alternative criteria may also need to be used or developed to evaluate language skills. In developing alternatives, caution must be exercised to assure that procedures have a high likelihood of being used by speech and language clinicians in typical school settings.

Criteria Selected. Damico has described 17 pragmatic criteria (Damico, 1985) but recommends using only 7 of these (Figure 1) to analyze language samples. Studies conducted by Damico and Oller (1980) and Damico et al. (1983) indicate that these 7 criteria contribute to a more accurate descriptive profile of a child's communicative difficulties. In analyzing children's conversations, one question which has surfaced is whether these 7 are the most effective in distinguishing normal from abnormal language acquisition. For example, a frequent behavior of the SLH subjects was that they failed to respond to interviewers' questions or comments. While delay before responding (DR) is one of the seven criteria, failure to respond is not. Consequently, perhaps significant pragmatic errors were missed in the analysis. Another example is that because linguistic nonfluencies (LNF) occurred so frequently across all groups, many students would qualify as handicapped on the basis of this criterion alone. It is likely that limited-English-proficient students, handicapped and nonhandicapped, lack fluency in English production and that the testing situation increases the students' dysfluencies in the native language as well. The category of LNF thus may not be an appropriate category for screening for possible handicapping conditions for this group of students.

Counting of Errors. Analysis of student performance is based on the number of utterances containing at least one error rather than on the total number of errors made by the subject in the conversation. Thus, there is no distinction made between an utterance that has one pragmatic error and one that contains multiple errors. The net effect is that this procedure may mask any differences between handicapped and nonhandicapped students and may make the language production of SLH students appear more normal.

Weighting of Errors. An additional concern is that the seven pragmatic criteria described by Damico (1985) receive equal weight although some types of error appear more serious than others (e.g., delays before responding versus inappropriate responses). Analysis by type of error must be conducted to determine whether some errors tend to be more characteristic of one group than another.

Time Involved in Analysis. Analysis of language using pragmatic criteria is very time consuming. Typically, a complete evaluation of children's conversational samples in English and in Spanish, including transcribing, editing, segmenting, and identifying and counting errors, requires approximately 15–20 hours. Since this may discourage use of the procedure, ways of streamlining the process should be explored. However, it is stressed that if results of this study support the use of pragmatic criteria for distinguishing normal from abnormal language acquisition, then time is better spent on assessment than on inappropriate intervention. This is particularly important given data indicating that, after initial placement, children are not usually reevaluated until 3 years later (Ortiz et al., 1985; 1986).

Codeswitching. Currently used assessment procedures, both discrete-point and pragmatic, assume that a child speaks English *or* Spanish. The speech of many of the subjects included codeswitching, the inter- and intra-sentential mixing of both languages: 3.8% of the utterances in the subjects' English language samples were mixed, and 9.93% of the utterances in the subjects' Spanish samples were mixed. Procedures for evaluating codeswitching using pragmatics must be developed.

Lack of Appropriate Assessment Instruments. Effective identification of handicapped Hispanics on the U.S. mainland continues to be hampered by a lack of appropriate assessment instruments. As the language minority population increases, this will become an even greater issue as districts struggle to achieve nondiscrimination in testing. Until such instruments are available, assessment personnel will be unable to distinguish handicapping conditions from linguistic difference using norm-referenced procedures.

Developmental Sentence Screening. The lack of data related to the acquisition of both English and Spanish language skills among LEP students becomes evident immediately when one attempts to describe the acquisition of grammatical and syntactical structures and to judge whether children's acquisition is within the developmental norm. Guidelines for conducting such analyses will be an important contribution of the present study.

Summary

Preliminary results of this research indicate that analysis of Hispanic LEP students' relative proficiency in English and Spanish provide an essential set of information for determining both the choice of assessment procedures and language in which to conduct assessments, as well as in the diagnostic/prescriptive process. For all educators of LEP children, the examination of students' mastery of both English and the home language would appear to be crucial to identifying the child's specific disability and for the planning of appropriate intervention. The research being conducted by the HMRI highlights the complexities of assessing the language skill of both normal and handicapped students from dual language backgrounds. This research effort also promises to increase the understanding of the interaction of language proficiency and exceptionalities and to provide helpful suggestions to the field for improving current practice.

REFERENCES

Barrie-Blackey, S., Musselwhite, C. R., & Rogister, S. H. (1978). *Clinical oral language sampling: A handbook for students and clinicians*. Danville, IL: Interstate Printers.

Bloom, L. & Lahey, M. (1978). *Language development and language disorders*. New York: Wiley.

Carrow-Woolfolk, E. (1973). *Test for Auditory Comprehension of Language: English/Spanish*. Allen, TX: DLM Teaching Resources.

Celce-Murcia, M. (1978). The simultaneous acquisition of English and French in a two–year old child. In E. Hatch (Ed.), *Second language acquisition: A book of readings*. (pp. 38–53) Rowley, MA: Newbury House.

Cummins, J. (1982). The role of primary language development in promoting educational success for language minority students. In *California State Department of Education, Schooling and language minority students: A theoretical framework* (pp. 3–49). Los Angeles: Bilingual Education Evaluation, Dissemination, and Assessment Center.

Cummins, J. (1984). *Bilingual special education: Issues in assessment and pedagogy*. Clevedon, Avon, England: Multilingual Matters.

Damico, J. S. (1985). Clinical discourse analysis. A functional approach to language assessment. In Simon, C. (Ed.), *Communication skills and classroom success: Assessment of language-learning disabled students* (pp. 165–204). San Diego, CA: College-Hill Press.

Damico, J. S. & Oller, J. W., Jr. (1980). Pragmatic versus morphological/syntactic criteria for language referrals. *Language Speech and Hearing Services in Schools, 11*, 85–94.

Damico, J. S. Oller, J. W., Jr., & Storey, M. E. (1983). The diagnosis of language disorders in bilingual children. *Journal of Speech and Hearing Disorders*, 48, 285–294.

De Avila, E. A., & Duncan, S. E. (1981). *Language Assessment Scales*. San Rafael, CA: Linguametrics Group.

Dew, N. (1984). The exceptional bilingual child: Demography. In P.C. Chinn (Ed.), *Education of culturally and linguistically different exceptional children* (pp. 1–42). Reston, VA: The Council for Exceptional Children.

Dulay, H. C., Burt, M. K., & Krashen, S. (1982). *Language two*. New York: Oxford University Press.

Dulay, H. C., Hernandez-Chavez, E., & Burt, M. K. (1978). The process of becoming bilingual. In S. Singh & J. Lynch (Eds.), *Diagnostic Procedures in Hearing, Speech, and Language* (pp. 251–303). Baltimore: University Park Press.

Dunn, L. M., & Dunn L. M. (1981). *Peabody Picture Vocabulary Test*. Circle Pines, MN: American Guidance Service.

Dunn, L. M., Padilla, E. R., Lugo, D. E., & Dunn, L. M. (1986). *Test de Vocabulario en Imagenes Peabody/Peabody Picture Vocabulary Test*. Circle Pines, MN: American Guidance Service.

Holtzman, W. H., Jr., Ortiz, A. A., & Wilkinson, C. Y. (1986). *Characteristics of limited English proficient Hispanic students in programs for the mentally retarded: Implications for policy and practice*. Austin, TX: The University of Texas, Handicapped Minority Research Institute on Language Proficiency.

Juarez, M. (1983). Assessment and treatment of minority-language handicapped children: The role of the monolingual speech-language pathologist. *Topics in Language Disorders*, 3, 57–66.

Krashen, S. D. (1982). Bilingual education and second language acquisition theory. In *California State Department of Education, Schooling and language minority students: A theoretical framework*. Los Angeles: Bilingual Education Evaluation, Dissemination, and Assessment Center, School of Education, California State University.

Lee, L. (1974). *Developmental sentence analysis*. Evanston, IL: Northwestern University Press.

Manni, J., Winikur, P., & Keller, M. (1980). *The status of minority group representation in special education programs in the state of New Jersey: A summary report* (PTM No. 100.83). Trenton, NJ: State Department of Education.

Mattes, L. J., & Omark, D. R. (1984). *Speech and language assessment for bilingual handicapped*. San Diego, CA: College-Hill Press.

Mercer, J. R. (1976). Pluralistic diagnosis in the evaluation of Black and Chicano children: A procedure for taking socio-cultural variables into account. In C. A. Hernandez, M. J. Haug, & N. N. Wagner (Eds.), *Chicanos: Social and psychological perspectives* (pp. 183–195). St Louis, MO: C. V. Mosby.

Newcomer, P. L., & Hammill, D. D. (1982). *Test of Language Development-Primary*. Austin, TX: Pro-Ed.

Oller, J. W., Jr. (1983). Testing proficiencies and diagnosing language disorders in bilingual children. In D. R. Omark & J. G. Erickson (Eds.), *The exceptional bilingual child* (pp.69–88). San Diego, CA: College-Hill Press.

Ortiz A. A. (1984). Choosing the language of instruction for exceptional bilingual children. *Teaching Exceptional Children, 16*(3), 208–212.

Ortiz, A. A., Garcia, S. B., Holtzman, W. H., Jr., Polyzoi, E., Snell, W. E., Jr., Wilkinson, C. Y., & Willig, A. C. (1985). *Characteristics of limited English proficient Hispanic students in programs for the learning disabled: Implications for policy, practice, and research*. Austin, TX: The University of Texas, Handicapped Minority Research Institute on Language Proficiency.

Ortiz, A. A., Garcia, S. B., Wheeler, D. S., & Maldonado-Colon, E. (1986). *Characteristics of limited English proficient Hispanic students served in programs for the speech and language handicapped: Implications for policy and practice*. Austin, TX: The University of Texas, Handicapped Minority Research Institute on Language Proficiency.

Ortiz, A. A., & Maldonado-Colon, E. (1986). Reducing inappropriate referrals of language minority students to special education. In A. C. Willig & H. F. Greenberg (Eds.), *Bilingualism and learning disabilities* (pp. 37–52). NY: American Library.

Ortiz, A. A., & Yates, J. R. (1983). Incidence of exceptionality among Hispanics: Implications for manpower planning. *Journal of the National Association for Bilingual Education*, 7, 41–53.

Ortiz, A. A., & Yates, J. R. (1984). Linguistically and culturally diverse handicapped students. In R. Podemski, B. Price, T. Smith, & G. March, II (Eds.), *Comprehensive administration of special education* (pp. 114–141). Rockville, MD: Aspen Systems.

Toronto, A. S. (1976). Developmental assessment of Spanish grammar. *Journal of Speech and Hearing Disorders, 41*(2), 150–171.

Tucker, J. (1980). Ethnic proportions in classes for the learning disabled: Issues in nonbiased assessment. *Journal of Special Education, 86,* 351–360.

U.S. General Accounting Office. (1981). *Unanswered questions on educating handicapped children in local public schools.* (Report to the Congress of the United States, HRD–81–43). Washington, DC: Author.

Woodcock, R. W. (1982). *Bateria Woodcock Psico-Educativa En Espanol.* Allen, TX: DLM Teaching Resources.

Woodcock, R. W., & Johnson, M. B. (1977). *Woodcock-Johnson Psycho-Educational Battery.* Allen, TX: DLM Teaching Resources.

CHAPTER 5

Understanding School Language Proficiency Through the Assessment of Story Construction

Vicki A. Jax

Language is critical to achievement in school. It is important for basic interpersonal communication, but schooling requires a special set of institutionalized behaviors (Michaels & Collins, 1984) for autonomous or self-directed language tasks including speaking, reading, and writing. Yet, the literate competencies used as the standard of performance in the schools are closely tied to oral language competencies (Olson, 1982; Tannen, 1980). Mastery of grammatical language structures and mastery of discourse, how to combine and interpret both meanings and language forms, are critical competencies of language proficiency. For reading as for speaking, strategies are mapped onto underlying meaning (Olson, 1982). The strategies a child develops for accomplishing mapping begin in interpersonal communication and evolve to literate language use in self-directed academically oriented tasks. Relying on the acquisition of a literature style of interpersonal communication in the home, schools have typically assumed the responsibility for teaching reading and writing (Olson, 1982), as opposed to emphasizing speaking and understanding the language of schools. Results of an assessment of school language proficiency through the use of story construction tasks indicate the discourse structures used by the child in an autonomous, academically oriented task, as well as the oral or literate characteristics of the child's style of production.

LANGUAGE DEMANDS OF SCHOOLING

Research and clinical practice with children learning English as a second language have led to increased concern about the relationship between language proficiency and academic achievement (Ulibarri, Spencer, & Rivas, 1981). This issue is of particular concern because of rapidly increasing language minority populations (Bureau of Census, 1984); federal mandates to identify, assess, and place language minority children in instructional environments commensurate with their level of English language proficiency (Office of Civil Rights, 1977); and numbers of language minority children receiving special educational services (Cummins, 1982; Mercer, 1973).

Language minority children typically achieve at lower levels than majority children (U.S. Commission on Civil Rights, 1971; Brown, Rosen, Hill, & Olivas, 1980), and differences in achievement are especially noted in language related areas (Coleman et al., 1966; Gordon, 1968; Okada, Cohen, & Mayeske, 1969; Rueda, Cardoza, Mercer, & Carpenter, 1985). However, relatively little is known about the relationship between language proficiency and academic performance. Although it has been suggested that low academic achievement, particularly in language related areas, is due to language minorities students' difficulties in higher level information processing (Peal & Lambert, 1962), it is more likely that poor academic achievement is related to English language proficiency for academic use (Cummins, 1979).

A special set of institutionalized language behaviors, that is, a range of literate strategies, is required in school (Michaels & Collins, 1984), including development of a literate style of information presentation in the spoken and written mode of communication. Literate discourse strategies of school language use are for communication with an audience that is relatively unfamiliar to the child. As such, relevant background information must be provided in communication. Literate devices are used to signal thematic cohesion. Further, organization of the progression of extended texts is required for effective communication. Information conveyed through nonlexical channels in oral style discourse must be made explicit through the choice of lexical items and syntactic construction (Collins & Michaels, 1980; Gee, 1985; Michaels, 1981).

A communicative viewpoint on language proficiency offers a multidimensional framework that incorporates both an interpersonal communication dimension and an autonomous language dimension (Canale, 1983, 1984; Duran, Canale, Penfield, Stansfeld, & Liskin-Gasparro, 1985) and is a useful model for the assessment of school language. The communicative language dimension involves the social interpersonal uses of language (other-directed language production) through both spoken and written channels. The autonomous language dimension includes intrapersonal uses of languages (e.g., in problem solving, organizing one's thoughts).

There are four types of knowledge and competence areas involved in each dimension of language proficiency. These areas are grammatical competence, sociolinguistic competence, discourse competence, and strategic competence (Canale, 1983, 1984; Canale & Swain, 1980; Duran et al., 1985). Considering the influence of competence areas on communicative proficiency, grammatical forms and literal meanings receive less emphasis than the social meaning of language. In self-directed, autonomous language proficiency, both grammatical and discourse competence are more highly involved than sociolinguistic competence and strategic competence. The production and comprehension of literate-style spoken and written discourse are involved in the development of autonomous language behaviors. While self-directed language is imperative in language-related academic areas, the production and comprehension of the text structures of discourse are particularly important to achievement in reading.

DISCOURSE STRUCTURE

Discourse is a type of structure that exists in both spoken and written forms and involves communication of meaningful relations across sentence boundaries (Tannen, 1982). While meaning is certainly conveyed within individual sentences, discourse focuses on the structure of meaning that supercedes sentences and that pervades the text. The interpretation of any sentence is dependent upon the interpretation of other sentences within the text (van Dijk, 1980), since meaning of a total discourse is more than what can be interpreted from the sum of the meanings in the individual words and sentences (Westby, 1984). Thus, the text structure influences the meaning taken by the reader (Anderson, Hiebert, Scott, & Wilkinson, 1985).

Narrative is one type of discourse with particular relevance for academic language. Narrative discourse has been described in terms of high points (Labov, 1972; Labov, Cohen, Robins, & Lewis, 1968; Labov & Waletzky, 1967), episodes (Glenn, 1978; Mandler, 1978; Mandler & Johnson, 1977; Rumelhart, 1977; Schank & Abelson, 1977; Stein & Glenn, 1979; Thorndyke, 1977), and plot units (Botvin & Sutton-Smith, 1977; Sutton-Smith, 1981). High points described in a narrative are critical points to which the story line builds in the recapitulation of an event and from which resolution of the problem occurs. An episode consists of an event that causes a protagonist either to set a goal or respond to the situation, and is terminated by resolution of the activity (Peterson & McCabe, 1983). A plot unit delimits the action within the narrative through representation of the motivation for the action, subsequent action, and resolution (Botvin & Sutton-Smith, 1977). Stories typically represent narrative discourse in either spoken or written form. As such, they reflect the transformation of experience and depend on the use of informational units to recapitulate an event (Labov, 1972). In representing events, narrative discourse stories establish causal, temporal, and motivational relationships between people, things, and events.

The following seven types of narrative story structures emerged in the collaborative research of Glenn and Stein (Peterson & McCabe, 1983).

1. Descriptive sequences provide a description of character(s), setting, and habitual activity without indication of causal relationships.

2. Action sequences provide a chronological list of actions with no indication of causal relationships.

3. Reactive sequences indicate a circumstance that automatically causes change in a state of affairs with no planning.

4. An abbreviated episode presents the goals of the protagonist, but his/her planning is not indicated.

5. A complete episode provides evidence of planning in the description of purposive activity. Further, the complete episode must include consequences as well as two narrative components, i.e., events, motivating states, or attempts.

6. A complex episode provides elaboration of the complete episode by either embedding or multiple plan application.

7. An interactive episode describes the goals and attempts of two characters who influence each other and provides complete episodes from the perspective of each character.

These story patterns are considered logically ordered from the least to the most complex. Each level of complexity includes all of the functional and content categories of the level before and all of the relationships between those categories.

Narrative discourse structures are useful when considering the mastery of language behaviors on a continuum of oral-literate language competencies. In that regard, assessment of discourse behaviors in the spoken mode is important for understanding a child's development of school language, and approaches to the language proficiency testing deserve review.

APPROACHES TO LANGUAGE PROFICIENCY TESTING

Language proficiency tests represent a major source of information on which placement and instructional recommendations are made, and adequate performance on such tests results in placement in the regular classroom (Merino & Spencer, in press). Conventional language proficiency tests typically measure the syntactic proficiency of the language minority child. While this aspect of proficiency has been considered indicative of ability to communicate in the English language community, the value of syntactic proficiency as predictive of ability to function in classrooms where English is the language of instruction has been questioned (Cummins, 1979). Results of recent research with over 1,300 Hispanic children indicated that large numbers of language minority children who had passed conventional language proficiency tests did not achieve in the regular classroom and were referred for special education evaluation. The primary reasons for referral were low academic achievement, poor reading skills, and poor oral skills (Rueda, Cardoza, Mercer, & Carpenter, 1985). These findings suggest that proficiency instruments utilized in the diagnostic and placement process were not sensitive to the skills necessary to achieve in the English language classroom.

Since syntactic measures of language proficiency have not functioned as predictors of academic achievement, additional measures of language proficiency must be considered. One option is the evaluation of language use in the construction of spoken stories. Assessment of story construction should be a better predictor of performance on reading comprehension since organizational features of storytelling guide the individual in the construction of functional relationships between elements of a narrative. Further, the organizational features utilized in story construction guide to the comprehension of stories constructed by others, by activating cues presented in spoken or written stories. Ability to recognize and recall information from text is also dependent upon the availability of an organizing system.

Given the apparent relationship between spoken story construction and comprehension of written text, it is important to determine the relative effectiveness of conventional and story construction measures of language proficiency in predicting reading comprehension. One such measure of story construction is a modified language sampling procedure that allows the child to demonstrate English proficiency in story formulation. The storytelling task is typical of the literate style of interaction in the regular classroom—that is, the child is asked to tell a story about a book in which the story is presented only pictorially. While storytelling occurs interpersonally in conversation and/or oral interview, a mode of storytelling can be used in which the child produces a story independent of discourse cues provided in conversation. Based on spoken language samples, analysis of story construction can provide information on story setting, initiation of events, reaction, attempts, outcomes, and endings. Additionally, the type of story structure produced in the construction of narrative can be classified. The seven classifications of story structures (sequences and episodes) which emerged in the collaborative research of Glenn and Stein (Peterson & McCabe, 1983) are (a) descriptive sequences, (b) action sequences, (c) reactive sequences, (d) abbreviated episode, (e) complete episode, (f) complex episode, and (g) interactive episode.

Language performance assessed through story construction relates to reading comprehension with certain expectations. Those children who use descriptive sequences in their story construction have an organizational framework for comprehending setting information in text. Similarly, those children who formulate reactive sequences in story construction employ organizational frameworks for processing information on circumstances that automatically cause change in the state of affairs. Those children who formulate episodes (abbreviated, complete, complex, or interactive) employ organization frameworks that account for goals, plan applications, and temporal and causal relationships. It is predicted that children who achieve a higher level on the story construction tasks will achieve higher scores in reading comprehension than children who achieve lower story construction levels. Further, it is expected that story construction scores will be more predictive of reading comprehension level than conventional language proficiency scores.

EDUCATIONAL IMPLICATIONS

The implications of such research are important for educators, psychologists, and speech and language personnel. Their role in the public schools demands reconsideration of diagnostic strategies for evaluating the language use of minority children. In light of information about language use for academic purposes, it is necessary to consider language samples for the information they provide on a child's construction of stories, in addition to information on the individual's phonological, morphological, syntactic, semantic, and pragmatic proficiency. In the case of children learning English as a second language who are not succeeding in the regular classroom, appropriate diagnostic decisions and educational recommendations can be made only after language assessment that accounts for the relationship between language proficiency and academic performance. In the assessment of language proficiency as it relates to academic learning, the use of language sampling strategies that lead to the analysis of story construction can assist school personnel in the determination of special needs of language minority children.

REFERENCES

Anderson, R. C., Hiebert, E. H., Scott, J. A., & Wilkinson, I. A. G. (1985). *Becoming a nation of readers: The report of the Commission on Reading.* Washington, DC: National Institute of Education.

Botvin, G. J., & Sutton-Smith, B. (1977). The development of structural complexity in children's fantasy narratives, *Developmental Psychology, 13,* 377–388.

Brown, G. H., Rosen, N. L., Hill, S. T., & Olivas, M. A. (1980). *The condition of education for Hispanic Americans.* National Center for Education Statistics. Washington, DC: U.S. Government Printing Office.

Bureau of the Census. (1984, March). *Selected social and economic characteristics of persons in households by language spoken at home and ability to speak English: April, 1980, Detailed population characteristics United States summary* (pp. 18–19). Washington, DC: U.S. Department of Commerce.

Canale, M. (1983). A communicative approach to language proficiency assessment in a minority setting. In C. Rivera (Ed.), *Communicative competence approaches to language proficiency assessment: Research and application.* Clevedon, England: Multilingual Matters.

Canale, M. (1984). On some theoretical frameworks for language proficiency. In C. Rivera (Ed.), *Language proficiency and academic achievement.* Clevedon, England: Multilingual Matters.

Canale, M., & Swain, M. (1980). Theoretical bases of communicative approaches to second language teaching and testing. *Applied Linguistics, 1*(1), 1–47.

Coleman, J. S., Campbell, E. Q., Hobson, C. J., McPartland, J., Mood, A. M., Weinfeld, F. D., & York, R. L. (1966). *Equality of educational opportunity.* Washington, DC: U.S. Government Printing Office, U.S. Department of Health, Education, and Welfare, Office of Education.

Collins, J., & Michaels, S. (1980). The importance of conversational discourse strategies in the development of literacy. *Proceedings of the Sixth Annual Meeting of the Berkeley Linguistics Society.* Berkeley, CA.

Cummins, J. (1979). Linguistic interdependence and the educational development of bilingual children. *Review of Educational Research, 49*(2), 222–251.

Cummins, J. (1982). Tests, achievement, and bilingual students. *Focus, 9,* 1–7.

Duran, R. P., Canale, M., Penfield, J., Stansfeld, C. W., & Liskin-Gasparro, J. E. (1985). *TOEFL from a communicative viewpoint on language proficiency: A working paper* (Report No. ETS–RR–85–8). Princeton, NJ: Educational Testing Service.

Gee, J. P. (1985). The narrativization of experience in the oral style. *Journal of Education, 167*(1), 9–35.

Glenn, C. G. (1978). The role of episodic structure and of story length on children's recall of single stories. *Journal of Verbal Learning and Verbal Behavior, 17,* 229–247.

Gordon, C. W. (1968). *Educational achievement and aspirations of Mexican-American youth in a metropolitan context.* Los Angeles: University of California at Los Angeles, Mexican-American Study Project.

Labov, W. (1972). Translating experience in narrative syntax. In W. Labov, *Language in the inner city: Studies in the Black English vernacular* (pp. 354–396). Philadelphia, PA: University of Pennsylvania Press.

Labov, W., Cohen, P., Robins, C., & Lewis, J. (1968). *A study of the non-standard English of Negro and Puerto Rican speakers in New York City* (Vol. 2; Cooperative Research Project No. 3288). Washington, DC: Office of Education.

Labov, W., & Waletzky, J. (1967). Narrative analysis: Oral versions of personal experience. In J. Helm (Ed.), *Essays on the verbal and visual arts.* Seattle: University of Washington Press.

Mandler, J. (1978). A code in the node: The use of story schema in retrieval. *Discourse Processes, 1,* 14–35.

Mandler, J., & Johnson, N. (1977). Remembrance of things parsed: Story structure and recall. *Cognitive Psychology, 9,* 111–151.

Mercer, J. (1973). *Labeling the mentally retarded: Clinical and social system perspectives on mental retardation.* Berkeley: University of California Press.

Merino, B. J., & Spencer, M. (in press). The comparability of English and Spanish versions of oral language proficiency instruments. *NABE Journal.*

Michaels, S. (1981). "Sharing time": Children's narrative styles and differential access to literacy. *Language in Society, 10,* 423–442.

Michaels, S., & Collins, J. (1984). Oral discourse styles: Classroom interaction and the acquisition of literacy. In D. Tannen (Ed.), *Coherence in spoken and written discourse.* Norwood, NJ: Ablex Publishing Corporation.

Office of Civil Rights. (1977). Task force findings specifying remedies available for eliminating past educational practices ruled unlawful under *Lau* v. *Nichols* (1975). In T. Oakland (Ed.), *Psychological and educational assessment of minority children* (pp. 159–168). New York: Brunner/Mazel.

Okada, T., Cohen, W., & Mayeske, G. W. (1969). *Growth in achievement for different racial, regional and socio-economic groupings of students* (Technical Paper No. 1).

Olson, D. R. (1982). The language of schooling. *Topics in Language Disorders, 2*(4), 1–12.

Peal, E., & Lambert, W. E. (1962). The relation of bilingualism to intelligence. *Psychological Monographs, 76*, 546.

Peterson, C., & McCabe, A. (1983). *Developmental psycholinguistics: Three ways of looking at a child's narrative. New York: Plenum Press.*

Rueda, R., Cardoza, D., Mercer, J., & Carpenter, L. (1985). *Final report—longitudinal study 1 report: An examination of special education decision making with Hispanic first time referrals in large urban school districts* (Contract No. 300–83–0273). Washington, DC: U.S. Department of Education.

Rumelhart, D. E. (1977). Understanding and summarizing brief stories. In D. LaBerge, & S. A. Samuels (Eds.), *Basic processes in reading: Perception and comprehension* (pp. 265–303). Hillsdale, NJ: Lawrence Erlbaum Associates.

Schank, R., & Abelson, R. P. (1977). *Scripts, plans, goals, and understanding.* Hillsdale, NJ: Lawrence Erlbaum Associates.

Stein, N., & Glenn, C. (1979). An analysis of story comprehension in elementary school children. In R. Freedle (Ed.), *New directions in discourse processing* (Vol. 2) (pp. 53–120). Norwood, NJ: Ablex.

Sutton-Smith, B. (1981). *The folkstories of children.* Philadelphia: University of Pennsylvania Press.

Tannen, D. (1980). Implications of the oral/literate continuum for cross-cultural communication. In J. Alatis (Ed.), *Georgetown University Round Table on Language and Linguistics: Current issues in bilingual education* (pp. 326–347). Washington, DC: Georgetown University Press.

Tannen, D., (Ed.). (1982). *Analyzing discourse: Text and talk.* Georgetown University Round Table on Languages and Linguistics 1981. Washington, DC: Georgetown University Press.

Thorndyke, P. W. (1977). Cognitive structures in comprehension and memory of narrative discourse. *Cognitive Psychology, 9*, 77–110.

Ulibarri, D. M., Spencer, M. L., & Rivas, G. A. (1981). Language proficiency and academic achievement: A study of language proficiency tests and their relationship to school ratings as predictors of academic achievement. *NABE Journal, 5*(3), 47–80.

U.S. Commission on Civil Rights. (1971). *The unfinished education: Outcomes for minorities in the five western states.* Washington, DC: U.S. Government Printing Office.

van Dijk, T. (1980). Story comprehension: An introduction. *Poetics, 9*, 1–21.

Westby, C. E. (1984). Development of narrative language abilities. In G. P. Wallach & K. G. Butler (Eds.), *Language learning disabilities in school-age children* (pp. 103–127). Baltimore: Williams & Wilkins.

CHAPTER 6

Characteristics of Learning Disabled, Mentally Retarded, and Speech-Language Handicapped Hispanic Students at Initial Evaluation and Reevaluation

Alba A. Ortiz
James R. Yates

There is a strong rationale for all educators to be concerned with handicapped language minority students who are the focus of these studies. The rationale is simple and specific: a dramatically changing demography. The Census Bureau has reported that since the 1980 census, the Hispanic population in the United States increased by 30%, almost ten times the growth rate of the general population. Reich (1986) projects that, by the year 2080, the Hispanic population will have increased from 7% to 19%. In Texas, to cite a state where these changes are dramatic in terms of their effect upon schools, 38% of the general population is minority. Of interest is the fact that 34% of public school students in Texas are Hispanic, and approximately half of all kindergarten students are Hispanic.

Demographic changes such as these are not strictly, nor uniquely, a Texas phenomenon. Chicago, for example, is the third most populous Hispanic center in the United States (Fiesta Educativa, 1984). The average age of White women in this country is 32 years; Black women, approximately 25 years; and Hispanic women, 22 years. Hispanic women are not only the largest population group in the childbearing age range for the near future, but also have the highest birth rate of any ethnic group. Yes, there will be another baby boom, but this baby boom of the future will be Hispanic (Hodgkinson, 1985).

Population characteristics are shifting, and those elected to positions of power reflect a shift to larger numbers of minorities. In 1986, 6,000 elected officials were Black; in 1987, there were 3,314 elected Hispanic officials (Trevino, 1987).

When placed in perspective, these shifts in demography and in the power configurations represent critical information to special educators. No longer can special educators be concerned solely with the nature of the handicapping condition and/or the appropriate match of instructional procedures to that handicap. Special educators must also be concerned with a range of other characteristics of the population they will be serving, specifically, unique features such as linguistic, cultural, and other background characteristics.

Despite the dramatically increasing number of language minority students in special education, there is limited research focusing specifically on the exceptional limited-English-proficient or bilingual student. The Handicapped Minority Research Institute on Language Proficiency (HMRI) at The University of Texas at Austin has conducted the only programmatic research studies to date aimed at describing the interaction of language proficiency and handicapping conditions. The findings of these studies serve as the backdrop in this paper to describe the state of practice in serving exceptional limited-English-proficient (LEP) Hispanic students; to identify major issues in service delivery; and to develop recommendations for improving policy and practice for students who qualify for both special education and for special language programs, such as bilingual education or English as a second language (ESL).

CHARACTERISTICS OF LIMITED-ENGLISH-PROFICIENT HISPANIC STUDENTS SERVED IN PROGRAMS FOR THE LD, SLH, OR MR

The findings reported here are those of a series of *ex post facto* investigations of the initial referral, assessment, and placement of limited-English-proficient (LEP) Hispanic students served in programs for the learning disabled (Ortiz et al., 1985), mentally retarded (Holtzman, Jr., Ortiz, & Wilkinson, 1986), and speech and/or language handicapped (Ortiz, Garcia, Wheeler, & Maldonado-Colon, 1986). A total of 519 students in grades 2–5 comprised the sample; 334 were classified as learning disabled (LD), 124 as communication disordered or speech and language handicapped (SLH), and 61 as mentally retarded (MR). To select the subjects, lists of Hispanic students enrolled in special education and of students classified as limited English proficient in three large urban school districts in south central Texas were cross-referenced to identify second-, third-, fourth-, and fifth-grade Hispanics in LD, MR, or SLH programs who were also classified as LEP. Students are considered LEP if their primary language is other than English and their English proficiency, as measured by a standardized oral language achievement test, is such that they have difficulty performing ordinary classwork in English (Texas Bilingual Education Act, 1981). These students met federal and state eligibility criteria for bilingual education and/or ESL programs.

Data retrieved from special education eligibility folders by trained coders included: (a) linguistic, sociocultural, and other demographic characteristics of LEP students at the time of their initial referral to special education; (b) reasons for referral; (c) performance on tests administered; (d) individuals most frequently involved on placement committees; (e) subjects' primary and secondary handicaps at initial placement; and (f) amount of time recommended for special education instruction. Data were analyzed for indicators that distinguished behaviors characteristic of handicapping conditions from those suggestive of linguistic, cultural, or other unique student characteristics.

FINDINGS RELATED TO LD POPULATIONS

One of the dilemmas when an LEP student is referred to special education is that the characteristics of second-language learners are similar to behaviors associated with certain categories of exceptionality, including learning disabilities and communication disorders (Ortiz & Maldonado-Colon, 1986). Ortiz (1984) suggests that many language minority students are referred to special education because educators are unable to distinguish individual differences from handicapping conditions. For instance, "problem behaviors" such as difficulty following directions, poor eye contact, inattention, and daydreaming could be associated with a handicapping condition, but they could also reflect a lack of English proficiency. If educators are not aware of this, a LEP student's academic difficulties might be inaccurately attributed to cognitive or intellectual deficits, thus triggering a special education referral.

Teachers gave 31 reasons for referring limited-English-proficient Hispanic students to special education for suspected learning disabilities (Ortiz et al., 1985). The most frequently cited were: (a) attention/behavior; (b) poor academic progress in general; (c) poor progress in reading; (d) poor academic progress in one or more areas (other than reading); and (e) problems related to language.

To explore the possibility that referrals might be related to limited English proficiency, attention/behavior problems which could also be characteristics of second-language learners were regrouped under the category of language problems. Upon re-analysis, the language problem category became the most frequent reason for referral of LEP. The new data suggested that more than half of all referrals of LEP students were related to limited English proficiency. Data from a related study by Wilkinson and Ortiz (1986) provide support for this finding. They compared a sample of LEP and nonLEP students and found that limited English proficiency influenced referrals. Language problems were the most frequent concern for LEP students, with 53% of the LEP sample having at least one language-related referral reason; on the other hand, the most common reason for referral of nonLEPs was poor academic progress. This suggests a need to train regular classroom teachers to better distinguish between characteristics of normal second language acquisition and true learning handicaps to prevent the referral of students whose achievement difficulties result from inadequate language proficiency.

Grade and Age at Referral

The majority of LD students were between 7 and 8.5 years of age when they were referred. The largest number were in the second grade, followed by those in the first grade. Approximately 45% of the students had been retained at least once prior to referral. The high rate of retention raises questions as to the nature and appropriateness of prior attempts to improve student performance in the mainstream.

Language Background at Home and at School

There was little correlation between dominant language reported by teachers and dominant language reported by parents on the Home Language Survey, the screening instrument used by districts to identify students who are potential candidates for bilingual education or English-as-second-language instruction. The Home Language Survey indicated that Spanish was the primary home language for two thirds of the students. Teachers, however, reported that English was the predominant language for half of the sample. That so many students who were classified as English-dominant in school but from Spanish-dominant or bilingual homes supports literature which suggests that language dominance is dependent upon the communication context or situation, the topic, and the interactors (Erickson & Omark, 1981). Therefore, it may be possible for a child to be Spanish-dominant at home, but English-dominant in school.

It is possible that the ratings of language dominance at school reflect that: (a) these children are able to communicate well in English and that ratings were based on teachers' perceptions that the child had mastered the surface structures of English (Cummins, 1984); (b) the subjects perceived that they were supposed to speak English at school; (c) English was the child's *preferred* but not necessarily *dominant* language; or (d) students were English-proficient in the use of language for interpersonal communication, but were not able to handle the language requirements of academic work (Cummins, 1984).

Comprehensive Individual Assessment

Tests of intelligence, achievement, and perceptual/motor development were the most frequently administered, followed by language proficiency and developmental/readiness tests. The most commonly used instruments were the Wechsler Intelligence Scale for Children-Revised (WISC-R) (1974); Woodcock-Johnson Psychoeducational Battery (1977); Wide Range Achievement Test (Jastak & Jastak, 1978); and the Bender Visual Motor Gestalt Test (Koppitz, 1964). Assessment procedures for LEP students were essentially the same as those used for Anglo students.

While districts are not specifically required to conduct a formal language proficiency assessment as part of the individual evaluation, they are required by state and federal law to conduct assessments in the child's dominant language. This implies that information on the student's language dominance or proficiency should be available to determine the language to be used in test administration. Despite this requirement and the need to rule out lack of English language proficiency as a cause of learning problems, very little information on language was actually included in the initial assessment. Only 25% of the assessments contained evidence of current language proficiency testing; results of prior testing tended to be approximately one year old.

Students' scores on the WISC-R were usually one standard deviation below the mean on Verbal and Full Scales, but closer to, or at the mean, on the Performance Scale. A consistent discrepancy was found between Verbal and Performance Scale scores. Such a discrepancy is quite common among bilingual populations (Cummins, 1984; Kaufman, 1979). The performance of LEP Hispanic students on tests of achievement also revealed low levels of functioning, generally around the first-grade level. These scores support the initial reason for referral to special education, that is, poor academic performance. However, one must consider that achievement was tested in English. Because LEP students receive initial instruction in their native language, (i.e., they learn to read and write in Spanish), measurement of these skills in English constitutes an unfair assessment practice. Moreover, the lack of data on native language functioning makes it impossible to determine whether a child has a discrepancy in achievement and is therefore learning disabled.

Placement in Special Education

There appeared to be little adaptation of decision-making processes when LEP students were considered for special education eligibility. Placement committee membership usually reflected state requirements for representation (representatives of administration, assessment, instruction, and the parent). Of the 334 cases deliberated, there was complete agreement among the members on 97.6% of committee decisions. This high percentage of agreement suggests that the signatures are a reflection of group decision processes, rather than individual opinions about cases.

FINDINGS RELATED TO LEP STUDENTS
WITH COMMUNICATION DISORDERS

Identification of speech and language handicaps has traditionally been based on the examinee's ability to use surface forms of speech, often the morphological and syntactical elements of language (Oller, 1983). Emphasis on surface structures, however, creates serious problems when the child being tested is limited English proficient. It is difficult to determine whether the child makes errors in English because of a disorder, whether errors are developmental in nature, and/or whether they indicate that the student is in the process of normal second language acquisition (Damico, Oller, & Storey, 1983).

Because of differences in exposure and experience, it is normal for LEP students to demonstrate lower levels of English proficiency (i.e., greater error rates) than their monolingual English-speaking peers, particularly on standardized language tests. This performance alone is not sufficient to conclude that the child is disordered or to justify special education placements. Rather, a child should be judged to have speech and language deficits only if presenting behaviors which are atypical of peers from the same cultural group who speak the same dialect and who have had similar opportunities to hear and use language (Mattes & Omark, 1984). Moreover, children should not be considered handicapped if the problem is documented in English, but not in the native language (Juarez, 1983; Ortiz, 1984). Identification of communication disorders can only be made by comparing the child's ability to communicate in both languages in meaningful speaking contexts (Oller, 1983).

Referrals

Analysis of data on the subjects included in the study of communication-disordered Hispanics (Ortiz, Garcia, Wheeler, & Maldonado-Colon, 1986) revealed that the majority of referrals

(82%) were made by classroom teachers. For the most part, the 23 reasons they cited for seeking special education assistance were related to students' communication behaviors: (a) speech (30%); (b) poor language development (18%); (c) articulation (18%); (d) achievement difficulties (17%); (e) unintelligible speech (14%); and (f) articulation and language (7%). The majority of students were referred between the ages of 5 and 7 years. Those between the ages of 5 and 6 constituted 31% of the referrals; those between 6 and 7 years of age composed 29% of the sample.

Comprehensive Individual Assessment

The Goldman-Fristoe Test of Articulation (GFTA) (Goldman & Fristoe, 1969) was the most frequently administered. The most commonly used language tests were the Peabody Picture Vocabulary Test (PPVT) (Dunn, 1965) in English and Spanish, the Test for Auditory Comprehension of Language (TACL) (Carrow, 1973) in English and Spanish, and the Test of Language Development (TOLD) (Newcomer & Hammill, 1977). A language sample was obtained for 40% of the subjects.

Performance on Tests Administered

Articulation. Articulation errors were tabulated for each consonant sound tested ($n = 23$) by type of error (substitution, omission, distortion) and by position (initial, medial, and final). These data revealed a pattern of misarticulated sounds which must be interpreted in light of two important student characteristics—LEP status and age at assessment.

Since all students in the sample were LEP, and the majority of them were from homes where Spanish was the primary language, the results of articulation testing were compared with phonological characteristics of Spanish speakers who acquire English as a second language. For example, Saville and Troike (1975) predicted that Spanish speakers learning English as a second language would have difficulty discriminating and pronouncing the following sounds correctly: /ch/ - /sh/; /s/ - /z/; /n/ - /ng/; /b/ - /v/; /t/ - /soft th/ - /s/; /d/ - /hard th/; and /y/ - /j/. The sounds identified by Saville and Troike were the sounds most frequently misarticulated by LEP students in this study. The most frequent types of errors were substitutions, followed by omissions, and then distortions.

Additionally, the most frequently misarticulated sounds were categorized as either developmental, if the child's age was at or below the developmental norm for mastery of the sound (Sander, 1972), or as indicative of a possible disorder, if the child's age was greater than the developmental norm. As a group ($n = 39$) for whom both age and assessment results were available, there was a higher percentage of students for whom errors appeared to be normal developmental errors. This is to be expected given that 60% of the subjects were referred between 5 and 7 years of age. Thus, sounds for which the developmental age of mastery is 3 years were rarely misarticulated, while the error rate for those which have a developmental norm of 7 to 8 years was high. Errors made by LEP students are even more likely to be developmental since they are in the process of acquiring English as a second language.

There was limited testing of Spanish language skills, making it impossible to compare communicative competence in the two languages as a means of ruling out lack of knowledge of English as the cause of speech and language problems. According to Anderson (cited in Mattes & Omark, 1984):

> Assessment for the purpose of identifying speech disorders should always be done in the first or dominant language of the child. At present, there are no reliable means to determine whether a child's articulation errors in the second language reflect the child's interlanguage phonology, or whether they are evidence of a speech disorder. Consequently, testing for articulation disorders in the second language could result in labeling a normal child as handicapped. In addition, a program of speech therapy might interfere with the child's normal interlanguage development (p. 6).

Language Development. Subjects' scores on tests of language development revealed low patterns of functioning in English and trends toward even lower levels of performance in the native language. For example, available scores on the English TACL ($n = 40$) yielded a mean age equivalent of 5 years, 2 months, with scores ranging from 3 years, 2 months to 6 years, 7 months. Reported scores from Spanish administrations were lower, with the mean at 4 years, 4 months, and ranges from 3 years, 0 months to 6 years, 10 months. However, because there are no Spanish norms for the TACL, speech pathologists based age equivalents on available English norms, a practice which makes test results suspect. While scaled scores were generally low, score patterns on language tests reflected higher levels of comprehension than knowledge of surface structures such as syntax and grammar. This pattern is also descriptive of second language acquirers. Low scores, however, appear to be used to justify recommendations for special education intervention, rather than to validate the students' limited-English-proficiency status.

Language Samples. Language samples were obtained for 39% of the subjects. The samples tended to be brief and did not meet criteria for length of samples recommended in the language assessment literature. According to Mattes & Omark (1984), a minimum of 30 minutes of conversation should be recorded for analysis. Other researchers maintain that a minimum of 100–200 utterances must be obtained (Damico, Oller, & Storey, 1983; Prutting, 1982; Tyack & Gottsleben, 1974), while others recommend 200 or more (Muma, 1978). Obtained samples were also limited in terms of the context or topic of conversation. In most instances, one English sample was obtained. It was, therefore, not possible to compare students' communicative competence in English to that in Spanish. Consequently, language sample data offered no more elucidation as to whether the child's language performance was normal or disordered.

Placement

Language therapy was the most frequently recommended service for eligible students, followed closely by articulation therapy. This is an interesting finding in that reasons for referral suggested that teachers were more concerned about articulation skills. One hour of therapy was recommended for 69% of the SLH students; 14% were to receive 1 1/2 hours, and 10 were to receive 2 hours of intervention weekly. This suggests that students were mildly handicapped. As with LD students, the most frequent representatives on placement committees were representatives of administration, assessment, instruction, and parents. Of the 116 cases for whom information on this variable was available, there was complete agreement among members in 97% of the cases.

CHARACTERISTICS OF MENTALLY RETARDED LEP STUDENTS

As described previously, three school districts participated in this study. When the MR sample was selected, however, there were some interesting district differences. There were no eligible mentally retarded LEP students in one district and only seven in the second, despite the large number of LEP students served in all three. As will be seen by the patterns described in the third district, it appears that local education agencies have become extremely reluctant to identify and serve language minority students in the category of mental retardation. While there are some obvious advantages to this caution, there are some disadvantages as well. There are some mentally retarded students in need of services who have not been identified; others are being served under the wrong classification (most likely learning disabilities) and may not be receiving appropriate services. Given the limited availability of subjects, the MR findings will be discussed only briefly for the purpose of describing trends in service delivery for this population.

Referrals

The mean age of MR subjects at the time of referral was 7 years, 4 months. At least 44% of the students had been retained at least once; because data were not available for a third of the subjects on this variable, it is possible that the percentage of retention exceeded 50%. Poor academic progress in general was the most commonly cited reason for referral (49%). Language problems of various types were cited as reasons for referral for 26% of the subjects.

Language Background

Teacher ratings, which indicated that students had very low language proficiency, were corroborated by results of administrations of the Language Assessment Scales (LAS) (DeAvila & Duncan, 1977). Of 40 students for whom LAS scores were available, 35 were categorized as nonspeakers of English. Results of Spanish testing were virtually identical to English results, with scores being low enough for students to be classified as nonspeakers of Spanish as well.

Comprehensive Individual Assessment

The most frequently administered tests were the WISC-R, Stanford-Binet Intelligence Scale (Terman & Merrill, 1960), Peabody Individual Achievement Test (Dunn & Markwardt, 1970), Wide Range Achievement Test, and the Bender Visual Motor Gestalt Test. The Vineland Social Maturity Scale (Doll, 1965) was the most frequently administered adaptive behavior scale. Assessment results indicated that students were low functioning across all areas tested. For example, on the WISC-R Verbal Scale, subtest scores, in almost all instances, were more than two standard deviations below the mean of 10. Performance Scale subtest scores were somewhat higher but were still very low. Seventy-five percent of the students obtained age-equivalent scores that were below the 6-year level on the adaptive behavior scale. While not all subjects performed poorly on achievement tests, scores in most cases fell well below the mean.

The pattern of very low IQs, combined with low adaptive behavior and achievement scores, suggested that the subjects were, in fact, mentally retarded. Students were classified as mentally retarded only when scores on these measures left little doubt that the classification was appropriate. However, limited assessment in the native language leaves open the possibility of inaccurate placements.

CHARACTERISTICS OF LEP LD STUDENTS AT REEVALUATION

In a related study, Wilkinson and Ortiz (1986) examined practices used in the reevaluation of LEP Hispanic students and how these impact continued special education eligibility. The sample included 72 learning disabled Hispanics. Half of the students were classified as LEP and were drawn from the same population as the LD study previously cited (Ortiz et al., 1985). LEP students were then paired with nonLEP subjects, using initial special education placement data. Both members of a pair had been referred and placed in special education while in the same grade and during the same school year.

Interestingly, although reassessments can be requested at any time by committees which review student progress annually, reevaluations of both LEPs and nonLEPs took place almost exactly 3 years after the initial assessment. Early reevaluation occurred for only 3% of the LEPs and 6% of the nonLEPs. This means that students identified as handicapped typically spend at least 3 years in that placement, making even more critical ensuring that initial decisions are accurate.

While the total number of tests administered ($n = 6$) did not change for either LEPs or nonLEPs between the initial assessment and reevaluation, the composition of test batteries did. Significantly fewer IQ tests were given at reevaluation. Unlike the initial assessment, which usually included two intelligence tests, one of which was nonverbal, more projective testing was done at reevaluation.

Teachers' ratings of children's dominant language at school were reported much less frequently at reevaluation than at initial assessment. Among children whose language dominance was perceived to have changed at reevaluation, 90% of LEPs and all nonLEPs moved in the direction of greater English usage. Reevaluations were characterized by more testing conducted in English.

Past research (Oakman & Wilson, 1986; Vance, Blixt, Ellis, & Debell, 1981) has suggested that handicapped children's scores on the WISC-R are fairly stable over time. However, both Verbal and Full Scale WISC-R IQs decreased significantly between administrations for this group of Hispanic students. The magnitude of score decreases was greater for LEPs than nonLEPs, although differences between the two groups were not significant.

Achievement scores were difficult to compare, in that few students received the same test during both evaluations. However, results which were available for the Woodcock-Johnson Psychoeducational Battery showed that math, reading and written language scores were approximately equal at initial placement and at reevaluation. The students' achievement did not change in respect to the achievement of their peers, despite specialized intervention. This fact raises questions about the efficacy of special education for this population.

The majority of students (66% of LEPs and 64% of nonLEPs) were assigned the same primary and secondary handicapping condition following reevaluation as assigned at initial evaluation. Rates of dismissal from special education were similar for the two groups: 11% for LEPs and 18% for nonLEPs. Placement committees recommended significantly more time in special education for students who were not dismissed, regardless of LEP status.

INDIVIDUALIZED EDUCATION PLAN (IEP)

One of the most important aspects of the special education process is the development of the Individualized Education Plan (IEP). In the case of linguistically different students, specialized services must not only be appropriate to handicapping conditions, but must also accommodate students' levels of native language and/or English proficiency as well.

Goals and Objectives for LEP Students

Wilkinson, Willig, and Ortiz (1986) investigated the IEPs written for the LD and MR subjects in their study. Goals relating to reading, written expression, and spelling were the most frequently specified for learning disabled LEP and nonLEP Hispanics across districts. The most frequently listed objectives were all reading related. Although the most frequently selected goals for the LEP MR students were in academic areas such as reading and language arts, the most frequent set objectives were in oral expression/expressive language.

Language of Instruction

None of the IEP forms used by any of the districts provided space or direction to specify the language of instruction. This may explain why so few references to language were found. Of the 396 IEPs examined, for both LEP and nonLEP students, eight (2%) stated that some instruction would be provided in the native language.

It appears that there is little difference between the goals and objectives included in the IEPs of limited-English-proficient Hispanic students and those specified for English-proficient students. Additionally, little difference was found between the content of IEPs written for language minority students and that of IEPs written for non-minority students as described in other studies (e.g., McCormick & Fisher, 1983; Pyecha et al., 1980; Turner & Macy/cited in Safer & Hobbs, 1980). These findings suggest that a child's language background and proficiency have little effect on the selection of goals and objectives by IEP committees.

Committee recommendations, with very few exceptions, assumed that handicapped LEP students profit from instruction delivered totally in English.

POLICY AND PRACTICE IMPLICATIONS

The results of the studies reported are a reflection of current practice in special education. While mandates aimed at ensuring that handicapped LEP students receive an appropriate education are embodied in policy, law, and judicial decisions (e.g., P.L. 94–142 of 1975; Diana vs. State Board of Education, 1970; Lau versus Nichols, 1974), districts need guidance to effectively implement existing safeguards. These findings and the effects emerging from them suggest specific policy and/or practice implications.

Policy and Practice Implications Associated with Assessment

1. It becomes clear from the results of these studies that there must be a requirement for an assessment of the competence of the student in the area of language prior to any other assessment. These assessments should not be confined to proficiency in English, but must also include assessment of competence in the student's native language. For referred students, such language assessment, because of its implications relative to the determination of handicapping conditions, must be the responsibility of special education and cannot be left to bilingual education and/or some other programs. Because language proficiency is critical to the determination of whether special education services are truly required, it must be assessed prior to any other assessments. Once the assessments traditionally used to determine entrance into special education have been accomplished, it is too late in the decisioning process to go back and determine language competence of the student in the native language and in English.

2. It must be recognized that to be truly handicapped, a child must be handicapped in his/her native or dominant language, not merely in the English language. The logic seems overwhelming that policy must be formulated which states that a student who is not handicapped in the native language is not a handicapped student.

3. Due to the paucity of standardized instruments and/or other measures available for students of limited English proficiency and/or bilingual students, it is necessary to utilize adaptations of assessment procedures and instruments. The specific policy practice implications are, however, that all such adaptations of assessments, procedures, and instruments must be documented and described within the students' records. These descriptions must become a part of reports utilized by the various special education decision-making committees. It is not uncommon for assessment personnel who make assessment adaptations to be absent from an Assessment, Review, and Dismissal (ARD) or IEP committee meeting. Therefore, it cannot be left to chance that adaptations and/or modifications in standardized procedures will be documented.

4. In addition, it must be recognized that scores obtained on assessment instruments and/or through assessment procedures for language minority students are most often a minimal, rather than a maximal, indication of abilities. For a variety of reasons, second language learners will score less than their potential. It is incumbent upon assessment personnel to be sensitive to this obvious fact and to articulate, both in assessment reports and in decision-making contexts, that the assessment results probably represent minimal evidence of abilities.

5. Although there is often a shortage of such personnel, it is incumbent upon special educators, parents of language minority children, and regular educators to insist upon the use of assessment personnel fluent in the student's dominant language. Without such insistence,

there will be limited movement on the part of administrators to hire bilingual professionals or for training institutions to train them.

6. Assessment is the "gearwheel" which drives placement into and out of special education. Special education must become more intimately involved with, and linked to, assessment personnel training and/or development. Special education is ordinarily not considered a major component of university preparation programs for assessment personnel, nor is it often a topic of professional development for assessment personnel. Without linkages to special education, the appropriate feedback loop associated with the effects of assessment of language minority students for special education will remain ineffective.

7. The traditional special education concept of an annual and/or 3-year follow-up assessment is often inappropriate for language minority students. These students are continuously enhancing and improving both their English and their native language skills. Assessment results for language minority children are, therefore, greatly influenced by time. Results obtained at initial assessment must lead to appropriately sequenced, and more frequent, follow-up assessments.

Policy and Practice Implications for Special Education

1. Special education instructional adaptations must also include adaptations appropriate for students of different cultures and languages. This is a unique and, at this time, relatively rare response on the part of special education instructional personnel. As the percentage of language and cultural minority students within special education programs increases, special education cannot remain truly special without these particular adaptations.

2. The findings of these studies highlight the critical need for personnel with specialized language skills to help with the adaptation and/or instructional process for language minority students placed in special education. Special education must have bilingual special education personnel available to serve language minority students, or, at the very least, special educators trained in English-as-a-second-language instructional techniques. Institutions of higher education must train such professionals.

3. The education profession is limited in the number of bilingual personnel and language specialists also trained as special educators. Therefore, it is particularly critical at the level of practice that special education utilize, within instructional, assessment, and decisioning processes, educational specialists from other program areas, specifically bilingual education. The integration of these complementary disciplines becomes critical to appropriate assessment, placement, and instruction for handicapped language minority students.

Policy and Practice Implications for Regular Education

1. The mismatch between instructional needs of the language minority child and the general educational system at this time destines many language minority students to a general lack of achievement, not necessarily indicative of a need or requirement for special education services. There must be universal policy statements articulating that responding to this general lack of achievement is not the exclusive responsibility of the special education system.

2. In order to enhance the probability of accurate identification and placement of language minority students into special education, regular education must institute prereferral processes which give the system the opportunity to adapt instructional programming to the language minority student. Certain models (Adelman, 1970; Ortiz & Garcia, see Chapter 2) hold promise for the regular educator in this critical area of practice.

3. Regular education must more clearly define and make more generally available to teachers and others in the system the criteria to be applied when placing language minority students

in special education. Understanding of these criteria are critical to preventing inappropriate allocation of special education resources to the student who is not, in fact, handicapped.

4. Regular educators must make generally available to the regular education system information which describes the developmental stages for second language acquisition. Information about other student characteristics, such as culture and socioeconomic status, which influence student behavior and which can be inaccurately interpreted as deviant, should also be part of the knowledge base of regular educators.

Finally, research and development efforts must focus upon the development of instruments and procedures appropriate for second language learners. Demographic data suggest that the need for such assessment tools will increase, rather than diminish, in the future.

The findings and effects of the studies reported must be viewed as formative for special educators. These findings are presented in order to raise points of concern and issues of policy and to point the direction of future practice for special education personnel.

REFERENCES

Adelman, H. (1970). An interactive view of causality. *Academic Therapy, 6*, 43–52.

Carrow, E. (1973). *Test for Auditory Comprehension of Language: English/Spanish*. Hingham, MA: Teaching Resources.

Cummins, J. (1984). *Bilingualism and special education: Issues in assessment and pedagogy*. Clevedon, Avon, England: Multilingual Matters.

Damico, J. S., Oller, J. W., & Storey, M. E. (1983). The diagnosis of language disorders in bilingual children. *Journal of Speech and Hearing Disorders, 49*, 285–294.

DeAvila, E. A., & Duncan, S. E. (1977). *Language Assessment Scales (LAS), Level 1*. Corte Madera, CA: Linguametrics Group.

Diana v. State Board of Education. C.A. No. 70–37 R.F.P. (N.D. Cal. filed Feb. 3, 1970).

Doll, E. A. (1965). *Vineland Social Maturity Scale: Manual of Directions* (Rev. ed.). Minneapolis: American Guidance Service.

Dunn, L. M. (1965). *Peabody Picture Vocabulary Test*. Circle Pines, MN: American Guidance Service.

Dunn, L. M., & Markwardt, F. C., Jr. (1970). *Peabody Individual Achievement Test*. Circle Pines, MN: American Guidance Service.

Education for All Handicapped Children Act of 1975 (Public Law 94–142, 28 Nov., 1975).

Erickson, J., & Omark, D. R. (1981). *Communication assessment of the bilingual bicultural child*. Baltimore, MD: University Park Press.

Fiesta Educativa. (1984). La familia en marcha: Final report. Chicago: Author.

Goldman, R., & Fristoe, M. (1969). *Goldman-Fristoe Test of Articulation*. Circle Pines, MN: American Guidance Service.

Hodgkinson, H. L. (1985). All in the system: Demographics of education—kindergarten through graduate school. Washington, DC: Institute for Educational Leadership.

Holtzman, W. H., Jr., Ortiz, A. A., & Wilkinson, C. Y. (1986). *Characteristics of limited English proficient Hispanic students in programs for the mentally retarded: Implications for policy, practice, and research*. Austin, TX: The University of Texas, Handicapped Minority Research Institute on Language Proficiency.

Jastak, J. F., & Jastak, S. (1978). *Wide Range Achievement Test*. Wilmington, DE: Jastak Associates.

Juarez, M. (1983). Assessment and treatment of minority language handicapped children: The role of the monolingual speech-language pathologist. *Topics in Language Disorders, 3*, 57–66.

Kaufman, A. S.(1979). *Intelligent testing with the WISC-R*. New York: John Wiley & Sons.

Koppitz, E. M. (1964). *The Bender Gestalt Test for Young Children*. New York: Grune & Stratton.

Lau v. Nichols. (1974). 414 U.S. 563, 39 L. Ed. 2d 7, 94 S Ct. 786, 38.

Mattes, L. J., & Omark, D. R. (1984). *Speech and language assessment for the bilingual handicapped*. San Diego, CA: College-Hill Press.

McCormick, P. K., & Fisher, M. D. (1983, February). *An analysis of individualized education program goals for learning disabled students*. Paper presented at the International Association for Children with Learning Disabilities Conference, Washington, DC. (ERIC Document Reproduction Service No. ED 235 644).

Muma, J. R. (1978). *Language handbook*. Englewood Cliffs, NJ: Prentice-Hall.

Newcomer, P. L., & Hammill, D. (1977). *Test of Language Development*. Austin, TX: Pro-Ed.

Oakman, S., & Wilson, B. J. (1986, April). *Stability of WISC–R intelligence scores: Implications for three-year re-evaluations of learning disabled students*. Paper presented at the meeting of the American Educational Research Association, San Francisco, CA.

Oller, J. W., Jr. (1983). Testing proficiencies and diagnosing language disorders in bilingual children. In D. R. Omark & J. G. Erickson (Eds.), *The exceptional bilingual child* (pp. 69–88). San Diego, CA: College-Hill Press.

Ortiz, A. A. (1984). Choosing the language of instruction for exceptional bilingual children. *Teaching Exceptional Children, 16*(3), 208–212.

Ortiz, A. A., Garcia, S. B., Holtzman, W. H., Jr., Polyzoi, E., Snell, W. E., Jr., Wilkinson, C. Y., & Willig, A. C. (1985). *Characteristics of limited English proficient Hispanic students in programs for the learning disabled: Implications for policy, practice and research*. Austin, TX: The University of Texas, Handicapped Minority Research Institute on Language Proficiency.

Ortiz, A. A., Garcia, S. B., Wheeler, D. S., & Maldonado-Colon, E. (1986). *Characteristics of limited English proficient students served in programs for the speech and language handicapped; Implications for policy, practice, and research*. Austin, TX: The University of Texas, Handicapped Minority Research Institute on Language Proficiency.

Ortiz, A. A., & Maldonado-Colon, E. (1986). Recognizing learning disabilities in bilingual children: How to lessen inappropriate referrals of language minority students to special education. *Journal of Reading, Writing, and Learning Disabilities International, 2*(1), 43–56.

Prutting, C. A. (1982). Pragmatics as social competence. *Journal of Speech and Hearing Disorders, 47*, 125–134.

Pyecha, J., Cox, J. L., Conway, L. E., Hocott, A., Jaffe, J., Pelosi, J., & Wiegerink, R. (1980). *A national survey of individualized education programs (IEP's) for handicapped children: Vol. 3 Basic survey findings*. (ERIC Document Reproduction Service No. ED 199 972).

Reich, K. (1986, September 26). Hispanic population likely to double by 2020. *Austin American Statesman*, A–4.

Safer, N., & Hobbs, B. (1980). Developing, implementing, and evaluating individualized education programs. *School Psychology Review, 9*(3), 212–220.

Sander, E. K. (1972). When are speech sounds learned? *Journal of Speech and Hearing Disorders, 37*, 55–63.

Saville, M. R., & Troike, R. C. (1975). *A handbook of bilingual education*. Washington, DC: Teachers of English to Speakers of Other Languages.

Terman, L. M., & Merrill, M. A. (1960). *Stanford-Binet Intelligence Scale*. Boston, MA: Houghton-Mifflin.

Texas Bilingual Education Act (1981). Senate Bill 477.

Trevino, J. (1987, September 21). Hispanic political clout gaining. *Austin American Statesman*, A–9.

Tyack, D., & Gottsleben, R. (1974). *Language sampling, analysis, and training*. Palo Alto, CA: Consulting Psychologists Press.

Vance, H. B., Blixt, S., Ellis, R., & Debell, S. (1981). Stability of the WISC–R for a sample of exceptional children. *Journal of Clinical Psychology, 37*(2), 397–399.

Wechsler, D. (1974). *Manual for the Wechsler Intelligence Scale for Children-Revised*. New York: Psychological Corporation.

Wilkinson, C. Y., & Ortiz, A. A. (1986). *Characteristics of limited English proficient and English proficient learning disabled Hispanic students at initial assessment and at re-evaluation*. Austin, TX: The University of Texas, Handicapped Minority Research Institute on Language Proficiency.

Wilkinson, C. Y., Willig, A. C., & Ortiz, A. A. (1986). *Goals and objectives targeted in individualized education programs developed for exceptional limited English proficient and English proficient Hispanic students*. Austin, TX: The University of Texas, Handicapped Minority Research Institute on Language Proficiency.

Woodcock, W. R., & Johnson, M. B. (1977). *Woodcock-Johnson Psychoeducational Battery*. Hingham, MA: Teaching Resources Corporation.

CHAPTER 7

Educational Assessment of the Culturally Diverse and Behavior Disordered Student: An Examination of Critical Effect

George Sugai

The Education for All Handicapped Children Act (P.L. 94–142, 1975) is one of public education's most important pieces of legislation. It has occasioned significant changes in how handicapped children and youth are perceived and served in America's schools. As a result, special education programs have become commonplace in most public school buildings. The effect of these changes on the roles and responsibilities of special education, however, have been debated actively in recent months (Lily, 1986; Wang, Reynolds, & Walberg, 1986; Will, 1986). Madeleine Will, Assistant Secretary for the Office of Special Education and Rehabilitative Services, has delineated a number of challenges that face special educators in the next decade. They include the following:

1. The categorical nature of special education programs reinforces a presumption that students with learning problems cannot be taught in regular education settings.
2. The diverse number of special education programs has made it difficult to define how special and regular education are different and to determine who should receive what services.
3. Special education programs tend to focus on learning problems which in turn cause students to perceive themselves as inadequate and incompetent.
4. Categorical special education programs tend to limit services for handicapped students to those services associated with the handicapping category. As a result students are underserved.

These problems are particularly apparent when working with students who display behavior problems. Seriously emotionally disturbed or behaviorally disordered (BD) students represent one of the special education's most un- and underserved handicapped populations (Grosenick & Huntze, 1980; Kauffman, 1985). The BD student is more likely to be removed from the mainstream and to be placed in more restrictive settings than students with less intrusive handicaps. According to findings reported in the Eighth Annual Report to Congress on the Implementation of the Education of the Handicapped Act (U.S. Department of Education, 1986), 68% of all handicapped students in the United States were served in regular classroom settings, 25% in separate classes, and 7% in separate schools or other settings. In contrast, 44% of behaviorally disordered students were educated in regular classroom settings, 37% in separate classes, and 19% in separate schools or other settings.

Since 1977, when 3,704,915 special education students were served, there has been a 17.6% increase in the number of students receiving special education services (in 1984–1985, 4,363,031 students were served). In contrast, the number of BD students has increased 32%

(283,072 to 373,207), the highest categorical increase except in the learning disabilities area (131%). Despite these increases, the percent of identified BD students in the total school age population (3–21 years of age) is 0.5%. A survey of state directors of special education (Schultz, Hirshoren, Manton, & Henderson, 1971) indicated prevalence estimates that ranged from 0.5% to 15%. Kauffman (1985) suggested that a reasonable estimate should be 6%–10%. Using a very conservative figure of 2%, special education programs might be serving 1,373,880 BD students. This discrepancy between the actual and expected number of BD students suggests that a significant number of students are not being served in special education. A further inference is that many students with emotional or behavioral problems are being served effectively (or ineffectively) in general education settings.

These service delivery and identification problems are further confounded by cultural diversity. In different regions of the country, some culturally different students are overrepresented in special education programs for behavior disordered students (e.g., Black, Hispanic), while other groups are underrepresented (e.g., Asian). New immigrant populations from Pacific rim countries pose even greater problems to schools that are based on more traditional majority curricula and practices.

The purpose of this chapter is to review and describe classroom-based assessment and evaluation strategies that can be used when working with culturally diverse, BD students. In describing these strategies a context for educating culturally different, BD students is developed. Guidelines for making sound educational decisions within the context of cultural diversity and behavioral deviance are also presented. An interventionist approach to assessment and evaluation is recommended.

FIRST ORDER CHANGE

This discussion is based on the premise of first order change, or change at the behavior and classroom levels. Second order, or system level change, is not discussed directly because solutions involve complex political, legislative, and attitudinal modifications beyond the scope of this chapter.

First order change emphasizes the role of classroom teachers and acknowledges their ability to make accurate diagnoses about student performance. Gerber and Semmel (1984) recommended that teacher suspicions should not be viewed as a call for validation "testing" but as a valid test in and of themselves. Teacher identification is based directly on the working characteristics of the classroom, that is, nature of instruction, classroom economics, behavior management, student performance, etc. They also indicated that it is inappropriate, misguided, and potentially harmful to base identification of handicapped students on psychometric measurement. This norm-referenced approach enables teachers to divorce themselves from ownership of an instructional problem. The school's failure to tolerate and accommodate individual differences frequently shapes a student's handicaps, not deviations based on psychometric measurements or cultural, learning, or behavioral differences.

FOUNDATIONS

Before beginning this discussion on assessment and evaluation practices with culturally different, behavior disordered students, some basic questions should be discussed.

What Is a Minority?

Many definitions have been used to describe a "minority." For the purposes of this discussion, a definition by Brantliner and Guskin (1985) will be utilized. Based on their definition, a minority individual has three basic characteristics: (a) "politically excluded from proportionate roles and responsibilities in the major institutions of power" (p. 1), (b) "receive less than their share of goods, services, values, rewards, power, prestige, and prerogatives" (p. 1), and (c) perceived by the dominant institutions as "deviant, difficult, inferior, or wrong" (p. 1) (or somewhat more positively, different or interesting).

What is Competence?

"Competence" does not equal dominance, but equals power, skill, knowledge, and ability to cause change. Power in this case refers to the ability to engage in objective and functional decision making that results in an increase in the individual's ability to achieve proactive change, that is, to access the goods, resources, services, etc. of the dominant society.

What is the Role of Language in Student Learning?

Language is a major factor contributing to a student's success (or failure) in U.S. public school classrooms. A student's language system represents the vehicle by which culture, knowledge, and competence are communicated within and between cultures.

> Language is unique in its dual role as an intrinsic component of culture and as a medium through which other aspects of culture, including the content of formal education, are expressed and transmitted. Language is an intricate part of selfhood, and the way others respond to it affects the child's self-concept and feelings towards self. (Brantlinger & Guskin, 1985, p. 7)

HOW DOES CULTURE AFFECT STUDENT BEHAVIOR?

The relationship between culture and student behavior or performance can be described in a simple six-component configuration (see Figure 1). In general, a family's cultural beliefs reflect the values and standards of the larger culture within which the family exists. These cultural beliefs have a strong influence on the values incorporated into the basic family unit. This set of culturally based values, in turn, affects child management practices used by family members within the home. Childrearing practices influence the child's academic, social/emotional, and behavioral development and how he or she responds to the demands and expectations of the school and community. When cultural beliefs are diverse or in conflict with the dominant community or school environment, social development and educational opportunities are affected. The existence of a handicapping condition, especially a learning or behavioral problem, influences the student's movement through the six components.

What Factors Determine Behavioral Normalcy/Deviancy?

Determining how a student's culture interacts with the school culture and when a student is behaviorally disordered is very difficult. Such decisions tend to be based on norm-referenced standards that are setting or culturally referenced. This condition can be described in a four-component structure that organizes the major factors that contribute to determinations of normalcy and deviancy (see Figure 2). Predisposing factors consist of those conditions which predispose or make a student susceptible to exhibiting a set or class of behaviors. These conditions are frequently biologically or genetically based (e.g., physical attributes, race) or described in more covert terms (e.g., emotions, thoughts, feelings). Behaviors consist of those language and action events that students (or teachers) emit to operate or act on the environment. We use student behaviors to make inferences and decisions about the student.

The third component of this structure includes those precipitating factors or antecedent conditions that trigger a class of behaviors. Events and objects in the social or instructional settings are included—for example, setting contexts, rules, norms, expectations, attitudes, curricula, etc. Precipitating factors that impinge upon a student's learning are biased by the predisposing characteristics of the teacher and school climate. The fourth component consists of contributing factors which are consequence conditions that become associated with a given class of behaviors. They include events and objects in the social environment that immediately

FIGURE 1

The Relationship Between Culture and Student Behavior

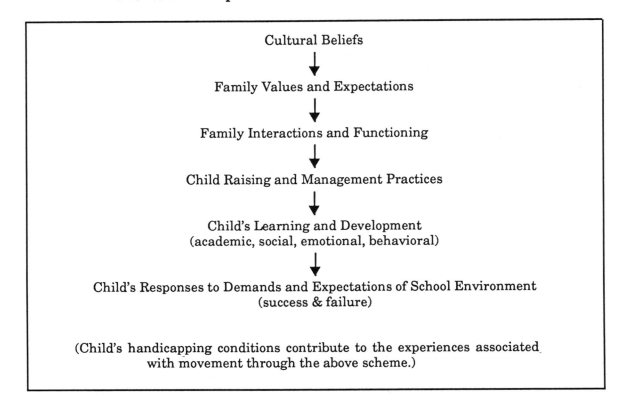

Cultural Beliefs

↓

Family Values and Expectations

↓

Family Interactions and Functioning

↓

Child Raising and Management Practices

↓

Child's Learning and Development
(academic, social, emotional, behavioral)

↓

Child's Responses to Demands and Expectations of School Environment
(success & failure)

(Child's handicapping conditions contribute to the experiences associated
with movement through the above scheme.)

follow a student's learning or responses, for example, social reactions, reinforcement, punishment.

When assessing the learning and behavioral characteristics of the culturally different student, all behaviors and predisposing, precipitating, and contributing factors from the school, community, and home settings should be considered. Kauffman (1985) has described five basic school-based contributions to determinations of deviancy: (a) "insensitivity to children's individuality"—failure to acknowledge a student's expressions of individuality which are predisposed by culture and learning history; (b) "inappropriate expectations"—self-fulfilling prophecies held by teachers and school building staff; (c) "inconsistent management"—unequal treatment across individual students and discrepant behavior and classroom management; (d) "instruction in nonfunctional and irrelevant skills"—failure to engage students in learning and creating artificial reasons for learning; (e) "nefarious contingencies of reinforcement"—inconsistent use of reinforcement and feedback for both appropriate and inappropriate behaviors; and (f) "undesirable models"—inappropriate behaviors modeled by peers and adults.

The outcomes associated with a failure to consider predisposing, precipitating, and contributing factors and failure to change school contributions to deviancy can be dramatic for the culturally different student. Four outcomes can be delineated (Chinn & McCormick, 1986). First, minority children are expected to have higher incidences of handicaps than other groups. Second, minority children are judged as less competent than their peers. Third, disproportionate and erroneous numbers of minority children are referred for special education evaluation. Fourth, teachers tend to refer children who bother them. In some cases migrant and immigrant children tend to be referred sooner than other children, frequently before they

FIGURE 2

**A Four-Component Structure that Organizes the Factors
Contributing to Normalcy and Deviancy**

Precipitating Factors	Predisposing Factors	Behaviors	Contributing Factors
Events and objects in the social environment; setting contexts, rules, norms, expectations	Biologic make-up, genetic endowment; physical attributes; cultural experiences, values, and norms; behavior repertoire; emotions, thoughts, and feelings	Language and actions	Events and objects in the environment: effects, reactions, products

have had the opportunity to adjust to the new demands and expectations of a new system. In all these outcomes, the problem is a conflict between the teacher and student (and family) as to what constitutes acceptable behavior.

APPLIED PROBLEM

The goals of regular and special education are clear: (a) to assess and evaluate student learning; (b) to prepare students for the less restrictive learning environment; (c) to prepare students for community living; and (d) to increase students' opportunities for academic and social success. However, when working with students with divergent learning or behavioral histories, special educators must combat the effects of time, which is the applied problem (see Figure 3). As discrepancies between special pupils and their peers increase over time, opportunities for academic and social success are reduced. Without extremely powerful interventions, the kind and number of interfering or nonfunctional behaviors increase over time. The applied problem is further compounded when working with students from culturally different backgrounds whose behaviors are perceived as deviant.

The applied problem can be characterized as follows: (a) failure to acknowledge the classroom teacher as a "perfect test", (b) failure to accommodate individual differences in teaching and social interactions, (c) failure to examine the full range of factors that contribute to student performance, (d) tendency to separate assessment and evaluation practices from instruction, (e) tendency to view culturally different students as deviant and less competent than their dominant culture peers, and (f) failure to evaluate the effect of individual biases and values on educational decision making. The remaining sections of this chapter describe assessment evaluation practices that will respond to aspects of the applied problem.

PART OF THE SOLUTION: AN EXAMINATION OF CRITICAL EFFECTS

This attempt at a solution to the applied problem emphasizes an interventionist approach. It is based on three basic assumptions that are founded on theories of social learning and applied behavior analysis. First, the interventionist approach is based on the assumption that behavior or student performance can be described in understandable terms. Second, behavior

FIGURE 3

The Applied Problem of Increased Learning Discrepancies Between
Special Pupils and Their Peers Over Time

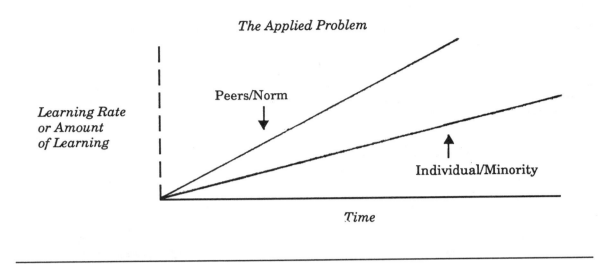

tends to occur in regular patterns that, when assessed adequately, can be predicted. Third, both appropriate and inappropriate behaviors are acquired in the same manner.

The interventionist approach has the following characteristics: (a) student and teacher share responsibility for successful and unsuccessful learning, (b) teachers actively participate in student learning, (c) assessment is an integral component of instruction, (d) the direct measurement of student performance is the focus of teaching, (e) assessment and evaluation is centered on the immediate contexts of learning, (f) socially important behaviors and educational goals are stressed, and (g) principles of applied behavior analysis are emphasized.

Fundamentals

Before addressing assessment and evaluation practices directly, it is important that we discuss some fundamental and underlying concepts. Traditionally, assessment is linked directly to the measurement of student performance, that is, strengths and weaknesses. Effective assessment and evaluation practices, however, are grounded in a multidisciplinary team approach that enables teachers, parents, and students to communicate, be accountable, and make reliable and valid decisions. The team approach also can set the occasion for analytic thinking and problem solving, which decrease the effects of irrelevant factors contributing to poor educational decisions.

Effective assessment and evaluation practices also consider the contexts in which student performance is displayed. The effective teaching movement has documented many important instructional pinpoints that must be assessed. A summary of these contextual factors is included in Figure 4. More detailed discussion on the effective teaching research can be found in other sources (e.g., Bickel & Bickel, 1986; Good & Brophy, 1984; Wittrock, 1986).

The point of this discussion is that student assessment should be viewed as an indicator of performance under conditions of predisposing, contributing, and precipitating factors. The student comes to the learning experience with a set of predisposing factors that must be assessed, but assessed within the context of contributing and precipitating factors governed by the instructional conditions provided by the teacher. If we fail to consider the contributions

FIGURE 4

Characteristics of Effective Teaching

Presented curriculum
Performance feedback
Validated instructional procedures
Formative assessment and evaluation practices
Emphasis on academic learning time
      Student engaged with curriculum
      Brisk instructional pace
      Increase learning opportunities
      High success rate
      Time allocated to learning
Training for generalized responding
Fundamental classroom management strategies
      Continuous monitoring
      Predictable structure
      Sound pacing and scheduling
      Communication of academic and social
        expectations for achievement
      Safe, orderly, and academically focused work environment

of the whole range of factors on student learning, we are not being efficient in our attack on the applied problem.

Assessment and Evaluation Practices: An Interventionist Perspective

When culturally different students are assessed because their behaviors deviate from their "normal" peer group, reliable assessment and evaluation practices must be used. In general, four basic levels of assessment may be described: (a) archival, or previous observations, reports, and data on past performance; (b) verbal report, or interviews with the student and others who are familiar with the student; (c) standardized/norm-referenced testing, or contrived statistically based contexts to which the student responds, with student performance subsequently being compared to a norm group; and (d) direct observation, or observing the student in natural contexts. Of these four, the first three will not be discussed because they contribute relatively little to first order, or behavior, change. Direct observation procedures produce information about current levels of functioning, are not as vulnerable to reporting biases, and are not limited by the contexts of standardized testing formats.

The following discussion addresses basic guidelines for assessment and evaluation from an interventionist perspective. More detailed descriptions of specific direct observation techniques can be obtained from other sources (e.g., Alberto & Troutman, 1986; Wolery, Bailey, & Sugai, in press; Kerr & Nelson, 1983). Two basic questions are addressed here: Is there a problem? What is the nature of the problem?

Is There a Problem?

Determining whether there is a problem is one of the most important decisions that teachers and parents must make. An answer to this question can have a significant influence on the student's future educational experiences. The observation that a student is not learning is sufficient to suggest that a problem exists; however, the real question is whether special instructional modifications are required, that is, is special education needed? To answer this question, the relative contribution of extraneous factors must be determined. In the case of the student who is culturally predisposed to be different (e.g., family, values), failure to succeed may be associated with nonhandicapping conditions. It is particularly important that nonbiased practices be employed.

Identifying *who* views the situation as troublesome is useful in determining the severity of the problem and, ultimately, whether special education is required. Generally, teachers and school building administrators indicate that a problem exists; however, it is not uncommon for parents and students to pinpoint difficulties and request assistance. If special education is being considered, several independent referrals should be received, or independent validation of the initial indication should be conducted. Although many questions can be asked to verify the existence of a problem, the following represents a sample of the kinds of questions that should be asked:

1. Have several independent referrals been made?
2. How is the problem operationalized or defined?
3. Is the behavior functionally different from some comparison or standard, for example, peer group?
4. Have there been dramatic changes in the individual's behavior in relatively short periods of time?
5. Have there been any significant life events in the student's or family's recent history?
6. Does the behavior interfere with the student's academic progress? Peer or adult relations? Community functioning?
7. Is the behavior destructive of property or injurious to other people?

This problem identification stage provides an excellent opportunity to conduct prereferral interventions. The prereferral intervention model is a consultation variation to service delivery (Graden, Casey, & Bonstrom, 1983; 1985; Graden, Casey, & Christenson, 1985). The emphasis is placed on the identification and definition of the student's presenting problem and, if necessary, the development and implementation of possible interventions before the actual student referral for special services. The prereferral intervention approach has evolved from concern for the increasing number of special education referrals. Algozzine, Christenson, and Ysseldyke (1982) and Sevick and Ysseldyke (1986) estimated that approximately 90% of the school age children who are considered for special education are evaluated formally. About three-quarters of that number are labeled and receive special services.

The advantages of the prereferral intervention model for the culturally different student who displays emotional or behavioral problems are numerous. First, regular education teachers are given a level of assistance that enables them to keep the student in the mainstream and to avoid creating a "pull-out" situation. Second, the likelihood of inappropriate and/or highly segregated placements can be reduced. Third, the quality of the educational programming available in the general education setting can be enhanced. Fourth, the focus of educational interventions is retained in the regular education classroom or setting. Finally, the cooperative relationship between regular and special education is reinforced.

What is the Nature of the Problem?

If there is confirmation that a problem exists, the character of the problem should be determined. This step requires a determination of possible testable explanations or hypotheses. A systematic examination of these testable explanations follows to ascertain the functional nature of the relationship between the behavior and other precipitating, predisposing, and contributing factors.

Functional Analysis and Functional Relationships. One of the most useful assessment procedures is the functional analysis (Bijou, Peterson, Harris, Allen, & Johnston, 1969;

Skinner, 1953). It enables teachers to analyze the nature of a problem in an objective and unbiased fashion by emphasizing direct observation under prevailing response conditions. Teachers who conduct a functional analysis measure (a) student behavior, (b) teacher behavior, and (c) setting or contextual conditions.

A functional analysis is simple to execute. The observer divides a piece of paper into three columns and labels them "antecedents," "behaviors," and "consequences" (see Figure 5). After noting the setting conditions in which the observation is being completed, the observer notes each behavior displayed by the target student. Any events that precede (antecedents) or follow (consequences) a given behavior are also noted. Sequences or chains of events and behaviors can be highlighted by placing a check in the appropriate column.

After completing the functional analysis observation, recurring behaviors, antecedents, and consequences are examined. Hypotheses are generated that describe the relationship between the behaviors and preceding or following events. These hypotheses are called "testable explanations," and are defined as specific statements about possible functional relationships between two variables. Some examples of testable explanations follow:

- "Whenever the teacher has a transition between lessons that exceeds 5 minutes, the number of talkouts emitted by Julio increases threefold."

- "If Cleo sits next to Caesar during English class, Caesar finishes half the number of assignments he normally completes."

- "Kiam turns away and does not interact with others when she is corrected publicly for making an error during oral reading."

It is important to note that in each of these testable explanations both variables (i.e., student behavior and antecedent/consequence events) are described in terms that can be observed and validated by another person. This degree of specificity enables an objective and systematic implementation of possible manipulations to test the integrity of the testable explanation. Statements that do not contain manipulatable components are called "explanatory fictions"; for example, "Whenever Gordie is hyperactive, he talks back to the teacher," or "Cleo fails to make friends because of her home situation." In these examples, "hyperactivity" and "home situation" are not described in observable terms and are not manipulatable or testable.

If the manipulation of components from a testable explanation produces consistent and predictable changes in the student's targeted behaviors, the testable explanation is said to be a statement of a "functional relationship." A functional relationship describes the nature of the problem and gives the teacher a starting point for the development of possible interventions. When working with culturally different students who display disordered behavior, our job as teachers is to change nonadaptive functional relationships and replace them with more adaptive ones. If the difference is cultural in nature, students must be taught a larger repertoire of skills to increase their opportunities for success without sacrificing individual differences.

Empirical and Social Validity. When a problem has been identified and its characteristics delineated, teachers must validate it both empirically and socially. Empirical validation refers to the systematic testing of the relationship between the student's problem behaviors and the contextual conditions that are associated with it. Empirical validation requires that the teacher collect direct observational data on the occurrence of the problem behavior under a variety of preplanned conditions. If the behavior changes only when the conditions are manipulated, and if other confounding factors can be accounted for, the stronger the validation. When teachers can predict the behavior change under different conditions, then a sound functional relationship has been described. For example, Kiam's teacher can change the error correction procedure so that it is not public. If Kiam subsequently interacts more and turns away less, the functional relationship is confirmed. If the public error correction procedure is reinstated, and the problem behaviors recur, the teacher has further evidence as to the empirical validity of the functional relationship statement.

FIGURE 5

Functional Analysis Format

FUNCTIONAL ANALYSIS

Observer _____

Student _____

Date _____

Setting Characteristics:

Time	Antecedents	Behaviors	Consequences

Empirical validation is useful, but if the functional relationship is not viewed as a problem by relevant others, it may not require special attention. An examination of social validation enables teachers to obtain more subjective information about the nature of the problem. Two basic forms of social validation data can be obtained (Kazdin, 1977). Subjective evaluation information is collected from the student and/or relevant others who are familiar with the student, for example, parents, other teachers, school building staff. This information is obtained through simple interview procedures. The second form of social validation data is determined by comparing the student's behaviors to the performance of his or her peers. In the case of the culturally different student, two peer group comparisons should be considered: the majority peer group and the student's culturally similar peer group.

Wolf (1978) suggested that social validation procedures examine three major instructional areas. The first is an examination of the social significance of the goals or expectations that have been established for a student. The question is whether the student's specific educational goals represent what the classroom, school, family, and community really want and value. Second, the social appropriateness of the instructional procedures available to the student must be assessed. Given that the goals are important, do the ends justify the means; that is, do teachers, students, parents, and other consumers consider the instructional procedures and treatments acceptable? The last area is an evaluation of the social importance of the changes in the student's behavior. Teachers, parents, and the student should ask whether the student is satisfied with the degree of change observed in both desirable and undesirable outcomes.

Communicative Function of Behavior. A powerful complement to the systematic determination of functional relationships is the analysis of the communicative function of behavior (Donnellan, Mirenda, Mesaros, & Fassbender, 1984). Regardless of the kind of overt behaviors displayed by a student, the communicative intent that "motivates" student responding may be difficult to determine. Donnellan and associates suggested that there are two basic categories of behavioral function: interactive and noninteractive. Interactive functions may communicate requests, negations, or declarations/comments. Noninteractive functions include self-regulation, rehearsal, habitual, and relaxation/tension release.

It is important to consider that students with different learning histories or diverse cultural backgrounds may have different "behavioral indicators" to communicate their functional intents. When working with students, especially those who are predisposed with diverse cultures and family value systems, it is important to evaluate behaviors from within the context of their communicative function. Donnellan et al. suggested that three basic intervention approaches be considered based on the behavior observed and its inferred communicative intent: (a) teach replacement communicative responses, (b) use functionally related alternative response procedures, and (c) manipulate antecedent conditions. Assessing the communicative function of behavior will increase the teacher's ability to make objective and nonbiased assessments of the nature of a problem.

Critical Effect Principle. When examining the communicative function of a behavior, the focus is on the inferred motivation and intent that drives a behavior. Teachers working with culturally diverse students also must attend to the types of behaviors displayed and the critical effects associated with them (Neel, 1983). As we have emphasized throughout this paper, the types or forms of behavior emitted by a student are learned and culturally based. A given context or situation sets the occasion for different students to display different forms of behavior that frequently are associated with the same critical effect. For example, if Crystal is thirsty, the critical effect she attempts to achieve is to get a drink of water and satisfy her thirst. Crystal can achieve this critical effect in classroom settings in a number of ways: (a) raise her hand and ask for permission to get a drink, (b) not raise her hand and say that she is thirsty, (c) demand that another person bring her a glass of water, (d) be noncompliant or aggressive toward another person, earn a trip to the office, and get a drink on the way...and the list goes on. Which behavior she actually displays will be directed by her learning and cultural history. The situation is further compounded by the same behavioral forms being used to create different critical effects. For example, Crystal also uses noncompliance to avoid working on math problems, and she asks permission to get a drink in order to visit her locker.

The critical effect concept is important to the objective and accurate assessment of student behavior and the development of appropriate intervention strategies. Teachers must remember that behavioral forms and critical effects will vary with setting and contextual conditions. The traditional practice of looking at a student's behavior in isolation from the environmental or predisposing conditions increases the likelihood of intervention error and biased referral and placement decisions. When assessing behavioral forms and critical effects, the following types of questions should be considered:

1. What are the behavior forms that are in the student's repertoire?
2. What are the critical effects that are associated with these forms?
3. What are the critical effect requirements of the less restrictive or natural environment of the individual student?
4. What are the form expectations of the less restrictive environment that are required to achieve these critical effects?
5. What contexts (setting events) predict a given form/critical effect functional relationship?
6. What type of student learning/performance problem exists?

CONCLUSION

The purpose of this chapter was to develop a context for working with culturally diverse students who display behavioral problems. In this discussion, an attempt was made to describe how cultural diversity affects educational decision making and to describe a sampling of educational assessment and evaluation strategies that can reduce the bias associated with more traditional assessment practices. This paper was developed on the premise that teachers are valid and appropriate professionals to be engaged in the assessment and evaluation of student performance. It was recommended that the use of psychometrically based, indirect assessment procedures be replaced by curriculum-based practices that focus on the educational process rather than on student performance only.

When teaching the culturally diverse student, teachers should be systematic and objective when attempting to identify and examine the nature of a problem behavior or situation. A prereferral approach to problem identification was described as a possible structure for increasing cooperative and efficient problem solving. The focus of this discussion was on direct observation assessment methods, including functional analysis, empirical and social validation, communicative function of behavior, and behavioral forms and critical effects.

Although the intent of this paper was to describe these assessment and evaluation principles, a more important purpose was to emphasize that schools must acknowledge and understand how cultural diversity provides a context for academic and social behavior learning and change. For some minority groups the influence of culture can decrease access to the academic and social success that is governed and evaluated by the norms and values of the dominant culture. The greater the difference, the more difficult access will be and the greater the probability of referral for alternative educational experiences. Objective assessment and evaluation practices were stressed to decrease the influence of irrelevant factors or biases on sound educational decision making.

REFERENCES

Alberto, P. A., & Troutman, A. C. (1986). *Applied behavior analysis for teachers* (2nd ed.). Columbus, OH: Merrill.

Algozzine, B., Christenson, S., & Ysseldyke, J. E. (1982). Probabilities associated with the referral to placement process. *Teacher Education and Special Education, 5*, 19–23.

Bickel, W. E., & Bickel, D. D. (1986). Effective schools, classrooms, and instruction: Implications for education. *Exceptional Children, 52*, 489–500.

Bijou, S. W., Peterson, R. F., Harris, F. R., Allen, K. E., & Johnston, M. S. (1969). Methodology for experimental studies of young children in natural settings. *Psychological Record, 1*, 174–191.

Brantlinger, E. A., & Guskin, S. L. (1985). Implications of social and cultural differences for special education with specific recommendations. *Focus on Exceptional Children, 18*, 1–12.

Chinn, P. C., & McCormick, L. (1986). Cultural diversity and exceptionality. In N. G. Haring & L. McCormick (Eds.), *Exceptional children and youth* (4th ed.) (pp. 95–117). Columbus, OH: Merrill.

Donnellan, A. M., Mirenda, P. L., Mesaros, R. A., & Fassbender, L. L. (1984). Analyzing the communicative functions of aberrant behavior. *Journal of the Association for the Severely Handicapped, 9*, 201–212.

Gerber, M. M., & Semmel, M. I. (1984). Teacher as imperfect test. *Educational Psychologist, 19*, 137–148.

Good, T. L., & Brophy, J. E. (1984). *Looking in classrooms* (3rd ed.). NY: Harper & Row.

Gollnick, D. M., & Chinn, P. C. (1986). *Multicultural education in a pluralistic society* (2nd ed.). Columbus, OH: Merrill.

Graden, J. L., Casey, A., & Bonstrom, O. (1983). *Prereferral interventions: Effects on referral rates and teacher attitudes*. (Research report number: 140). Minneapolis, MN: Institute for Research on Learning Disabilities.

Graden, J. L., Casey, A., & Bonstrom, O. (1985). Implementing a prereferral intervention system: Part II. The data. *Exceptional Children, 51*, 487–496.

Graden, J. L., Casey, A., & Christenson, S. L. (1985). Implementing a prereferral intervention system: Part I. The model. *Exceptional Children, 51*, 377–384.

Grosenick, J. K., & Huntze, S. L. (1980). *National needs analysis in behavior disorders: Severe behavior disorders*. Columbia, MO: University of Missouri, Department of Special Education.

Kauffman, J. M. (1985). *Characteristics of children's behavior disorders* (3rd ed.). Columbus, OH: Merrill.

Kazdin, A. E. (1977). Assessing the clinical or applied importance of behavior change through social validation. *Behavior Modification, 4*, 427–452.

Kerr, M. M., & Nelson, C. M. (1983). *Strategies for managing behavior problems in the classroom*. Columbus, OH: Merrill.

Lily, M. S. (1986). The relationship between general and special education: A new face on an old issue. *Counterpoint, 6*, 10.

Neel, R. S. (1983). *Teaching autistic children: A functional curriculum approach*. Seattle, WA: University of Washington.

Ogbu, J. U. (1985). Research currents: Cultural-ecological influences on minority school learning. *Language Arts, 62*, 860–869.

Paul, J. L. (1985). Where are we in the education of emotionally disturbed children? *Behavioral Disorders, 10*, 145–151.

Schultz, E. W., Hirshoren, A., Manton, A. B., & Henderson, R. A. (1971). Special education for the emotionally disturbed. *Exceptional Children, 38*, 313–319.

Skinner, B. F. (1953). *Science and human behavior*. New York: Macmillan.

Sevick, B. M., & Ysseldyke, J. E. (1986). An analysis of teacher's prereferral interventions for students exhibiting behavioral problems. *Behavioral Disorders, 11*, 109– 117.

U.S. Department of Education (1986). *Eighth Annual Report to Congress on the Implementation of the Education of the Handicapped Act*. Washington, DC: Author.

Wang, M. C., Reynolds, M. C., & Walberg, H. J. (1986). Rethinking special education. *Educational Leadership, 44*, 26–31.

Will, M. (1986). *Educating students with learning problems: A shared responsibility*. Washington, DC: U.S. Department of Education, Office of Special Education and Rehabilitative Services.

Wittrock, M. C. (Ed.) (1986). *Handbook of research on teaching* (3rd ed.). New York: Macmillan.

Wolery, M., Bailey, D., & Sugai, G. (in press). *Effective teaching: Principles and procedures of applied behavior analysis with exceptional children*. Boston, MA: Allyn & Bacon.

Wolf, M. M. (1978). Social validity: The case for subjective measurement, or how applied behavior analysis is finding its heart. *Journal of Applied Behavior Analysis, 11*, 203– 214.

CHAPTER 8

Finding and Nurturing Potential Giftedness Among Black and Hispanic Students

Donnelly A. Gregory
Waveline T. Starnes
Arlene W. Blaylock

Paul Torrance said in 1970 that the greatest source of untapped talent in the nation lies among the disadvantaged minority population (Torrance, 1970). The information in this chapter is intended to cast light on the thorny problem facing school districts across the nation, the historic underrepresentation of Black and Hispanic youngsters in programs for the gifted and talented. Over a period of 5 years, efforts by the school system in Montgomery County, Maryland, to increase the participation of Black and Hispanic students in such programs were largely unsuccessful. This is a large suburban school system with minority enrollment of approximately 30%. The minority population in individual schools, however, ranges from a low of 6% to a high of 90%. To address the inequity in gifted programs more boldly, a research effort was initiated over 6 years ago (Johnson, Starnes, Gregory, & Blaylock, 1985).

During the developmental period of this project, an effort was made to find out as much as possible about unrecognized minority students who are gifted and talented or who possess the potential to be gifted. It became apparent that these students are not a homogeneous group. Many of these youngsters have the ability to be identified as gifted and talented and would be successful in existing programs. Refinement and consistent implementation of the multiple criteria identification process and provision of a support system for schools has fostered the recognition and selection of some of these students as gifted and talented. This gradual improvement in the participation of Black and Hispanic students, however, does not yet ensure equity of opportunity for these students.

Some practitioners in the field of gifted education have looked toward the emergence of a new test as a potential solution to inadequate minority identification. The experiences of this project indicate that the problem is much too complex to be resolved by a new assessment instrument (Gregory, 1985). The Program of Assessment, Diagnosis and Instruction (PADI) was developed to pursue the exploration of ability among a much larger group of minority students, those not yet at the level of giftedness. The approach taken by PADI is grounded in the belief that potential giftedness can be found among a very diverse group of youngsters—among students with deficits in their basic skills, among students with limited English proficiency, among disadvantaged and minority students whose experiences may distance them from the mainstream. They might be characterized as a group of children who come to school in kindergarten and first grade less ready to profit from the school experience. School may not be a comfortable environment for them, and their strengths and abilities may not easily translate into school activities. They are often prevented from refining and extending their skills because of barriers to their development such as poverty, lack of early enrichment experiences, developmental delays, and differences in languages or culture (Gregory, 1987). If they are slow in learning to read and write, recognizing their potential becomes even more difficult (Whitmore, 1980). Frequently, their abilities are not evident in their daily classroom performance.

As challenging as discovering these students may be, it is only the first step. They require an approach that focuses on early identification and nurturing. Regardless of their abilities, they cannot be placed in existing gifted programs because they do not have the skills to be successful.

This program tries to go beyond simply increasing the numbers of gifted minority students. PADI is pursuing an overall goal that relates more broadly to increasing minority achievement. In fact, PADI is interested in making these youngsters effective learners so that they can profit from all that school has to offer them. PADI is not a program for the gifted. It is a program to identify and foster potential which also enables "hidden" gifted students to emerge and refine their skills sufficiently to move into programs for the gifted.

THE DIAGNOSTIC BATTERY

It is obvious that before students with potential can be nurtured instructionally, they must be identified. The first task in PADI was to develop a process for uncovering these students. This section deals with that process.

PADI proceeded with the notion that the potential ability or hidden giftedness of these students could be tapped, if it were assessed in subtle and nontraditional ways. One of the real strengths of PADI lies in the time and care taken to assess the strengths of each individual child through a special diagnostic battery. The battery itself is a unique tool because it teases out information on students' reasoning and creativity with little dependence on their academic skills. There was a deliberate effort to find assessment techniques that give evidence of these abilities while bypassing any limitations posed by language and experience.

The diagnostic battery was refined by extensive experimentation, implementation, and subsequent validation. Approximately 400 children originally participating in the diagnostic battery activities were also given the WISC-R (Wechsler Intelligence Scale for Children-Revised) performance scale. This served as the criterion measure for validation of the battery. Some measures were discarded because they did not contribute to the prediction of WISC-R scores. A thorough discussion of the validation procedure is contained in an article in *The Journal of Negro Education* (Johnson et al., 1985). The version of the battery which resulted consists of seven assessment activities. These activities are generally conducted in the regular classroom with all students participating. A specially trained team of testing assistants administers the diagnostic battery over a period of 1–2 weeks. A brief description of each assessment activity follows.

Cartoon Conservation Scale

This paper-and-pencil test, developed by Edward DeAvila, uses a cartoon format to assess Piagetian conservation concepts (DeAvila & Havassy, 1975). It measures the child's mastery of conservation of number, length, substance, distance, horizontality of water, conservation of volume, egocentricity, and probability.

Diagnostic Thinking Tasks

Informal thinking tasks have long been advocated as an adjunct to the Montgomery County Public Schools' identification procedures for gifted and talented students. These informal activities are a useful technique for gaining additional information about the way children reason, think creatively, and solve problems (Gregory, 1985). It is also relatively easy to use tasks that are not content based or heavily dependent on language skills. The items included in the Diagnostic Thinking Tasks are as follows:

- Design Completion—Completing an incomplete pattern formed by geometric shapes.
- Block Counting—Counting seen and unseen blocks in a simple structure.
- Triangles—Counting triangles in an embedded figure.
- Missing Numbers—Finishing an incomplete number sequence.
- Creatures—Identifying attributes among imaginary creatures.

Student Interview/Peer Survey

Peer judgment is a useful tool in the identification of able students (Granzin & Granzin, 1969). Some school systems have had success soliciting peer information in an interview format with young children in grades K–3. Testing assistants interview students in small groups of six to eight, discussing questions such as "Which boys and girls are the first to explain to others how games are played or how things are done?"

Rating Student Potential Checklist (RSP)

This particular teacher checklist was developed by the project based on specific cultural strengths highlighted in the literature. Most of the characteristics were suggested by the work of Paul Torrance with disadvantaged Blacks and of Ernest Bernal with Hispanic students (Bernal, 1978; Torrance, 1969).

Coloured and/or Standard Progressive Matrices (Raven)

This assessment instrument uses figural analogies to tap logic and reasoning (Raven, 1938). It does not require reading. More recent norms representative of U.S. populations are now available.

Circles Activity

This activity is adapted from Paul Torrance's Minnesota Test of Creativity (Torrance, 1964). Pilot use of this activity was conducted in order to determine the optimum size and number of circles for a particular age level. Children use pencil to draw on nine large circles on a single page in order to create something. They can either make something different out of each circle or they can use several circles together to make something.

Draw-a-Person

This paper-and-pencil drawing task assesses maturity and developmental level. It is a test which is often used in cross-cultural studies (Harris, 1963). The project uses the expanded scoring format developed by Dale B. Harris.

After the total diagnostic battery has been implemented in the spring of Grade 1, local standards of performance are computed for each activity at each individual school. This ensures that students will be compared only to peers in their own schools. Students already identified as gifted and talented are not potential PADI candidates. All remaining students are ranked from highest to lowest performance on the seven activities. Each assessment activity carries equal weight in the evaluation of student performance. Those students demonstrating strong performance, at least one standard deviation above the mean, on three or more activities are candidates for placement in PADI. There is also provision for the administrative placement of students for whom strong evidence of potential ability exists. This provision is most often used to place limited-English-proficient students whose language skills may inhibit their performance on the diagnostic battery.

PADI has been implemented only in schools with a combined Black and Hispanic enrollment of 30% or more. Some PADI schools have minority enrollment of close to 80%. Once a school is selected to participate in the project, race is not a factor in the selection of students. Occasionally more students may qualify than can be accommodated in the PADI class, and minority students may be placed ahead of majority students with the same performance on the diagnostic battery. This is seldom necessary, however. Figure 1 compares overall elementary enrollment in Montgomery County by race to participation in gifted and talented programs and participation in PADI. Clearly race is not a barrier to participation in PADI. The diagnostic battery taps potential across ethnic groups and helps to uncover potentially gifted students previously unrecognized by their schools.

INSTRUCTIONAL PROGRAM

The heart of PADI is the instructional program that has been developed to nurture the potential of students with hidden strengths primarily in grades 2 through 4. Initially discovered through their performance on the diagnostic battery, these students give further

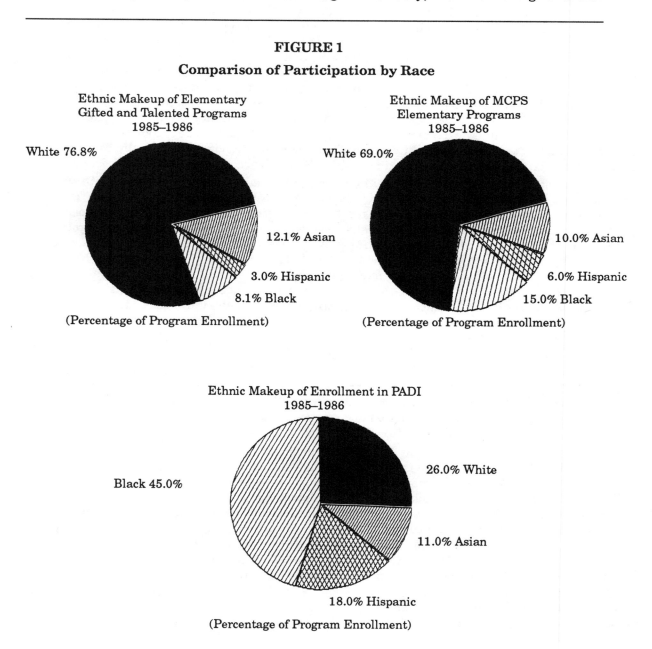

FIGURE 1

Comparison of Participation by Race

Ethnic Makeup of Elementary Gifted and Talented Programs 1985–1986

White 76.8%

12.1% Asian

3.0% Hispanic

8.1% Black

(Percentage of Program Enrollment)

Ethnic Makeup of MCPS Elementary Programs 1985–1986

White 69.0%

10.0% Asian

6.0% Hispanic

15.0% Black

(Percentage of Program Enrollment)

Ethnic Makeup of Enrollment in PADI 1985–1986

Black 45.0%

26.0% White

11.0% Asian

18.0% Hispanic

(Percentage of Program Enrollment)

evidence of their abilities as they interact daily with the instructional demands of the program. This is an approach to assessment the project calls "identification through teaching." Rather than identifying gifted students at one specific time, staff members can refine their judgments about how individual PADI students meet the cognitive demands of the program, based on observations over time. PADI, then, has a commitment to long-term nurturing of these students. The self-concept and learning problems of most PADI youngsters cannot be resolved in a few months or even in a year. In contrast, in an early childhood program in Illinois, students are moved out after one year if they have not been identified as gifted (Karnes, Bertschi, 1978). The changes and growth many disadvantaged/minority students must make will take more time.

What is special about the PADI instructional program? Most nurturing programs designed for minority students focus on language arts. PADI is somewhat unique in the selection of social studies and science as the content vehicles for the program. These students, in particular, need a program which emphasizes an area of the curriculum where they are not experiencing difficulty. Since social studies and science instruction does not require a basal text, students are much less hindered by low reading skills. These content areas also build on a natural interest and curiosity disadvantaged children frequently have about their own environment (Stallings, 1972). Social studies and science also promote the hands-on participation of students PADI requires. Daily writing for fluency on topics related to current study is incorporated into PADI instruction. Students have frequent opportunities to read for information about subjects they are highly motivated to investigate further. In addition, PADI uses interdisciplinary extensions to all units so that students pursue activities involving art, music, movement, drama, and literature. Daily learning activities continually reinforce students' language skills, though the primary focus is on science and social studies.

PADI is designed, then, to provide daily instruction in social studies and science. With the exception of two half-time teachers funded by the project, the remaining 33 teachers come from regular staff in the PADI schools. These teachers all assume responsibility for the social studies and science instruction of the specially selected PADI students. Most schools regroup students in the afternoon in order to set up the PADI class. Several teachers at a grade level may exchange students in order to gather the PADI students into a single group with the PADI teacher. Some of the students may have this same teacher in the morning for reading/language arts and math. Others have one classroom teacher in the morning and the PADI teacher in the afternoon. Each PADI class strives to meet for 90 minutes of social studies and science instruction each day. The consistency of this daily instruction promotes the long-term nurturing of student potential.

As Figure 2 illustrates, the *basis* of instruction in PADI, shown in the lower circle, is the school system curriculum in social studies and science. PADI students work on the same objectives and many of the same units as other students at their grade level. Instruction differs in the special emphasis placed on the three thinking skills indicated in the left-hand circle: classifying, hypothesizing, and making transformations. More time may be spent in a PADI class on activities promoting these skills.

The right-hand circle presents the expectations or product outcomes of PADI instruction. As shown in the enlargement of this circle in Figure 3, an important outcome of PADI instruction is the active involvement of students in their own learning. Social studies and science guarantee this involvement, the manipulation of concrete objects, and frequent opportunities to collect and analyze data. Responding to and posing questions is a natural outgrowth of group discussions in PADI. Although such activities are time consuming, it is critical for these students to refine their thinking through reflection and dialogue on the various concepts explored. These expectations are all designed to promote improved self-concepts for learners and growth in both academic and critical thinking skills.

PADI uses a select group of teaching strategies or activities which promote thinking and discussion and which demonstrate the integration of the content, the thinking skills, and the expectations of PADI instruction. They are referred to as exemplars. They are a particular

FIGURE 2

Elements of PADI Instruction

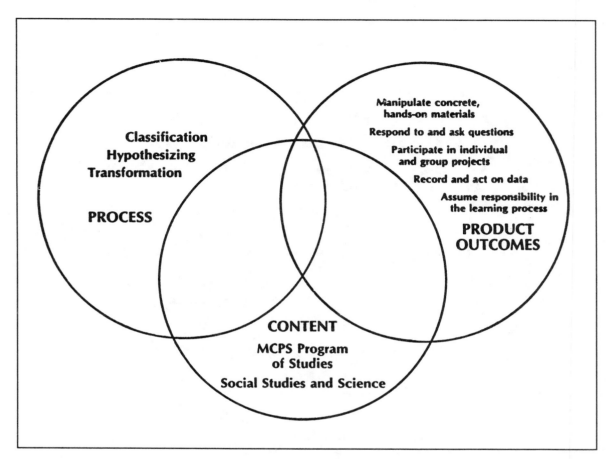

focus of the teacher training component which is discussed later. The eight PADI exemplars are listed below:

- Guess Box
- Collection
- Comparison Circles
- Picture Interpretation
- Music Interpretation
- Science Investigation
- Word of the Day
- Webbing

RESULTS

PADI has monitored the program's effectiveness through both formal and informal evaluation efforts. The first positive results stem from validation of the Diagnostic Battery with the WISC-R Performance Scale. The battery does indeed tap potential among a diverse group of youngsters regardless of their current academic performance. It identifies the most varied

FIGURE 3

Product Outcomes of PADI Instruction

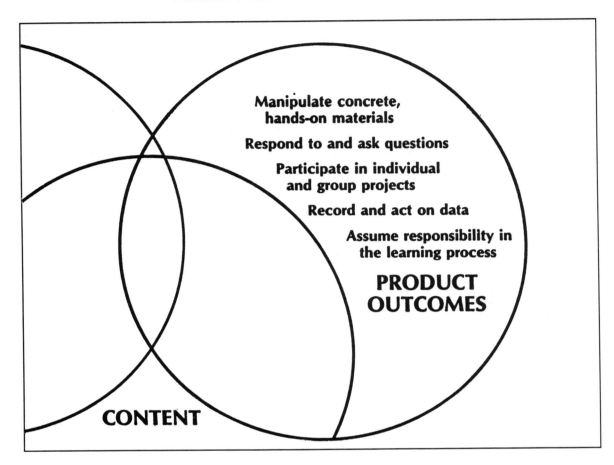

Manipulate concrete, hands-on materials

Respond to and ask questions

Participate in individual and group projects

Record and act on data

Assume responsibility in the learning process

PRODUCT OUTCOMES

CONTENT

group of students imaginable—diverse in ages, skills, and backgrounds, but similar in their ability to think and reason at a higher level. The time and effort required for the administration of this diagnostic battery is well worth it because many of these students are the very ones who would not be recognized and challenged, and whose potential giftedness might therefore be lost.

The second positive result grows out of the movement of students from PADI into gifted and talented programs. Continuous monitoring of PADI students has enabled the project to track students as they leave the program. Out of the first 400 PADI students, over 125 were identified as gifted and talented. Every year additional students have been identified as gifted, leaving the PADI class to participate in even more challenging instructional opportunities. Over the past several years the percentage of students making this transition seems to be holding at between 25% and 30%.

Equally exciting as the movement of students to programs for the gifted and talented has been the significant impact of this program on the students remaining in PADI. These students have changed their concepts of themselves as learners. Parents, classroom teachers, principals, and counselors have all reported dramatic changes in these students' attitudes toward school and learning. An advisory committee made up of parents, community members, and staff has guided the project for over 7 years. At PADI Advisory Committee meetings parents will comment that "PADI is the best school experience my son has had." "There is such a difference in how he feels about school." "She can't wait to get home to tell me what she did in PADI science class."

Through the formal evaluation component the project is collecting objective data to study growth in writing fluency and in skills in social studies and science. Following students over time to see how they are faring after their PADI experience will also provide valuable insights into the program's impact.

TEACHER TRAINING

Just as students need to participate in a long-term nurturing instructional program, teachers need training and support provided over a long period of time. Employment of new teachers in this district for a number of years has been minimal. This means that PADI teachers come from a pool of older, more experienced teachers. It takes time to change the way experienced teachers operate in the classroom. Intensive summer training, demonstrations by master teachers, periodic workshops during the school year, and practice of the instructional strategies with peer feedback make PADI a unique experience for the teachers as well as the students.

The work of Joyce and Showers (1982) influenced the project to adopt peer coaching as an important aspect of the staff development component. For the past 3 years, teachers have worked on the refinement of their PADI instruction with the assistance of a coaching partner. The coaching process begins with the presentation, demonstration, and discussion of a specific strategy. This is accompanied by a detailed written description of the strategy. Figure 4 gives a brief example of a statement taken from the description of Comparison Circles.

The next step involves joint planning by the two coaching partners of a lesson involving the strategy. This is a lesson that one partner will teach to her PADI class while the other partner observes. Figure 5 shows a sample of questions posed to assist in planning this lesson using comparison circles.

The last step involves observation of the lesson by the coaching partner, who provides feedback on specific elements of the strategy. Figure 6 shows two elements of a lesson using comparison circles on which feedback will be given.

PADI teachers have been very receptive to peer coaching. Several teachers have commented that it is the most professionally rewarding experience they have had in their teaching career.

FIGURE 4

**Comparison Circles
Description of the Strategy**

The purpose of the sorting activity, the size of the collection, and the number of students in the group are all factors which influence the size and kind of strings or circles to be used.

FIGURE 5

**Comparison Circles
Planning Sheet**

What items are to be sorted ? What kind of circles shall I use ? How shall the students be seated ?

FIGURE 6

Comparison Circles
Guidelines for Observing/Coaching

Elements of the Activity	Supporting Evidence
The teacher selects the appropriate set of circles: ___ large circles ___ small circles ___ circles on chalk board	
Students are seated in a way that enhances interaction with the activity	

One teacher commented recently, "The training and support you have given to us in PADI is much stronger than anywhere else. This is superior training. Then we give it back to the kids." Another said, "We have time to talk together about what works. During the summer and through coaching, a network is set up. We are not isolated." *Companionship* is an important key. A coaching partner, who is struggling to achieve the same instructional goals with the same kind of students, can provide collegial support not otherwise available. This long-term training process with peer coaching has been a significant factor in the success of PADI.

SUMMARY

PADI combines three critical factors: (a) subtle and nontraditional assessment, (b) long-term nurturing of students' academic and thinking skills, and (c) a sophisticated approach to teacher training and support. Five years of experience has seen the screening of approximately 8,000 students, the instruction of over 1,000 youngsters in PADI, and the training of more than 40 PADI teachers. These experiences confirm that early recognition and nurturing of potential among Black and Hispanic students provides immeasurable benefit to the students themselves and ultimately to society.

REFERENCES

Bernal, E. M. (1978). The identification of gifted Chicano children. In A. Y. Baldwin, G. H. Gear, & L. J. Lucito (Eds.), *Educational planning for the gifted: Overcoming cultural, geographic, and socioeconomic barriers* (pp. 14–17). Reston, VA: The Council for Exceptional Children.

DeAvila, E. A., & Havassy, B. E. (1975). Piagetian alternative to IQ: Mexican-American study. In N. Hobbs (Ed.), *Issues in the classification of exceptional children* (pp. 246–265). San Francisco: Jossey-Bass.

Granzin, K. L., & Granzin, W. J. (1969). Peer group choice as a device for screening intellectually gifted children. *Gifted Child Quarterly, 13,* 189–194.

Gregory, D. A. (1985). Assessment of the gifted. *Diagnostique monograph: Perspectives in special education assessment* (pp. 88–97). Reston, VA: The Council for Exceptional Children.

Gregory, D. A. (1987). Nuture, challenge, caring—A plea for young gifted children. *Communicator, 17*(1), 9–13.

Harris, D. B. (1963). *Children's drawings as measures of intellectual maturity: A revision and extension of the Goodenough Draw-a-Man test.* New York: Harcourt Brace Jovanovich.

Johnson, S. T., Starnes, W. T., Gregory, D., & Blaylock, A. (1985). Program of assessment, diagnosis and instruction (PADI): Identifying and nurturing potentially gifted and talented minority students. *Journal of Negro Education, 54*(3), 416–430.

Joyce, B., & Showers, B. (1982). The coaching of teaching. *Educational Leadership, 40*(2), 4–10.

Karnes, M. B., & Bertschi, J. D. (1978). Identifying and educating gifted/talented non-handicapped and handicapped preschoolers. *TEACHING Exceptional Children, 10*(4), 114–119.

Raven, J. C. (1938, 1947, 1962, 1976, 1977). *Raven Progressive Matrices.* San Antonio, TX: The Psychological Corporation.

Stallings, C. (1972). *Gifted disadvantaged children.* Storrs, CT: University of Connecticut Technical Paper.

Torrance, E. P. (1964). The Minnesota studies of creative thinking, 1959–62. In C. W. Taylor (Ed.), *Widening horizons in creativity* (pp. 137–169). New York: Wiley.

Torrance, E. P. (1969). Creative positives of disadvantaged children and youth. *Giftesd Child Quarterly, 13,* 74–81.

Torrance, E. P. (1970). Broadening concepts of giftedness in the 70's. *Gifted Child Quarterly, 14,* 199–208.

Whitmore, J. R. (1980). *Giftedness, conflict, and underachievement.* Boston: Allyn & Bacon.

CHAPTER 9

Cultural and Acculturational Commonalities and Diversities Among Asian Americans: Identification and Programming Considerations

Esther K. Leung

Asian Americans are a relatively small minority group in the United States, constituting about 2% of the total population. They have often been stereotyped, perhaps due to readily distinguishable outward appearance such as skin color and physical features. Yet they are an extremely diversified conglomerate of various Asiatic ethnicities, sometimes sharing only minority status. Contributing to the differences among Asian groups is their cultural and acculturational variance; while they are distinguished from other majority and minority groups by their shared cultural and acculturational variables. The purpose of this paper is to delineate some of these commonalities and diversities, to enhance special educators' sensitivity to and understanding of Asian minorities, and to present some suggestions for identification and programming.

DIVERSITIES AND COMPLEXITIES

Asian Americans differ in origin, immigration and settlement history, degree and type of acculturation, and current status.

Origin

Asian Americans came from Asia, which spans the Indian subcontinent, the Malay Peninsula and Archipelago, Southeast Asia, East Asia, and the Japanese and Pacific islands; it comprises 23–29 political entities (Chan, 1986; Cheung, 1985a), including Pakistan, India, Afghanistan, the Philippines, Indonesia, Sri Lanka, Singapore, Malaysia, Burma, Thailand, Vietnam, Cambodia, Laos, China, Hong Kong, Taiwan, Korea, Japan, Guam, and tribal groups like the Hmong, Meow, and Khmer in Southeast Asia.

Asians speak over 1,000 languages and dialects. Most have long established histories and cultures ranging from primitive to technical-industrial, and economies from dire impoverishment to the world's foremost exporter and creditor. Asian governments include democracy and totalitarianism. Asia is the birthplace of four of the world's seven leading religions: Hinduism, Buddhism, Confucianism, and Taoism; its people also practice atheism, animism, shamanism, Shintoism, Islam, and Christianity.

Immigration and Settlement History

Most Asians migrated to the U.S. through immigration and refugee processes. However, their histories and experiences are dissimilar.

Immigrants. Early immigrants came to the United States before World War II. Many were uneducated and of low socioeconomic status. They came as Chinese laborers, Japanese farmers, and Asian Indian merchants. As targets of discrimination and harsh treatment, they often clung together for support and protection, forming ethnic centers such as "Chinatowns" in metropolises.

Recent immigrants came after World War II, as students, professionals, entrepreneurs, and friends and relatives of older immigrants. Many are quite successful socially and economically, with no painful experience of vicious discrimination. They include a higher percentage of Filipinos, Indochinese, and Koreans (Butterfield, 1986); they have diverse settlement patterns. Usually they have settled near jobs and educational opportunities, although many still flock around highly concentrated ethnic centers.

Refugees. A number of Chinese and Koreans were admitted to the U.S. as refugees from Communism in the 1940s and 1950s. However, the bulk of refugees are from Southeast Asia, and emigrated as a result of the Vietnam War. Many of them are young, having come in the 1975 wave immediately after the fall of Saigon and the 1978–1981 wave when the Communists forced out their "undesirable" citizens. The first wave included the "baby-lift" children who came to live with foster parents. The second wave (1978–1981) refugees comprise a complex group, including the "boat people" who had to survive Communist gunfire, pirates, the treacherous seas, and lengthy waits in refugee camps for resettlement. Some had already lived through the trauma of wars, guerrillas, occupation, and prison camps prior to their journey. Schooling and other niceties may have completely eluded them. Many may have been permanently scarred by the hardships and cruelties of war and refuge. Subsequent development of young refugees and children of refugees in the U.S. may be linked to those experiences. There are determined and appreciative high academic achievers, and there are youthful combat-experienced gangs who have terrorized Asian American communities (Glamser & Myers, 1987; Owen, 1985).

The second wave refugees included the Laos, Kmer, Hmongs, and other tribal people who fled their homelands after Cambodia and Laos fell to Communism. Some of these tribes have no written language.

The settlement history of the Southeast Asian refugees is rather unusual. The youngsters who came in the first wave generally ended up in adoptive or foster homes with American parents. Many in the second wave had to wait for months or years in refugee camps before admission to this country. Once here, they were often sent to isolated parts of the United States, away from metropolitan areas where Asian Americans congregate. Amidst strange people and culture, and having to cope with adjustment and adaptation within, as well as misunderstanding or hostility without, many Southeast Asian refugees found initial settlement turbulent at best. Many eventually trickled back to urban centers to be near their kin.

Acculturation

Acculturation refers to Asian-American immigrants' adaptation to and adoption of mainstream American culture. The degree and effects of acculturation differ.

Types of Acculturation. There are several distinguishable acculturational patterns among immigrants (Lin & Masuda, 1983).

1. *Marginality* includes immigrants at the juncture of two cultures, no longer adhering to their "old" Asian values, nor having adopted the "new" American system. Without a definite conduct code, they may (a) develop such high levels of anxiety or depression that they become neurotic or paralyzed in their personal and social functions; or (b) ignore the dictates

of both cultures and become deviates and thus social rejects, with increasing feelings of alienation among their own ethnic group and/or in society at large.

2. *Traditionalism* generally involves older or adult immigrants who are aware of cultural differences. They may at first vacillate between the "old" ethnic and the "new" American cultures; however, when forced to choose identity, they feel more comfortable sticking to their old ways of life.

3. *Overacculturation* occurs most frequently among the young. Growing up in American culture and being socialized through schooling, many young Asians consciously or unconsciously reject their ethnic culture, and become extremely if not totally Americanized in order to join the mainstream.

4. *Biculturation* occurs when immigrants integrate both cultures and function efficiently in either setting. Cheung (1985a) called it functional acculturation, the optimal adaptation and adjustment, when minority immigrants are comfortable in both cultural environments, making progress in mainstream society without totally abandoning their ethnic identity. Biculturation enriches and enhances development and achievement. However, bicultural immigrants do at times experience conflicts, divided loyalty, a sense of loss, and problems of identity.

Factors Influencing Acculturation. The degree and type of acculturation depend on the following factors:

1. *Time.* Time diffuses the link to and the practices of one's old ways of life. The longer a family has been settled in America, the more "American" the members tend to be. Thus first generations tend to be steeped in ethnic views and traditions which are gradually abandoned or modified with succeeding generations (Lum & Char, 1985).

2. *Proximity.* Physical and social proximity to one's old culture and ethnic group deters acculturation. Asian Americans who live in or near metropolitan areas with a high ratio of their ethnic group tend to retain their ethnic identification longer.

   By contrast Asian Americans in small towns lack opportunities to socialize with ethnic members and to keep up with ethnic culture. Both adults and children in such a setting may have to Americanize quickly to sustain economic, social, and educational activities to avoid rejection and isolation. Hence "overacculturation" and "marginality" are common.

   "Marginality" and "overacculturation" also occur among Asians in close physical or social proximity to their ethnic groups, if there is undue pressure to conform to either culture. However, frequent association tends to encourage "traditionalism," which is one way to avoid adjustment problems.

3. *Age.* Because young people can adapt to another culture more readily than their elders, the generation gap in immigrant families may be compounded by a cultural gap. In addition to clashing values and behavior codes, some families are caught unprepared for role reversals. A family's more acculturated youngsters may have to assume financial and social responsibilities. Such contradictions to tradition may upset the family equilibrium, resulting in grave adjustment problems for everybody concerned (Morales, 1983).

4. *Birthplace.* Asians born and/or raised in the U.S. are easily initiated into the "American" way through the public school and the peer group. Schooling and early association with American peers affect the pace, magnitude, and the nature of acculturation.

   Generally speaking, as Asian children enter school and begin a prolonged association with mainstream American peers, they may experience culture shock, if their home environment is not Americanized. They may come to a sudden realization of their minority status, epitomized by their skin color, physical features, and linguistic difference. They must cope with the often conflicting and stressful demands from school, community, and home environments (Leung, 1981). Generally, children with inadequate social skills or unfavorable home/school/community environments may end up marginally acculturated. Those with adequate social skills but too much sensitivity to minority status may become overacculturated, while those not impeded by personal inadequacy nor environmental predicament may achieve biculturalism.

5. *Sex*. Asian females are more readily acculturated than males (Fong, 1973). Women may be conditioned to adapt to new environments; Asian women could have more to gain by forsaking male-dominant Asian cultures. In many first-generation homes, the wives and daughters tend to Americanize sooner, and are more likely to be either overacculturated or bicultural; husbands and sons are more likely to be traditional or even marginal.

6. *Intermarriage*. Acculturation accelerates in intermarriages. Most couples do not share identical culture, custom, and native tongue. They therefore generally adopt English as the functional language and contemporary American standards for child-rearing practices.

Current Cultural and Socioeconomic Status

Asian Americans are extremely diverse in contemporary American cultural and socioeconomic dimensions. They differ in:

Education. Asian Americans range from illiterates to Nobel laureates, from high academic achievers to dropouts. Because Asian Americans value education, a high proportion of their young finish high school and go on to higher education.

Language. Asian Americans may be monolingual or bilingual. The monolinguals may only speak (and write) in their own tongue or English. The bilinguals may have proficiency in both English and their native tongue, or only minimal competency in one or both languages.

Social and Economic Status. Certain groups of Asian Americans have increasingly attained middle-class status, though in general they still range from poverty to extreme affluence. The poor tend to be recent immigrants and refugees, who came with little or no wealth, education, and English proficiency (Chinn & Plata, 1986).

COMMONALITIES

Amid diversities, there exist distinct commonalities among Asian Americans, especially among those of East and Southeast Asian origin. They include the following:

Experiential Background and Minority Status

Experience related to minority status is shared by all Asian Americans and indeed all minorities. In addition to feeling a sense of inadequacy or inferiority inherent to the awareness of deviance, minorities may encounter discrimination intentionally or unintentionally imposed on them. These subjective and objective experiences forge a bond among all minorities. This bond is further strengthened among Asians by their similar physical attributes, culture, and migration, settlement, and acculturation history.

Culture

The dominance of Confucianism, Taoism, and Buddhism, the religious-philosophic systems that undergird all facets of Asian life, contributes to the resemblance evident in Asian Americans' world views, ethics, social norms, values, folk beliefs, and lifestyles. Some understanding of these systems is therefore prerequisite to appreciating their cultural commonalities. (For an in-depth presentation see Leung, 1987).

World Views. The preeminent Asian views on the world and life are based on the teachings of Confucius, Lao Tzu, and Buddha Gautama. They began as philosophy, but evolved into religious systems. Each has its unique emphasis, with Confucianism social-political, Taoism philosophical, and Buddhism personal. However, they are mutually compatible and

89

complementary, enabling Asians to integrate and entertain complex mixes of thoughts and faiths.

1. *Confucianism*. Confucius (551–479 B.C.) and followers stress ethics as the key to harmony and prosperity. In Confucius' feudalistic world, the Supreme Ruler of the spiritual realm destined earthly rulers to lead and to care for earthlings. Rulers were to nurture the masses for Heaven's sake, providing for their physical needs and serving as their conduct models.

   Confucianism also believes that the spirits of the deceased, especially those of one's ancestors, are to be revered and appeased. The head of each household must maintain a proper relationship between their families and their ancestry, just as rulers between their subjects and Heaven. Family heads are also responsible for feeding and educating their dependents by exemplary words and deeds.

2. *Taoism*. Lao Tzu (604–? B.C.) advocated the cultivation of inner strength, selflessness, spontaneity, and harmony with nature and man, rather than Confucius' group-oriented propriety and conduct codes. He also explained natural and social phenomena by incorporating the ancient theory of cyclical counterbalancing forces of Yang and Yin. Because of its mystical approach, Taoism soon turned into superstition, magic, divination, sorcery, and necromancy among the illiterate. As these mystical practices are similar to and compatible with animism, Popular Taoism has been widely accepted and perpetuated by the masses.

   But Taoism at its best is purely philosophic. It has deeply influenced the Asian character, shaping it towards serenity, simplicity, meekness, and tolerance, with an inner core of strength, suppleness, and creativity (Smith, 1965).

3. *Buddhism*. Buddhism was begun in India by Prince Gautama (560–480 B.C.). Its goal is for humans to attain "enlightenment" to realize "Nirvana," an altered state of awareness when all sufferings are transcended and the pains of birth, aging, sickness, death, and separation can no longer be felt. Motivated by compassion, Buddha took his message to the populace. Buddhism as such is very therapeutic and essentially empirical (Smith, 1965); it has drawn huge followings, first in India, then throughout Asia. Buddhist outlook is therefore very pervasive in Asia. Buddhism in the form of Zen, which stresses Taoistic meditation, is especially popular in Japan.

Values, Beliefs, Lifestyles, Traditions, and Customs. Asian Americans share many values, beliefs, lifestyles, traditions, and customs (Cheung, 1985a; Morales, 1983; Tseng & Wu, 1985). The degree of similarity is inversely proportional to the level of acculturation. Thus the cultural similarity among Asian Americans is really a reflection of the similarity among Asian cultures, embedded not only in religion and philosophy but also in history of civilization, economy, and social-political structure.

Most Asian nations have long histories of civilization which differs from the West in orientation. Their concepts and practices may indeed be rooted in antiquity, and sometimes entail unscientific or erroneous notions. But they are by no means categorically underdeveloped or primitive.

Asian countries have been basically agrarian. Customs and traditions are therefore geared toward agricultural productivity and become meaningful in that light. Industrialization came late to Asian countries. Nowadays, bright Asian youths overwhelmingly embrace science and technology, a trend mirrored by Asian Americans.

Asian societies have not been democratic in the European-American model. There is usually an elite ruling class, aided by scholars or religious professionals. Authoritarianism characterizes social relationship, which is still the norm in Asian American communities, mainly among the old and the less acculturated.

Several unique Asian values, beliefs, and lifestyles are prominent in countries dominated by Confucianism, Taoism and Buddhism. They still influence the attitudes and behaviors of Asian Americans from such countries, depending on the level of acculturation.

90

1. *Family and Ethics*. Asian families are close-knit, extended, patrilineal, hierarchical and authoritarian (Cheung, 1985b). A large family with plenty of male farm hands, or an extended family that compensates for small family size, are advantageous in agrarian society where collaboration is crucial for survival. The extended family and family influence have gradually expanded to include entire clans, villages and far-reaching kinship networks; while mutual dependence evolved to an art and virtue. Social obligation and responsibility have likewise extended to state, nation, and the universe. Asians are thus basically group centered rather than individualistic, with exact codes governing social interactions.

   The reciprocity of Confucius' ethics leads to filial piety. Besides owing their elders respect, loyalty, and obedience, the younger generation must care for them in their old age, to reciprocate the kindness their elders have bestowed on them. Filial piety also promotes the respect of age. In traditional extended families, the oldest generation rules.

   "Saving face" is another outgrowth of filial piety. As bringing honor to one's parents, elders, and ancestors is a duty, one must always consider one's family or group and avoid bringing shame to them. Moreover, one must try to save face or honor if one is in danger of discredit, even through death. One would not disgrace others by embarrassing them before outsiders. Not admitting problems, not talking directly about concerns, not confronting issues and people, and doing business through a third party are some of the means to prevent losing face.

2. *Education, Morals, and Society*. The family has been the primary socializing agent in Asia, as public school is not universal. Confucius emphasizes the moral aspect of education; parents are to teach their children to be upright and proper primarily by their own examples. Indecorous children imply irresponsible parents.

   Traditionally, education has become a means of upward mobility. For years scholars ranked highest in China's social scale regardless of their economic status.

   The reverence and status conferred on teachers and the social significance of scholarship have firmly established the value of education in China and other Asian countries. To traditionally responsible parents, nothing is too great a sacrifice to secure a good education for their deserving children. Scholastic achievement, on the other hand, is the greatest tribute one could bring to one's parents and family.

3. *Other Values and Personality Characteristics*. Other values and beliefs have left indelible marks on Asian personality and behaviors. Again, they are intricately related to Confucianism, Taoism, and Buddhism.

   Moderation, harmony, and peace are prized in social relations and as one interacts with nature. Dissonance and disagreement should be resolved through mediation and concessions. Confrontation with issues and problems are avoided, as they may subside or dissipate over time. Often, moderation and harmony are maintained at the cost of personal mental health and the integrity of the nuclear family.

   Because caution, conservativeness, and compliance are valued in Asian cultures, traditional Asians may appear to be indecisive, timid, overconforming, and unassertive by American standards.

   Confucianism emphasizes verbal, social, and emotional restraint, while Taoists and Buddhists believe that meditation transcends language, reason, and emotion. In essence, reticence is a virtue, as is moderation in emotion and ambition. Neither excessive nor public display of feelings is appropriate; one demonstrates affection by caring and providing, not by words and physical acts of endearment. Apparently, much self-control and temperance is exerted daily by Asians, a clue to their rather high incidence of "mild" neurotic depressive (Lin, 1985). Paradoxically, these values and lifestyle may also contribute to their inner strength and resilience.

   Asian culture also values endurance, tolerance, and accommodation. Asians may fatalistically accept adversities as consequences of past sins or bad luck. Thus resigned, few would orchestrate concerted efforts to bear upon problems and misfortunes such as handicapped children. Instead, they adapt or accommodate.

Other Asian virtues include hard work and responsibility, meekness and modesty, loyalty, pragmatism, and realism. They are valued and practiced by many Asians in America, although they are not always appreciated by contemporary mainstream Americans.

IMPLICATIONS

Asian Americans comprise a heterogenous minority group. They are of Asiatic origin, but have diverse geographic, linguistic, political, and cultural affiliations, as well as a myriad of socioeconomic and experiential backgrounds prior to and following their migration to the U.S. Ranging from generations of citizenship to recent immigrants, they also vary in their degree of acculturation. Many Asian Americans prosper here, but there are others who hover around poverty, uncertainty, and impotence, unable to cope with problems and anxieties related to migration and acculturation. Among preschool and school-aged Asian Americans, there is a wide spectrum of human potentials, behaviors, extent of acculturation, English proficiency, schooling experience, and family and socioeconomic conditions that may significantly affect the rate and state of learning and performance.

Asian Americans do share commonalities. The foremost is the minority status and its associated experience, which is similar to and understood by all minority group members. Then, among Asians whose long history of ethnic cultures are rooted philosophically in Confucianism, Taoism, and Buddhism, and socially in a basic agronomic economy, there are unmistakable common outlooks, values, beliefs, lifestyles, traditions, and customs. The most noticeable ones relate to family, ethics, education, responsibility, industry, endurance, restraint, moderation, modesty, and loyalty. Yet mingling with these ideals is the reality of shrewdness, materialism, superstition, and ignorance which may be unavoidable in the masses of humanity constrained by limited resources and education.

Some implications of the above on special education for handicapped Asian Americans are in the areas of identification, programming, and family involvement.

Identification

There are handicapped Asian Americans. Contrary to recent publicity on Asian students' academic feats, they are not all gifted nor even normal youngsters. Rather, they have their proportions of intellectual, social, and psychomotor deviances (Tseng & Wu, 1985). In some cases, anomalies may have been masked, confounded, or compounded by cultural differences on the part of the Asians and by misconceptions on the part of professionals.

Take the case of intellectual performance. Some Asian students tend to achieve academically at a very high level because of their cultural emphasis on education, industry, responsibility, and family honors. Even the slowest students may be pushed to their limit; mental retardation or learning disabilities, though existing, may not be readily suspected by professionals nor admitted by parents and students. Thus some students may miss the opportunity of an appropriate education to meet their unique needs due to specific cognitive disorders.

On the other hand, culturally different behaviors such as nonassertiveness, reticence, modesty, and self-deprecation may cloud perception of ability; because of English deficiency, inadequate schooling, and traumatic migration/settlement experiences which may interfere with academic performance, some Asian students may be misidentified as having intellectual disabilities. Caution must be exercised, therefore, in assessment and consequent intervention, if warranted. Some problematic Asian learners need appropriate services such as language, remedial education, counseling, and social or emotional skills for survival in American classroom and society, rather than inappropriate special education for the mentally disabled. With this in mind, evaluation to determine eligibility for special education must do more than ensure that the item content of the assessment instruments is familiar to the testees and that assessment is conducted in the native tongue. The cultural and acculturational background of both the student and family must be a consideration in the selection of appropriate assessment procedures and instruments and the interpretation of scores derived from such instruments.

Asian Americans have been underserved in mental health services aimed at social and emotional handicaps (Cheung, 1985a; Tseng & Wu, 1985). The stigma of being deviant or mentally "sick" and the difficulty of distinguishing social and emotional disorders from common human phenomena are the major reasons for the underidentification and underrepresentation of Asian students in behavioral- or emotional-disordered classes. Furthermore, many Asians are conditioned to be compliant, reserved, restrained, modest, and moderate in their verbal and nonverbal behaviors. Emotional distress may not be noted nor tended as such until it has surfaced as severe psychosomatic symptoms. Even at the diagnostic stage such distress may not be identified.

Another problematic area in the affective domain relates to recent Southeast Asian immigrants and refugees. A high percentage of them are school-aged. While many have the ability and the incentive to become remarkable scholars, some of them also harbor tremendous emotional problems because of wartime, refuge, and settlement experiences (Carlin, 1983). They may become, if they are not already candidates for special education in the areas of behavioral disorders and/or emotional disturbance. Again, their customary demeanors may have disguised them, preventing them from having their problems discovered and receiving timely intervention. Unfortunately, there is no easy formula to improve the identification of behavioral/emotional handicaps among Asians. Perhaps the only way is through the trained eyes of professionals who are cognizant of the complex Asian American cultural and acculturational situations and ramifications, who have won their clients' respect and confidence, and who could therefore more readily differentiate disabilities from culture-specific demeanors.

Culture may also affect the identification and treatment of Asians with physical or sensory impairments. For example, ignorance and the face-saving tradition which might keep parents from realizing and acknowledging cognitive and affective deficits, could have a similar effect on psychomotor dysfunctions. Parents may resort to magic and superstition to "cure" a physically handicapped child, thus keeping him/her from early identification and early intervention. They may choose to ignore, endure, tolerate, or accommodate handicaps on philosophical, religious, or superstitious grounds. Not only are handicapping conditions not corrected, remediated, or alleviated, but other interrelated and secondary disabilities may develop because of delayed action. Again, knowledgeable and trusted professionals will be capable of discerning risks and disorders, and assisting families to seek early treatment.

Programming

Programming for Asian Americans' handicaps should be culturally and acculturationally relevant. As with other minority groups, professionals are ethically responsible for students' educational, emotional, and social needs in their home and ethno-cultural environment; as well as their acceptance by and ability to function effectively in school and mainstream society. For instance, a teacher may plan to modify the "low self-concept" of an Asian student who frequently emits self-berating remarks, refuses to attempt new tasks, and gives up too easily on school assignments. However, the parents may be very conservative, modeling self-effacement and insisting on modesty at home and in their ethnic social circle. A program that considers both the youngster's emotional and social needs would teach and foster appreciation of what each cultural system values, then help the youngster acquire and maintain appropriate behaviors specific to each setting.

Indeed, self-concept, emotional well-being, or social skills—call it what you will—should be of major concern in the education of minority students in general and Asian Americans in particular, for reasons that have been discussed in this chapter. Because a learner's cognitive, affective, and physical conditions are inextricably related, minority students who tend to endure stress and anxiety in their growing years are vulnerable socially and emotionally; this vulnerability may impede their other areas of learning and growth. Therefore, concerned educators should provide supportive, preventive, or corrective measures to promote minority students' healthy emotional and social development.

Useful measures include open discussion about cultures or minority status; counseling (Alley & Deshler, 1979); peer support groups; simulation activities to develop insight and empathy; bibliotherapy; curricular units on minority cultures and cultural events; and involving parents and minority persons in academic and extracurricular programs. Seeing family members, role models, or prestigious people in one's ethnic group amidst one's peers and teachers is especially inspiring to youngsters in identity crisis. However, the measures themselves are not as crucial as the attitudes of the significant others. Educators who can subscribe to the notion that Asian values and traditions are not inferior to Euro-American cultures, and who know what it takes to function efficiently in both the mainstream and the ethnic environment, can program for Asian Americans to help them achieve successful functional acculturation.

Family Involvement

Most Asian Americans respect authority and value education. Parental cooperation with educators is seldom a problem. Real collaboration, however, may be difficult to achieve. Out of respect for education and educators, Asian parents are likely to listen carefully and acknowledge affirmatively whatever teachers say. But attention and affirmation may only mean courtesy and propriety; parents do not wish to contradict the authority figures and cause them to lose face. Therefore a "yes" is not equivalent to a promise of adherence to the counsel or direction, especially if it is at odds with the Asian's knowledge base, belief, or value system. Moreover, when matters concern the external affairs of the family or clan, counsel and approval must come through other chains of command. Final authority often rests with the father of the household, the grandparents of the extended family, or the elders of the clan (Morales, 1983).

Even when approval is certain, a teacher who is a stranger and who has not demonstrated understanding of Asians in general and the family involved in particular may still be respected at a distance. The teacher's counsel and opinion regarding a handicapped child may not be accepted and followed through by the family. Trust occurs when contact with the teacher or professional has been initiated or affirmed through the networking of friends and relatives, or when familiarity has been developed. When there is trust, compliance will be almost guaranteed. To achieve collaboration, then, teachers and professionals must win trust through acquaintance, credentials, and sensitivity. Credentials may be gained by virtue of one's position, accomplishments, performance, or by word-of-mouth. Sensitivity will develop only from a nonbiased attitude and adequate knowledge about the Asian Americans.

Beyond collaboration, teachers and authority figures should also anticipate loyalty and the intention of establishing a permanent obligatory relationship. This should not be mistaken for an inclination toward dependence. Asians simply tend to "revere" teachers and to remember their benefactors. Moreover, Asians establish horizontal relationships only with those who do not impose their authority, knowledge, and value systems on them. Therefore, if special educators really desire mutual collaboration and open communication with Asian American parents, they must cultivate friendly relationships just as Asians would among themselves, by being modest, faithful, and above all, trustworthy or confidential in terms of keeping family secrets from "outsiders."

Finally, in involving the family, professionals must not forget about Asian family structure and ethics. In traditional and extended families, consistency in interventions for handicapped youngsters can be achieved only when the whole family, especially those in authority positions, agree to participate. In other words, if grandparents live in the same household, they too, must understand and cooperate in the implementation of a school-home or center-home program.

CONCLUSION

Some cultural and acculturational commonalities and diversities among a very small yet extremely complex minority, the Asian Americans, have been delineated in this chapter. Their implications on the identification, programming, and family involvement of handicapped Asian youngsters have also been discussed. As in all special education situations, systematic individualization from preplacement evaluation to program implementation is the only way to enhance accurate identification and appropriate services. A thorough understanding of the cultural and acculturational backgrounds of the Asian Americans as a group and specific handicapped Asians individually is imperative for successful effective individualization (Leung, 1987).

REFERENCES

Alley, G., & Deshler, D. (1979). *Teaching the learning disabled adolescent: Strategies and methods*. Denver: Love Publishing Co.

Butterfield, F. (1986, August). Why Asians are going to the head of the class. *The New York Times*, pp. 18–23.

Carlin, J. E. (1983). Southeast Asian refugee children. In R. F. Morales (Ed.), *Bridging cultures* (pp. 259–269). Los Angeles, CA: Asian American Mental Health Training Center.

Chan, S. (1986). Parents of exceptional Asian children. In M. K. Kitano & P. C. Chinn (Eds.), *Exceptional Asian children and youth* (pp. 36–53). Reston, VA: The Council for Exceptional Children.

Cheung, F. (1985a). *Cultural factors influencing diagnosis, disposition and treatment of Asian clients*. Washington, DC: Center for Minority Group Mental Health Programs, NIMH. Unpublished manuscript.

Cheung, F. (1985b). *Therapy with Asian families*. Washington, DC: Center for Minority Group Mental Health Programs, NIMH. Unpublished manuscript.

Chinn, P., & Plata, M. (1986). Perspectives and educational implications of Southeast Asian students. In M. K. Kitano & P. C. Chinn (Eds.), *Exceptional Asian children and youth* (pp. 12–28). Reston, VA: The Council for Exceptional Children.

Confucius. *Ta Hsueh (The Great Learning)*.

Confucius. *Chung Yung (Central Harmony)*.

Fong, S. (1973). Assimilation and changing social roles of Chinese Americans. *Journal of Social Issues, 29*(2), 115–127.

Glamser, D., & Myers, J. (1987, June). USA marvels at minority's winning way. *USA Today*, 1,2.

Leung, E. K. (1981). *The identification and social problems of the gifted bilingual-bicultural children*. Paper presented at The Council for Exceptional Children's Conference on the Exceptional Bilingual Child, New Orleans, LA. (ERIC Document Reproduction Service No. ED 203 653)

Leung, E. K. (1987). *Commonalities and diversities among Asian Americans for considerations in special education and related services*. Paper submitted to ERIC Document Reproduction Service.

Leung, E. K., Sultana, Q., & Andrews, J. (1987). *The effects of teacher organismics and articulation on listening comprehension*. Unpublished manuscript.

Lin, K., & Masuda, M. (1983). Impact of the refugee experience: Mental health issues of Southeast Asian refugees. In R. F. Morales (Ed.), *Bridging cultures* (pp.32–54). Los Angeles, CA: Asian American Mental Health Training Center.

Lin, Tsung-yi (1985). Mental disorders and psychiatry in Chinese culture, characteristic features and major issues. In W. Tseng & D. Wu (Eds.), *Chinese culture and mental health* (pp. 369–388). Orlando, FL: Academic Press.

Lum, K., & Char, W. F. (1985). Chinese adaptation in Hawaii: Some examples. In W. S. Tseng & D. Wu (Eds.), *Chinese culture and mental health* (pp. 215–226). Orlando, FL: Academic Press.

Morales, R. F. (Ed.). (1983). *Bridging cultures*. Los Angeles, CA: Asian American Mental Health Training Center.

Owen, T. C. (Ed.). (1985). *Southeast Asian mental health*. Washington, DC: U.S. Department of Health and Human Services.

Smith, H. (1965). *The religions of man*. New York: Perennial Library.

Tseng, W. S., & Wu, D. (Eds.). (1985). *Chinese culture and mental health*. Orlando, FL: Academic Press.

CHAPTER 10

Enhancing the Involvement of Black Parents of Adolescents with Handicaps

LaDelle Olion

Research pertaining to the involvement of Black parents of adolescents with handicaps is conspicuously absent from the literature. Despite the large number of Black adolescents with handicaps whose needs are not being met in the schools, and the proven relationship between effective parent involvement and the teaching and learning process (Comer, 1986; Marion, 1981), few studies have addressed this important area.

Recently there has been speculation about why more research studies have not been conducted on the involvement of Black parents with their adolescent children; however, the reasons are not fully known. Banks (1980) has noted that in the past, research and thinking about Black Americans was almost nonexistent because of a long history of discrimination. He further contends that the problems of Blacks were ignored or minimized by professionals because for years they were seen as relatively powerless and of low status. The Task Force on Black Academics and Cultural Excellence (1984), has pointed out that there is a lack of research on Blacks and their families because African-Americans have been lumped together with all others, with no recognition of the unique problems they have encountered and continue to experience. McAdoo (1981) adds that research in specific areas, such as the Black father's role in the socialization of his children, rarely occurs in social science literature. Others have questioned the appropriateness or the need for research or discussion articles on Blacks or in this case the involvement of Black parents of adolescents with handicaps.

Are Black parents really different from any other parents who have an adolescent with a handicap? Is involving parents of a young Black child with a handicap any different from trying to involve parents of an older child with a handicap? These and many more questions remain unanswered and primarily unaddressed in the literature. This chapter discusses the unique features of parenting older Black students with handicaps and offers some proven strategies that professionals may use to improve the involvement of Black parents of adolescents with handicaps.

UNIQUENESS FEATURES

Parenting is defined as the process by which the family socializes its children into the gender, cultural, and economic roles that the parents and/or society deem appropriate. Being the parent of any child (young or old) may involve problems and a certain amount of stress; however, parenting is seen as a more demanding task for Black families than for majority families, given the lowered expectations for achievement, economic discrimination, inferior medical services, and lower quality of life faced by many Black families (McAdoo, 1978). Jacobs (1986) states that over 40% of Black families are now headed by single females and that among families headed by females, 54.6% were considered to be living below the poverty level. For Black families with two parents, the poverty rate was 17.4%. Jacobs concludes that 66.2% of all Black children living in a household headed by a female were living below the poverty level in 1984.

Pierce (1969), a Harvard psychiatrist, also agrees that many Black Americans are different, and he states that "Black Americans live in a unique but mundane extreme environment of subtle-to-overt racism" (Peters, 1981, p. 220). Peters (1981) notes that:

- These oppressive environmental forces influence how Black families live and rear their children.
- Research on parenting in Black families demonstrates that the behavior and lifestyles of many Black people are different from those of Whites.
- Child rearing priorities, attitudes, and patterns of behaviors have developed out of the exigencies of the unique economic, cultural, and racial circumstances in which Blacks have lived.
- Most Black parents socialize their children to become self- sufficient, competent adults as defined by the society in which they live.
- For some Black families in the United States, socialization occurs within a cultural heritage that is both Afro-American and Euro-American and espouses both democratic equality for all citizens and caste-like status for its Black citizens.

On the other hand, like other parents, many Black parents are not prepared to be the parents of a child with a handicap; just like other parents of children with handicaps, Black parents frequently operate under tremendous physical, financial, emotional, and marital stress (Peters, 1981). In other words, in some respects parenting Black children or adolescents with handicaps may be no different from parenting any other child or adolescent with a handicap. Nevertheless, some Black parents are unique in that they face additional problems as a result of their culturally diverse status.

It is important to note that not all Black parents are alike, and that Black parents come from a variety of cultural groups in Africa and America. Lifestyles, values, and experiences vary a great deal within the Black community; however, members of the Black community have generally had the common experience of economic isolation, prejudice, and legally reinforced racism (McAdoo, 1978). Black parents first face the challenge of having dark skin color in many cases. Even today race and color are factors which influence education and affect one's identity and behavior in this country (Erikson, 1968). Likewise, the color and race of parents plays an important role in the whole process of parent participation, a premise that is supported by Comer (1986). Comer states that many schools simply do not want parents present and are reluctant to become involved with them because of racial, income, and educational differences.

The second challenge that many Black parents face is being the parent of a handicapped child. Marion (1980) mentions the similarities of Black parents who have handicapped children; however, he points out the following differences in being a Black parent of a handicapped child. First, many parents of culturally diverse handicapped children express anger and dismay at the overinclusion of their children in classes for the mentally retarded and emotionally disturbed. Many feel desperate and confused and express their anger at an educational system that they feel has promoted these two categories (mentally retarded and emotionally disturbed) as the only appropriate depositories for their children (Marion, 1979). Second, many of the frustrations of parents of culturally diverse populations have revolved around the condition of schooling for adolescents. He states that parents are concerned that many culturally diverse adolescents have been mislabeled because of their culturally different mannerisms.

The third challenge that many Black parents face which makes them unique is being the parent of an adolescent who has a handicap. Adolescence has been defined as a period when there is a struggle between independence and dependence; it is marked by a break from childhood, culminating in psychological maturity (Sabatino, 1980). Sabatino also defines adolescence as a period of (a) rapid physical growth, (b) newfound concerns for a place in an enlarged world, (c) establishment of sex role relationships, and (d) intense pressures from without to accept the adult world and declare an earned place in it. Jacks (1978) comments that adolescence does not miraculously bypass the student with a handicap. Add to these developmental dimensions the specific problems of teenage pregnancy, substance abuse, achievement motivation, high unemployment, suicide, juvenile delinquency, and an excessive dropout rate. Finally, combine these problems with the factors of race and handicapping conditions, and hopefully one can clearly see the complexities and uniqueness of problems surrounding Black families parenting adolescents with handicaps.

As a result of the uniqueness of the experiences of Black parents of adolescents with handicaps, many Black parents may require a different approach to get them involved and to meet their specific needs (Olion, Gillis-Olion, & Holmes, 1986).

STRATEGIES FOR ENHANCING INVOLVEMENT

In discussing or recommending techniques and strategies to be used to involve Black parents with handicapped adolescents, the lack of valid research to support such recommendations is often mentioned as a major criticism. As a result, only recommendations that have been made by authors or organizations that are knowledgeable, sensitive, and experienced in working with Black parents and handicapped students are included here. The recommendations to professionals are as follows:

1. *Respect Black parents.* Although respect is a courtesy that should be given to all parents, some professionals forget this when they interact with Black parents. In fact, lack of respect is often mentioned by Black parents as one of the reasons why they have refused to be involved in the schools (Marion, 1981). It should be noted that the problem is not totally racial; some Black parents have accused Black professionals of the same lack of respect. Professionals should note that unless there is respect for Black parents, there is little hope for successfully involving them in their children's education.

2. *Listen to Black parents and establish rapport.* Marion (1981) points out that professionals should be able to listen to parents without building up value judgments by using the following techniques:

   * Relax physically and center attention on the parents.
   * Use eye contact to help focus upon the parents and to communicate to them that they are being heard.
   * Understand what the parents are saying.

     Marion contends this is important because Black parents are often not afforded the courtesy of being heard. After listening to Black parents, it will be easier to establish rapport. If parents are not talkative, ask them what their views are about school. What do they feel you should be doing with their adolescent with special needs? Ask the parents about their practices in rearing their adolescent. What are their problem areas? Give them opportunities to express anxieties. These are some questions that may open up the discussion; however, remember the importance of listening to the parents. Marion (1981) points out that Black parents stop listening and talking when they are not heard.

3. *Develop interpersonal relations.* Parents should feel comfortable talking with professionals. However, the social struggles that have taken place over the last two decades have increased distrust between school personnel and parents. When parents sense neglect or exclusion, or when their children are having difficulty in school, they often become defensive, and the parent/school relationship is further complicated. Feelings of support, understanding, and caring must be sincerely conveyed by professionals to Black parents.

4. *Give Black parents straight answers.* If professionals are going to persuade Black parents to become involved, we must give them facts and straight answers to specific questions about their adolescent's needs and how the school intends to meet them. Unfortunately such answers seem to be difficult to get, sometimes for good reasons, but more often because nonspecific communication has become a parent/management tactic. General reassurances are not reassuring. Trust is not established by saying "Trust us" (Morton & Hull, 1976). As professionals we must be open and honest if we want to improve the involvement of Black parents.

5. *Actively involve Black parents.* Some schools give lip service to the importance of parent involvement, but do not give parents the opportunity to play a meaningful role. In some schools, Black parents are called only when there is a problem with their adolescent child. Some Black parents, who recall similar difficulties while they were in school themselves, are not eager to be involved. In attempting to actively involve Black parents we must discuss parent roles. Roles and responsibilities should be openly discussed in order to avoid misunderstanding (Minority Leadership Consortium of the Handicapped Children's Early Education Program, 1981). Black parents should be made to feel that they are *an active part of* the planning team rather than *the object of* the team's planning. Parent participation must be well-thought-out and well-structured. When this is not done, parent's concerns about teaching methods, the goals of the school, and even the competence of the staff can lead to conflict (Comer, 1986).

6. *Make a special attempt to involve Black fathers.* When Black parent involvement is examined, one finds that the mother is the parent most often involved. As a result, Young (1983) points out, some professionals view the father as unimportant. He asserts that the role of parenting is changing and that many Black fathers want to be involved. Working with Black fathers is an excellent suggestion, and perhaps if we focused on involving Black fathers of adolescents with handicaps, we would have identified another overlooked resource that could be used to improve parent participation. Young (1983) also states that meeting with fathers on Saturdays and training them as tutors of their handicapped children have been types of programs that have been successfully used with Black fathers in the Atlanta area.

7. *Contact Black fraternities and sororities.* Black fraternities and sororities represent substantial human and financial resources that could be used to improve parent participation, and to improve the skills of Black adolescents with handicaps. Black fraternities and sororities are numerous and can be found on campuses of historically Black and major institutions across the country (see Figure 1). An example of the type of project a fraternity or sorority might undertake is demonstrated by Omega Psi Phi, a predominantly Black fraternity. In one of the local chapters in Fayetteville, North Carolina, a Saturday enrichment program has been started that focuses primarily on adolescents with learning problems. The project has been in existence for approximately 5 years, and teachers and parents refer adolescents who need assistance to the program. The program serves regular students primarily; however, some of the fraternity members have expertise in special education and the program is now serving some adolescents with handicaps. The program has been so successful that other local fraternity and sorority chapters have now become involved, and the services have been expanded.

Black sororities and fraternities may also be willing to pay for limited child care services, allowing Black parents to participate in school programs. In addition, these organizations may be tapped to aid in understanding the Black family value system, or members may be used as tutors or as trainers of handicapped adolescents. Fraternity and sorority members could also be used to help alleviate the unnecessary referrals of some adolescents for special education services. The important point is that members of these organizations are knowledgeable and well-trained professionals, who are looking for opportunities to serve their communities. Involving Black fraternities and sororities with Black parents is a potential area of community service that should be investigated at each local level (Olion, 1982).

FIGURE 1

List of Black Fraternities and Sororities

Black Fraternities	Black Sororities
1. Omega Psi Phi	1. Delta Sigma Theta
2. Kappa Alpha Psi	2. Alpha Kappa Alpha
3. Alpha Phi Alpha	3. Sigma Gamma Rho
4. Phi Beta Sigma	4. Zeta Phi Beta

8. *Use local ministers.* Transportation has been listed as a major deterrent to the involvement of Black parents of handicapped children (Patton & Braithwaite, 1984). Local ministers should be contacted, as many churches have vans and buses that may be available to help transport parents to meetings. Churches may also be used for parent meetings.

9. *Develop a partnership.* The current upsurge of interest in school reform is bringing renewed interest in a variety of plans to increase parent participation in education. One such proposal is the partnership concept. The idea is that the education of students should be viewed as a partnership between the school and the home; that students and parents are co-producers of education, not simply passive recipients of educational services. Advocates of partnerships see them as a way to organize resources inside and outside the school system (Davies, 1985). The partnership concept places the responsibility for learning on students, parents, and the broader community as well as on teachers (Seely, 1981). Activities that may be included in a partnership program include home tutoring, homework helper and homework hot line projects, home visitor programs, parent education, and parent volunteer programs.

    An example of a partnership program in action is found in the Cumberland County Schools, in Fayetteville, North Carolina. The program was proposed in 1986 and implemented in 1987. It is a university-public school program that includes Black parents of handicapped adolescents. Fayetteville State University, a local university, adopted E. E. Smith, a senior high school. As a result, E. E. Smith Senior High School currently sends a number of its students to Fayetteville State University to receive reading instruction and other training. Parents of "adopted" students have also been included, and plans are now being made to conduct parenting workshops for parents who have various needs. It should be noted that the partnership program in Cumberland County is not designed exclusively for Black adolescents or Black parents. However, the project currently serves a large number of Black parents and their adolescent children. The partnership concept is a viable strategy that should be tried in an effort to improve the participation of Black parents.

10. *Develop Black parent advocacy programs.* Professionals must take a stronger and more programmatic interest in alleviating the problems that affect Black students and their parents. Professionals and Black parents must raise issues of nutrition, education, and employment needs if they are to be met for Black students (Edelman, 1981). Professionals must become well informed about the needs of Black adolescents with handicaps, must be persistent, and must focus energy on real issues, not symbolic ones. Goals must be set, thinking must take place about how to achieve goals, and means must be chosen to reach these goals. The premise in developing Black parent advocacy programs is that some Black parents may feel powerless, and as a result they may need the support of strong, well trained advocates. For example, an advocate might accompany parents to meetings to

discuss assessment results and eligibility for special education. Advocates could also assist adolescents and their parents with other school related problems.

11. *Use peer parents and paraprofessionals.* The job of peer parents or paraprofessionals would be to relate strategies that they have used successfully with their handicapped teenagers to other Black parents (Marion, 1980). Boone and Smith (1981) suggest that we identify community persons who can serve as informal intermediaries between the home and school. Retired teachers, church members, ministers, and extended family members could be trained to relay information to parents in an informal setting, or they could be used to assist in identifying adolescents with special needs.

12. *Make home visits.* Home visits should be made for the purpose of trying to relate to men and women who are significant to the adolescent. Professionals should try to find out about the parents' satisfaction or dissatisfaction with the school environment (Boone & Smith, 1981). Professionals should also try to get an idea of the parents' expectations as they relate to goals for their handicapped adolescent. These visits should not be evaluative in nature.

13. *Use recorded telephone messages.* Chapman and Howard (1982) suggest that recorded telephone messages be used to improve communication between parents and teachers. They state that the recorded message is a nonthreatening way to get parents actively involved in the student's academic assignments and in the activities of the school. Although Chapman's and Howard's suggestions were not designed specifically for Black parents of handicapped adolescents, the nonthreatening facet of the recorded messages makes their suggestion a very promising method to initiate participation of Black parents.

14. *Use role-playing and media training techniques.* Role playing is an important technique that has been successfully used to train parents. Role playing keeps the participants involved and motivated, and parents can be taught skills through role-playing interactions that may include individual education plan development or how to design and implement an intervention strategy (Olion, 1982). Media such as videotapes, slide presentations, and films can also assist in motivating Black parents and aid in maintaining interest. The biggest problem, however, is to locate material on handicapped adolescents that is relevant to Black parents.

15. *Involve Black parents in nontraditional ways.* For example, a parents day may be held when parents are invited to share a cultural activity with a class or parents might be asked to bring their favorite dishes to a pot luck dinner. This should be a relatively inexpensive way to get better acquainted with Black parents (Minority Leadership Consortium of the Handicapped Children's Early Education Program, 1981).

SUMMARY AND CONCLUSIONS

Black parents of adolescents with handicaps come from a variety of cultural and economic groups; therefore, in some cases strategies to involve Black parents in education would be no different from strategies used to involve any other parents with adolescents who are handicapped. On the other hand, parenting is seen as a more onerous task for Black families than for majority families, given their often lowered expectations for achievement, economic discrimination, inferior medical services, and a lower quality of life (McAdoo, 1978). Jacobs (1986) has pointed out that many Black families are headed by Black females and that 66.2% of all Black children living in a household headed by a female live below the poverty level. Additionally, it has been pointed out that Black parents face problems because of their skin color. Erickson (1968) has asserted that educators must learn that one's race and color are factors that influence education, and that educators must learn that one's race and color affects one's identity and behavior in this country. Comer (1986) has also concluded that many schools simply do not want parents present and are reluctant to become involved because of racial, income, and educational differences. Additional problems associated with being an adolescent and having a handicap have also been identified as problems that Black parents face in parenting. As a result of these unique differences, it was concluded that different approaches may be required to enhance parent involvement.

It has been noted that Black parents can make important contributions to the educational process, if they are actively involved and given the proper respect and opportunity. The effectiveness of Black parents with adolescents who are handicapped depends to a great degree on skillful professional guidance. Many more Black parents of adolescents with handicaps will get acquainted with schools and become better volunteers if they feel that they are welcome, know that their teenagers are treated fairly, are understood and listened to, and receive appropriate information on how to access the system when they are having problems.

The strategies suggested are not intended to be a panacea, nor will they be effective with all Black parents. In fact, none of the strategies recommended will have any significant impact on enhancing the involvement of Black parents with handicapped adolescents, unless professionals stop looking at working with Black parents as a step down or as a waste of valuable time. Responding to the specific needs of Black parents requires that professionals know and understand the culture from which parents come. Professionals must be aware of the unique qualities, values, and variations in lifestyle and structure found among Black families. We must learn to look at Black parents within the context of the parent's own cultural setting before any conjecture is made about their behavior. As professionals we must decide that we sincerely want to involve Black parents of handicapped adolescents, despite the many challenges that may be encountered in this endeavor.

REFERENCES

Banks, W. M. (1980). The social context and empirical foundations of research on black clients. In R. L. Jones (Ed.), *Black psychology* (pp. 283–293). New York: Harper and Row.

Boone, R., & Smith, P. (1981). *How much do black parents with exceptional children really know about P.L. 94–142 and its significance for them: A survey.* (ERIC Clearinghouse on Handicapped and Gifted No. ED 204 900).

Chapman, J. E., & Howard, W. L. (1982). Improving the parent-teacher communication through recorded messages. *Exceptional Children, 49*(1), 79–82.

Comer, J. P. (1986). Parent participation in the schools. *Phi Delta Kappan 67*(6), 442–446.

Davies, D. (1985, May). *Parent involvement in the public schools in the 1980s: Proposals, issues, opportunities.* Paper prepared for the Research for Better Schools, Inc., Conference: The Education Reform Movement: Impact on At-Risk Youth, Philadelphia, Pennsylvania.

Edelman, M. W. (1981). An advocacy agenda for black families and children. In H. P. McAdoo (Ed.), *Black families*, Beverly Hills, CA: Sage.

Erikson, E. H. (1968). Identity: Youth and crises. New York: W. W. Norton.

Jacks, K. B. (1978). A humanistic approach to the adolescent with learning disabilities: An educational psychological and vocation model. *Adolescence, 13*(49), 59–68.

Jacobs, J. E. (1986). An overview of black America in 1985. In J. D. Williams (ed.), *The state of black America 1984*, (pp. I–XI). Washington, DC: National Urban League, Inc.

Marion, R. L. (1979). Minority parent involvement in the IEP process: A systematic model approach. *Focus on Exceptional Children, 10*, 1–14.

Marion, R. L. (1980). Communicating with parents of culturally diverse exceptional children. *Exceptional Children, 46*(8), 616–623.

Marion, R. L. (1981). *Educators, parents and exceptional children.* Rockville, MD: Aspen.

McAdoo, H. P. (1978). Minority families. In J. H. Stevens & M. Matthews (Eds.), *Mother/child, father/child relationships,* (pp. 177–195). Washington, DC: The National Association for the Education of Young Children.

McAdoo, J. L. (1981). Involvement of fathers in the socialization of black children. In H. P. McAdoo (Ed.), *Black families,* (pp. 225–237). Beverly Hills, CA: Sage.

Minority Leadership Consortium of the Handicapped Children's Early Education Program (July, 1981). *Fostering parenting skills for mother and fathers of minority handicapped children: Awareness, acceptance and coping.* Workshop conducted by the Handicapped Children's Early Education Program of the U.S. Department of Education, Washington, DC.

Morton, K. A., & Hull, K. (1976). Parents and the mainstream. In R. L. Jones (Ed.), *Mainstreaming the minority child* (pp. 37–52). Reston, VA: The Council for Exceptional Children.

Olion, L. (1982). Working with minority parents of handicapped children: An overlooked issue. In Minority Leadership Consortium Monograph Series, *Dimensions of cultural diversity, strategies for serving minority handicapped children and their parents*, Washington, DC.

Olion, L., Gillis-Olion, M., & Holmes, R. L. (1986). Strategies for interacting with black parents of handicapped children. *The Negro Educational Review, 37*(1), 8–16.

Patton, J., & Braithwaite, R. L. (1984). Obstacles to the participation of black parents in the educational programs of their handicapped children. *Centering Teacher Education, 1*(2), 34–37.

Peters, M. F. (1981). Parenting in black families with young children: A historical perspective. In H. P. McAdoo (Ed.), *Black families* (pp. 211–224). Beverly Hills, CA: Sage.

Pierce, C. (1969). *The effects of racism.* Paper presented at the American Medical Association 15th Annual Conference cf State Mental Health Representatives, Chicago, IL.

Sabatino, D. A. (1980). Secondary special education: A case of benign neglect. In J. B. Jordan, D. A. Sabatino, R. C. Sarri (Eds.), *Disruptive youth in school* (pp. 87–101). Reston, VA: The Council for Exceptional Children.

Seely, D. (1981). *Education for partnership.* New York: Ballinger.

Task Force on Black Academic and Cultural Excellence. (1984). *Saving the African American child.* Washington, DC: National Alliance of Black School Educators, Inc.

Young, J. (1983, July). *Improving communications with parents of black students.* Presentation at National Conference and Training Workshops on the Exceptional Black Child, Atlanta, GA.

CHAPTER 11

California Bilingual Special Education Model Sites (1984–1986): Programs and Research

Jana Echevarria-Ratleff
Victoria L. Graf

The California State Department of Education (1983) reports that over 1 million language minority students are enrolled in California schools. This creates a need for programs that effectively serve culturally and linguistically different students.

In identifying components of a bilingual special education program that meets the needs of its students, Baca and Cervantes (1984, pp. 24, 271) suggest that the following be included:

1. An ongoing, broadly based, nonbiased assessment.
2. Prevention viewed as a priority.
3. Early intervention.
4. Some disabilities viewed as symptoms rather than disorders.
5. A broad range of special education services.
6. Instruction provided in the student's primary language.
7. Regular classroom teachers (including bilingual teachers) involved in the program planning and implementation.
8. A variety of special education services to meet the variety of disabilities.
9. Parents provided with maximum amounts of information in a language they understand and meaningfully involved in planning and reinforcing instruction.

This chapter reports the research findings of the Loyola Marymount University/SERN Bilingual Unit grant project with respect to effective bilingual special education programs. The research base was one of the California Bilingual Special Education Model Sites, the Bilingual Special Education Resource Specialist Program (RSP) at Paramount Elementary School in the Azusa Unified School District. This description is the first step in this project's determination of the effectiveness of instructional strategies in bilingual special education.

OVERVIEW OF MODEL SITES PROGRAM

Recognizing the importance of meeting the needs of culturally and linguistically different exceptional children (CLDE), the Programs, Curriculum, and Training Unit of the Special Education Division, California State Department of Education, authorized the funding of several school districts as Bilingual Special Education Model Sites. A committee of selected educators from throughout the state evaluated the proposals regarding the extent to which they represented promising practices in bilingual special education, such as those suggested by Baca and Cervantes (1984).

104

Six school districts were selected and funded as Bilingual Special Education Model Sites. These districts represented both urban and rural settings, as well as those serving both Hispanic and Asian populations. Each district was also selected for unique features such as nonpsychometric assessment process, prereferral bilingual student study team, parent as co-learner, and so forth. Table 1 shows the characteristics of the various sites.

BILINGUAL SPECIAL EDUCATION PERSONNEL PREPARATION PROJECT

In 1985, a personnel preparation grant was awarded by the Office of Special Education and Rehabilitative Services of the U.S. Department of Education to Loyola Marymount University and the Special Education Resource Network/Bilingual Unit (SERN/Bilingual Unit), an agency of the Programs, Curriculum and Training Unit of the Special Education Division, California State Department of Education. The intention of the project was to identify effective instructional strategies in bilingual special education, then integrate them into a special education preservice program at the university and to disseminate these strategies through subsequent SERN/Bilingual Unit training. The research component of the project involved the Model Sites. Selected sites were the primary source of data collection in terms of effective instructional strategies.

PROJECT DESIGN

An ethnographic approach was used to identify instructional practices in this Model Site through a description of the educational program as well as its development. This approach included field observation, interviews, and collection of work products. Data were collected over a 6-week period during the 1985–1986 academic year.

DISTRICT DEMOGRAPHICS

Azusa Unified School District is located 20 miles east of Los Angeles in the San Gabriel Valley. Median household income was $16,000/year, and 89% of the families were employed in skilled, semi-skilled and unskilled occupations. The major ethnic groups and their percentages represented by district students were as follows: (a) Hispanic, 52%; (b) Anglo, 43%; (c) Blacks, Asians, and Native Americans, 5%. Of the 600 students enrolled at Paramount School, approximately 70% were Hispanic, and 32% of these students were limited English proficient (LEP), as measured by the IDEA Proficiency Test or the Language Assessment Scales (LAS).

STUDENT CHARACTERISTICS

The Bilingual Special Education Research Specialist Program (RSP) involved 24 students in grades 1 through 6, with the majority being in grades 3 and 5. All students were average or above average in intellectual performance and qualified as learning disabled. As is characteristic of most learning handicapped programs, students' reading scores varied widely based on results from the Wide Range Achievement Test (WRAT). Based on the WRAT, reading performance ranged from kindergarten to seventh grade. Spelling performance ranged from first to third grades and math performance ranged from kindergarten to fifth grade.

Students were evaluated for their English language proficiency. Nine (38%) were identified as LEP and 15 (62%) were identified as fluent English proficient (FEP).

TABLE 1

Bilingual Special Education Model Sites

Model Sites	School	Population	Urban/Rural	Practices
Azusa Unified School District	Paramount	Hispanic	Urban	Bilingual Student Study Team, Parent as Co-Leader, Coordination of Special Education/Bilingual Programs, English/Spanish Computer Lab, Program Interventions/Modifications
San Joaquin County Office of Education		Hispanic	Rural	K–12 SDC Program, Referral, Assessment, Parent Involvement, Bilingual Communicatively Handicapped Class, Bilingual Learning Handicapped Class
Sweetwater Union High School District	Southwest High Southwest Jr.	Hispanic	Urban	Bilingual Parent Facilitator, Continuum of Interventions, Programming and Service Delivery, Bilingual SST, Grades 9–12
Winters Joint Unified School District	Waggoner	Hispanic	Rural	K–4 Program, Bilingual Student Study Team, Bilingual Staff/Specialized Staff Coordination, Utilization of Limited Resources
Oakland Unified School District		Chinese Indochinese Hispanic	Urban	K–6 Program, Bilingual Special Education Program, Assessment & Curriculum Instruction of Special Education
San Francisco Unified School District		Black Chinese Hispanic	Urban	Nonpsychometric Assessment Process, Bilingual Special Day Classes, K–12 Program

SCHOOL-WIDE APPROACH

A unique feature of this particular program was the extensive interaction among all school personnel and the commitment of the administration to fostering a cooperative school atmosphere. From interviews with administrators, regular education teachers, bilingual education teachers, and support personnel, it was apparent that there was notable staff involvement in all facets of the school's educational program.

This particular site implemented a school-wide approach to bilingual special education with a strong interface between the bilingual program and the special education program. As a result of administrative support, bilingual special education was an integral part of the school, not an isolated component.

The RSP classroom was located in the front of the school among other regular education classrooms. Students were served by the regular education program, the reading resource room, and the bilingual resource room, as well as the RSP. RSP students were instructed using the same curriculum and texts as the rest of the school in areas of reading, language, spelling, writing, and math. Students' programs were monitored by the RSP teacher until each was fully mainstreamed in a subject area.

INSTRUCTIONAL PROGRAMS

In describing instructional practices, it was important to consider the features of each student's class schedule (i.e., extent and nature of regular education, special education, bilingual education, etc.). The student's schedule was based on an Individual Education Program (IEP), which was both linguistically and academically appropriate to the student's needs. Language of instruction was designated on each IEP.

Reading Program

A significant factor contributing to the success of the instructional program included the use of a school-wide departmentalized reading program. All students were assigned to groups according to reading level. RSP students remained with their regular education class until their scheduled RSP reading instruction. While in the regular class, the student worked on materials provided by the Resource Specialist teacher, thus allowing participation in the school-wide schedule while receiving appropriate individualized reading instruction.

An important component of the reading program was the selection of the reading series. For FEP students, the Ginn series and Specific Skills series were used. Santillana and Specific Skills (Spanish version) were used for Spanish reading. For both language groups, the monitoring procedure was the same; end-of-unit and/or end-of-book tests were administered by the reading resource teacher (English readers) and the bilingual resource teacher (Spanish readers). These tests were the same as those taken by the regular school population. As with any other student in the school, if an RSP student failed some portion of the test, the appropriate resource teacher provided supplemental materials for the student to remediate his or her weak area.

A major area of interest in a bilingual special education program is the transition of LEP students from Spanish reading to English reading. In the Paramount program, LEP students received primary language instruction while learning English and were transitioned into an English program only when they met criteria. The criteria were (a) oral language proficiency in English as measured by the IDEA Proficiency Test or the LAS (must score LES or FES); (b) ESL/IDEA kit, Mastery Level IV or Rainbow Level, Intermediate Fluency (Stage 4); and (c) reading proficiency in Spanish as measured by Spanish Reading Keys, Mastery Level 6, Mi Mundo. In addition, teacher checklists for Spanish language proficiency and English language proficiency were used when determining transfer to English reading. The following are types of student behaviors listed on these checklists:

1. The child is speaking in sentences in Spanish using correct syntax.
2. The child is able to decode words and read in Spanish with comprehension.
3. The child is using his or her Spanish reading skills in creative writing.
4. The child is able to understand a variety of directions in English and follow them correctly.
5. The child is conversing with English peers in the classroom and playground.
6. The child is participating in ESL instruction.

It is noteworthy that an effort was made to use culturally and linguistically appropriate reading activities and curriculum. Often the teacher and the aides would try to elicit the students' personal cultural experiences relating to the lesson.

Language Program

In terms of language development, LEP students received instruction in English, Spanish, and English as a second language (ESL), as determined by the needs of the students. Anglo students could receive Spanish as a second language with parental permission. As with other academic areas, the language program for RSP students followed the language curriculum of the school. For example, with respect to ESL, the students used commercial as well as noncommercial materials. Some commercial materials included Santillana's "The Picture Collection" and the "Rainbow Collection"; the Peabody Language Development Kit; the Mots Worter "Language Treasure Kit"; and the "IDEA Kit." Various programs for the classroom's six computers were used extensively. To reinforce language development, Josten's Learning System, which included a voice synthesizer, was used by the students for independent practice of English language skills. In addition, some computer software packages included Binet International, LOGO Guided Discovery Kit, and Kidwriter SS (Spinnaker Software Corporation).

Spelling Program

The spelling program involved mastery of words which were derived from the reading curriculum, in both English and Spanish. Spelling tests, administered in the RSP classroom, were used to measure mastery.

Writing Program

Power Writing, a technique for developing written expression, was used in the RSP classroom as well as in the regular program. It was conducted in English and Spanish following specific rules for implementation. Kidwrite, a computer software program, was also adapted for use with Spanish-speaking students.

Math Program

The math program for the RSP students included basic computational as well as functional skills. The curricula, again, corresponded to the curricula used by the regular education program, that is, Addison-Wesley.

In addition, use of manipulatives was prevalent. Mastery was determined by end-of-unit and end-of-book tests administered by the Math Resource Specialist.

Delivery of Instruction

Instruction for the subject areas was conducted by the RSP teacher and aides, regular education teacher, bilingual education teacher (when appropriate), support personnel, and parent volunteers. The RSP classroom had four aides, three of whom were bilingual. The aides were trained through inservice training conducted by the County of Los Angeles and district and school site personnel. It was noted that the RSP teacher functioned as a master teacher in terms of her relationship with the aides. An example of this is the aides' involvement in the daily planning sessions. The RSP teacher led discussion of the following day's activities and aides gave suggestions, provided input/ideas, and identified problems the students were experiencing. While the aides played a significant role in planning, the RSP teacher maintained responsibility for final decisions.

The instruction in the RSP classroom was delivered by means of small group arrangement. The RSP teacher and each aide had responsibility for a group. These groups rotated approximately once a month, ensuring that each student received instructional time with the

RSP teacher. In addition, students received group practice in areas of need from the parent volunteers. Parents were trained through the Parents as Co-Learners program. Workshops were set up in which the parent and his or her child both benefited from the presentation—for example, nutrition and use of math manipulatives for home practice.

English and Spanish were used as the languages of instruction based upon the needs of the student. Content areas that were taught in Spanish included reading, writing, spelling, and math. At times, with the LEP students who had been transitioned into English instruction, Spanish was still the language of communication. To promote primary language development, student-teacher interaction was often in Spanish. This was observed in casual conversation, in clarification of concepts, and for classroom management. For example, the observer noted that during a math lesson devoted to helping students tell time in English, an LEP student used Spanish to request assistance. The teacher then explained the procedure in Spanish. In this instance, understanding of concepts was of primary importance with continual use of English being secondary.

PREREFERRAL INTERVENTIONS

One of the key elements which determined the district's designation as a Model Site was the school's Student Study Team (SST). This system was part of an attempt to intervene in areas of student need, thus possibly averting an inappropriate special education referral. When a student was having a problem in the regular classroom, the teacher was expected to implement and document at least eight of the academic or behavioral interventions shown in Table 2.

If those interventions did not prove successful, the student was then referred to the SST. This was a three-level process in which alternative interventions were considered before reaching Level 3, which was referral to special education.

Parent and student participation was encouraged throughout the entire process and an interpreter/translator was provided for non-English speaking individuals. If a student required special education assessment, it was provided in the student's primary language by both the bilingual psychologists and bilingual speech and language personnel.

Another preventive measure implemented at the school was a newly instituted developmental kindergarten where students who do not succeed in the first year of kindergarten are retained. If there is no progress the second year, steps are taken to provide early intervention, possibly through placement in special education after completion of the SST process.

As a function of the RSP teacher's role, it was observed that extensive consultation services were offered to all school personnel. The RSP teacher set up a conference schedule which included a time slot for every regular education teacher who had an RSP student. During this time, the RSP teacher noted progress and offered suggestions regarding strategies and curriculum. Much conferencing took place informally as well. It appeared that the efforts on behalf of the RSP teacher as coordinator/consultant fostered a relationship in which the regular teachers were willing to implement any intervention necessary in the interest of the RSP student.

SUGGESTIONS FOR REPLICATION OF THE PROGRAM

The program as presented in this chapter was in its third year of implementation. Interviews with administrators revealed that several factors were involved in the development of this program and need to be considered in the initiation of any similar bilingual special education program.

The most significant requisite is a strong interface among regular education, bilingual education, and special education staff. To initiate this interface, a high-quality, regular education program must be established as a foundation, with the building of strong bilingual

TABLE 2

Classroom Interventions Prior to Referral

1. Conference with student.
2. Parent involvement through conferencing, class visits, assists at home.
3. Change seat.
4. Study carrels.
5. Time-out.
6. Develop reward system/behavior modification.
7. Assertive discipline.
8. Special contract and/or agreement.
9. Emphasis on student strength by special recognition.
10. Provide buddy/tutorial system.
11. Modify assignments.
12. Academic regrouping.
13. Remedial reading.
14. Remedial math.
15. Classroom change for subject area.
16. After school help/counseling.
17. Use of different materials.
18. Tutoring (cross-age, classroom aide).
19. Reteaching.
20. Learner keeps study book.
21. Daily rehearsal of student expectation.
22. Classroom management.
23. Other learning modalities.

education and special education programs as the next step. This process should ensure a well-developed bilingual special education program.

Staff development is a key feature of a high-quality school program. This can be accomplished by using free services of local county agencies as well as district and state trainers such as the SERN/Bilingual Unit. Additional means might be consistent sharing with staff of current research and new developments in education as well as release time for faculty to visit other programs.

In order to build an expert staff, it was suggested that site administrators be involved in recruitment rather than relying only on district personnel offices. Furthermore, existing staff members should be treated as experts. One suggestion is to organize weekly leadership meetings in which selected faculty, that is, reading resource teacher, RSP teacher, and others, meet weekly with building principals to provide input regarding school business.

To create a positive atmosphere, the site administrator must have high expectations for staff, students, and community involvement. Professionalism and cooperation among staff should prevail. Derogatory statements by staff about students and their families should not be tolerated. Students should be expected to achieve their highest potential academically and socially. Parent/community participation in school activities and business should be expected and encouraged. Mutual respect among these groups can contribute to this atmosphere.

Finally, financial support can come from several sources. It is recommended that additional funds be sought out, such as state and federal grants or Title VII funds.

CONCLUSION

Observations, field notes, and interviews provide evidence that the Azusa Unified School District Bilingual Special Education program is addressing the components identified by Baca and Cervantes for effectively meeting the needs of culturally and linguistically different exceptional students. Furthermore, the program provided the students with the opportunity to be educated in the least restrictive environment, one that was culturally and linguistically sensitive to their needs.

As part of the Loyola Marymount University/SERN Bilingual Unit grant project, the findings discussed in this study, as well as data gathered at other sites, will be disseminated through the special education teacher training program at LMU and inservice training by the SERN Bilingual Unit.

REFERENCE

Baca, L. M., & Cervantes, H. T. (1984). *The bilingual special education interface*. St. Louis, MO: Times Mirror/Mosby College.

NOTE: Preparation of this chapter was supported in part by a U.S. Department of Education, Office of Special Education Rehabilitative Services Grant #G008535047 to Loyola Marymount University and the Special Education Resource Network/Bilingual Unit.

CHAPTER 12

The Need for Community-Based Special Education Programs in the Band-Operated Schools of Manitoba

Ron S. Phillips
Ford R. Cranwell

In federal, provincial, and band-operated schools throughout Canada the movement toward greater Indian involvement and control of Indian education has taken many forms as Indian people strive to ensure the transmission of their culture while providing meaningful, high-quality education. In this context, community-based, band-operated schools represent a unique opportunity for local bands to assume control of schooling in their communities.

In the course of furthering Indian control, little attention has been given to Indian children with special needs. Many of these children have exceptionalities or other learning problems that require specialized instruction, support services, materials, equipment, or educational settings. In circumstances where insufficient resources are available to assist students experiencing various kinds of learning difficulties, Indian children with special needs and their families are especially vulnerable and are at risk of not having their needs met.

This chapter examines the need for community-based special education programs in the band-operated schools of Manitoba. It reviews the current status of special education in band-operated schools, proposes a model for special education service delivery within Indian communities served by band-operated schools, and discusses the prospects for improved learning opportunities for Indian children with special needs.

SCHOOL JURISDICTIONS

In Canada, Indian children who live on reserves attend the following types of school jurisdictions:

- *Federal schools.* Located on reserves throughout Canada, these schools are operated by the federal government of Canada's Department of Indian and Northern Affairs Canada (INAC) for the education of 21,791 Indian students (INAC, 1982). In Manitoba, 4,363 Indian students attend federal schools (INAC–Manitoba, 1985).

- *Provincial schools.* These are public schools throughout Canada operated by local school divisions which receive tuition payments from INAC for the education of 38,489 Indian students (INAC, 1982). In Manitoba, provincial schools received tuition for 4,158 Indian students (INAC–Manitoba, 1985).

- *Band-operated schools.* These are local reserve schools that receive funds from INAC but are under the direction of locally elected education authorities. In Manitoba these local education authorities are in turn responsible to the Chief and Council of the reserve. Throughout Canada, 15,906 Indian students attended band-operated schools (INAC, 1982). In Manitoba, the figure is 3,970 Indian students (INAC–Manitoba, 1985). These students are served by 30 band-operated schools.

STATUS OF SPECIAL EDUCATION

Survey of Needs

The Manitoba Indian Education Association (MIEA) was created to support and promote the educational aspirations of Indian people on a province-wide basis. In 1984, MIEA surveyed 14 band-operated schools and 7 Tribal Councils (regional offices established to share resources), to ascertain the need for special education services (INAC, 1984a). Information on the needs of children and youth enrolled in band-operated schools or attending schools off reserve due to unavailable specialized services and on school-age children not in school was obtained through personal interviews with teachers, principals, directors of education, home/school coordinators and parents. The schools were selected on the basis of location and size to ensure that a good cross-section (high school, elementary, small and large enrollment, rural, isolated, and near urban settings) was surveyed.

The survey results indicated that 31% of the students were suspected of having one or more learning problems requiring specialized services (see Table 1). The teachers surveyed were almost unanimous in their dissatisfaction with the present lack of special education services. Needed services, personnel, and materials included: individual assessments, counseling, remedial teachers, special class teachers, consultative resource teachers, reading clinicians, school psychologists, speech and language pathologists, special education materials, and additional space. These results as well as a proposed action plan for establishing a provincial funding and service delivery system (INAC, 1984b) were given back to the schools in written form. There were also many presentations at school staff meetings, community (reserve) meetings, and school board/local education authority meetings.

Funding Limitations

During the early 1980s INAC had not as yet established a means to generate funds to support the establishment of special education programs and services within band-operated schools. In 1985, INAC included special education in its Directory of Services, which lists those programs for which funding will be provided. Special education is defined as follows:

> Instruction, instructional materials, student supplies, diagnostic testing and evaluation for students who have exceptional learning needs; student room and board and transportation may be provided where required. (INAC, 1985)

While this action was significant and legitimized special education as a band-operated school program, the level of funding to date has been inadequate. Schools receive special education funds based upon the following fiscal formula:

$$\text{amount per pupil } (\$268.24) \times \text{total number of enrolled students} = \text{total special education allocation}$$
(INAC–Manitoba, 1985)

The amount per pupil is presently $268.24. Of this amount the schools receive 75%, that is, $200.00 per pupil (INAC, 1986a, 1986b), with the remaining 25% divided between the Tribal Councils and MIEA for program coordination, training, and technical assistance (INAC–Manitoba, 1985). In 1985, the total amount of funds allocated to all the band-operated schools

TABLE 1

Students Suspected of Needing Services in Selected Band-Operated Schools of Manitoba by Grade Level and Special Needs Category

Grade	Special Needs Category*											Number of Special Needs**	Number of Students
	SPH	SVI	SHI	SP	SBP	IIA	LD	LDP	AGD	AT	G		
K	2	1		5	8	1	23	10		13	3	66	46
1	1		7	11	10	4	60	43	22	51	2	211	102
2	1	1	1	6	13	5	58	30	27	26	1	169	84
3		1	1	6	28	4	48	34	38	35	1	196	94
4		4	1	6	16	8	60	41	35	33	3	207	91
5		1	1	4	16	4	69	58	49	43	3	248	103
6		1	2	6	15	8	43	23	31	31	1	161	85
7	1		2	3	50	13	65	33	71	66	18	322	155
8	2	2		2	14	2	41	32	23	36	2	156	71
9					13	1	30	22	20	34	3	123	60
10				1	11	2	22	11	17	20		84	33
11				1	2		6	4	3	5		21	12
12					1			1		3		5	4
Special Class			2		2	6	13	5	11	18		57	29
Total Students	7	11	17	51	199	58	538	347	347	414	37	2,026	969

Number of students requiring special education assistance   969
Total number of students in surveyed schools   3,125
Percentage of students requiring services   31%

SPH   severe physical handicap
SVI   severe visual impairment
SHI   severe hearing impairment
SP   speech impediment

SBP   severe behavior problem
IIA   impairment in intellectual ability
LD   learning disabilities
LDP   language development problem

AGD   age-grade discrepancy
AT   attendance problem
G   gifted

*Special needs category
**Suspected special needs students may have more than one special need.

Note: From *Special Needs Data Base: Summary Report* by Indian and Northern Affairs Canada, INAC, 1984a, Winnipeg.

in Manitoba for special education was $1,609,392. The schools received approximately $1.2 million of this amount, while the Tribal Councils and MIEA received the remaining $409,000.

In comparison, a provincial school division similar to band-operated schools (in area, school size, and population) received $501.47 per student for special education. It should be acknowledged that the provincial schools in Manitoba have a well-defined system for receiving funds for special education students. There are both high and low incidence supports. The high incidence support is based on a formula with a grant of $23,000 for every 325 pupils. The low incidence support is designed to help those students who have severe to profound handicapping conditions. The amount of the low incidence supports ranges from Low Incidence I at $3,300 per pupil, Low Incidence II at $6,600 per pupil, to Low Incidence III at $13,200 per pupil. Additional funding is provided for clinical services and administration (Van Camp, 1986). The significantly higher level of fiscal support and the additional funding for administration and support services appears to provide adequate fiscal support for the development of comprehensive special education services that are noticeably absent in band-operated schools.

The level of special education funding provided by INAC has an especially debilitating effect in schools with small student populations. For example, during the 1985–86 school year a band-operated school with an enrollment of 116 students received $23,200 for special education. The cost of employing a qualified resource teacher and providing materials, however, was approximately $40,000.00 (Pine Creek, 1986).

Off-Reserve Placements

The lack of special education programs at band-operated schools also encouraged the placement of Indian children with significant special needs, for example, severely physically handicapped, autistic, severely hearing and visually impaired, etc., off reserve (INAC, 1978). Under such arrangements INAC pays the total cost of such placements. In 1985, INAC–Manitoba paid $2,712,000 to provincial schools for delivering special education services to 284 Indian students (average cost $9,549.21) (INAC, 1985). It has been estimated that approximately 100–125 of these children were from band-operated schools (McLeod, 1985). If these students were to attend a band-operated school, INAC would provide the school with only $200.00 per pupil (INAC–Manitoba, 1985).

COMMUNITY-BASED SPECIAL EDUCATION MODEL

The principles of parental responsibility and local control that guide the active participation of Indian people in the education of their children have relevance for special education as well. Community-based special education programs for Indian children with special needs ought to embody principles such as the following:

1. Equal access to school for Indian children with special needs regardless of the nature of their special learning needs.
2. Availability of appropriate, culturally sensitive special education and educational support services to all special needs Indian children.
3. Availability of early childhood special education opportunities for preschool children with special needs.
4. Opportunity for meaningful parental involvement (including informed parental consent with respect to permission to conduct an assessment, and special education placement) in all aspects of the educational decision-making process affecting their child.
5. Education of special needs Indian children with non-special needs peers within local community settings whenever appropriate.

The development and implementation of such a community-based special education program within band-operated schools will necessitate a clearer delineation of roles and responsibilities among schools, tribal councils, INAC, and other service providers. It will also require cooperation and collaboration among the Indian community, reserve school, tribal council, and the Education Support Services Unit (see Figure 1).

The remainder of this section describes how such a model might function in relation to various governmental levels.

Band-Operated Schools

Reserve schools would have resource room/special education teachers and early childhood special education teachers. Schools with fewer than 75 pupils would have access to a resource teacher on an itinerant basis. Teachers would receive assistance from the tribal council special education coordinator and clinicians as well as the clinicians and educational specialist from the Educational Support Services Unit. The band-operated school would also be active in home-based early intervention programs for children under 5 years of age.

Tribal Councils

Coordination of special education programs would occur through the tribal councils. Special education coordinators would arrange for clinicans as well as serve as the link between the reserve schools and the Educational Support Services Unit clinicians and specialists.

Educational Support Services Unit

The role of the Educational Support Services Unit would be to provide clinical and educational support to the band-operated schools, concerning identification, evaluation, and program development. Identification for special education eligibility is an important function that needs to be similar to provincial guidelines so that band-operated schools can be eligible for additional funding (Low Incidence Support) from INAC–Manitoba. This additional funding could be used to provide materials and/or aides for the special needs child.

The Educational Support Services Unit would also develop and disseminate information; provide training and information to parents and school personnel; identify service delivery gaps and needs in conjunction with schools and tribal councils; and establish demonstration projects on reserves. These functions and activities would enable Indian communities served by band-operated schools to have qualified "advice and assistance" in the area of special education.

INAC

The federal government of Canada, through its Department of Indian and Northern Affairs, Canada (INAC) would continue to provide necessary fiscal support. INAC would also be expected to ensure that band-operated schools, tribal councils, and the Educational Support Services Unit are accountable for delivering services. Equally important, INAC would support efforts to improve the quality of special education through the conduct of workshops, conferences, and demonstration projects.

PROSPECTS FOR IMPROVED SERVICES

Recognition of Needed Services

The lack of services for Indian children with special needs attending band-operated schools has in part been attributed to the fact that "native people in the past were not aware of services which were, and are available to handicapped individuals in urban areas" (INAC–Manitoba, 1982, p. 152). More recently, INAC Manitoba Region officials have indicated a need for bands to provide the Department with "specific figures identifying the number of special needs children" (Necheff, 1986, p. 5).

FIGURE 1

Community-Relevant Special Education Program

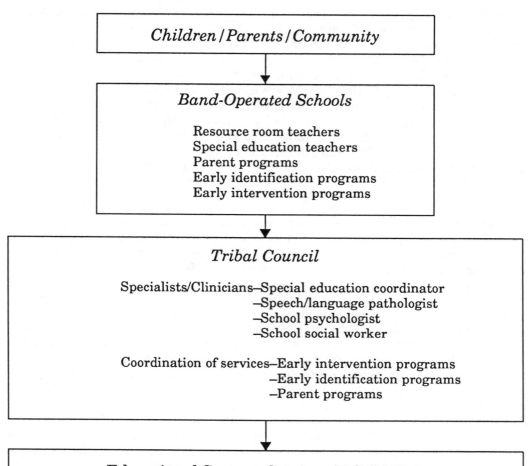

Children / Parents / Community

Band-Operated Schools

Resource room teachers
Special education teachers
Parent programs
Early identification programs
Early intervention programs

Tribal Council

Specialists/Clinicians–Special education coordinator
–Speech/language pathologist
–School psychologist
–School social worker

Coordination of services–Early intervention programs
–Early identification programs
–Parent programs

Educational Support Services (E.S.S.) Unit

Clinical Support

School psychologists
Speech and language pathologists
Reading specialist
School social workers
Physiotherapists
Occupational therapists

Educational Support

Special education consultant
Resource teacher consultant
Alternate program consultant
Gifted consultants
Vision impairment consultant
Hearing impairment consultant

Services

Coordination
Identify needs with reserve schools
   and Tribal Councils
Inservice–Parents, teachers
Dissemination of information
Demonstration projects

The lack of awareness about special education on the part of Indian people is understandable in light of previous efforts to serve these children which did not emphasize the development of services at band-operated schools. Rather, the practice of sending Indian children with significant special needs, for example, severely physically handicapped, autistic, severely hearing and visually impaired, etc., off reserve to placements elsewhere in the province (INAC, 1978) nullified the necessity to create special education programs within local reserve communities. As a result Indian people on the reserves were deprived of the opportunity to become acquainted with special education programs or professionals.

More recently reports, surveys, and proposals submitted to INAC from band-operated schools, tribal councils, and MIEA (INAC, 1984a; INAC, 1984b; MIEA, 1983; MIEA, 1985; MIEA, 1986; Pine Creek, 1986; West Region Tribal Council, 1986) have all indicated a consistent theme: the need to establish programs for special needs Indian children. In an era of increasing Indian involvement in Indian education these desires need to be recognized, considered, and responded to in a forthright, meaningful fashion by INAC.

Fiscal Support

While special education funding has improved over the last few years, it seems evident that the present level of fiscal support needs to be increased to be commensurate with provincial special education funding levels. Such a level of funding with annual adjustments for inflation would permit the orderly development and maintenance of services.

During the last year INAC–Manitoba, in response to the real need for additional special education funds for band-operated schools, ruled that the schools would receive 100% of the special education funds being generated, that is, $268.00 per student. The immediate effect of this action was an infusion of additional special education funds to the schools. In many instances, however, the extra funds remained insufficient to establish services or employ qualified personnel. On the other hand, the reallocation eliminated special education functions at the unit (MIEA) providing training and assistance to the schools as well as the coordination responsibilities carried out through the tribal councils. Thus, the reallocation deprives band-operated schools of qualified special education expertise and assistance in important areas such as program planning, development, and implementation.

Beyond the question of special education funding levels, consideration also needs to be given to the development of options on or near reserves for children with significant special needs. The present policy or practice of contracting with provincial schools to serve all of these students must undergo review and revision to encourage the establishment of additional options on or near reserve communities. This will entail careful planning on the part of parents, bands, INAC, and the province to ensure that these options are developed and implemented with minimal disruption to the children and youth and their families.

Personnel

Reserves, like many rural areas, experience severe teacher shortages and high mobility. The development of programs and services on reserves will also require the following:

1. The preparation of qualified personnel to work with special needs children, who are also able to effectively serve culturally diverse children and youth.
2. The preparation of Indian special education and other related support personnel.

The building of such a cadre of Indian and non-Indian personnel will require the collaboration of bands, INAC–Manitoba, and universities.

CONCLUSION

In recent years professionals, parents, band councils, and others associated with band-operated schools in Manitoba have increasingly voiced their concern about the need to serve children with special needs and their families. Prohibitive funding levels, policies encouraging the placement of certain special needs Indian children off reserve, and other organizational constraints are formidible barriers to the development of culturally appropriate special education programs in these schools.

The community-based special education model proposed reflects the current trend of Indian involvement and control of Indian education whereby the reserve community has an active role in shaping programs to meet the learning needs of their children. The future development of these programs will be dependent upon sustained advocacy on the part of special education and Indian education professionals, parents, and bands as well as commitment from INAC to support and assist in the development and improvement of reserve-based special education opportunities.

REFERENCES

Indian and Northern Affairs Canada, INAC. (1978). Educational Assistance Program, Manitoba Region, 1978–79, Student Services Section, Ottawa

Indian and Northern Affairs Canada, INAC, 1982. (1987). Nominal roll. In J. Hull, (Ed.), *An overview of the educational characteristics of registered Indians in Canada*. Winnipeg: W.M.C. Research Associates (Manitoba) Ltd.

Indian and Northern Affairs Canada, INAC. (1984a). *Special needs data base: Summary report*, June, Winnipeg.

Indian and Northern Affairs Canada, INAC. (1984b). An action plan for special education funding and service development in band-controlled schools, June, Winnipeg.

Indian and Northern Affairs Canada, INAC. (1985). *Education data base, call letter from Director General*, June, Ottawa.

Indian and Northern Affairs Canada, INAC. (1986a). Letter from Minister of Indian Affairs and Northern Development to Mr. Rod Murphy, M. P., March 7, 1986, Ottawa.

Indian and Northern Affairs Canada, INAC. (1986b). Letter from Minister of Indian Affairs and Northern Development to Chief Norman Bone, November 26, 1986, Ottawa.

Indian and Northern Affairs Canada, INAC–Manitoba. (1982). *Manitoba Region: Operational Plan 1983/84–1984/85. Winnipeg.*

Indian and Northern Affairs Canada, INAC–Manitoba. (1985). Educational Data Base, Fiscal Year 1985/86, Winnipeg.

Manitoba Indian Education Association, MIEA. (1983). *Rationale and Proposal for Special Education Services for Band-Operated and Federal Schools*. Manitoba Indian Education Association, Winnipeg.

Manitoba Indian Education Association, MIEA. (1985). *Educational Support Services Proposal-Pilot Project (DRAFT)*. Manitoba Indian Education Association, Winnipeg.

Manitoba Indian Education Association, MIEA. (1986). Letter from Charity and Minister of Indian Affairs, Manitoba Indian Education Association, Winnipeg.

McLeod, M. (1985). Personal conversation with Mrs. Muriel McLeod, April 14, 1985, Winnipeg.

Necheff, J. (May 2, 1986). Reserves lack resources to detect learning problems, conference told. *Winnipeg Free Press*, p. 5.

Pine Creek (1986). Meeting at Pine Creek Reserve, May 22, 1986, Pine Creek Reserve.

VanCamp, K. (1986). Presentation at Special Needs: Special Education and Native Children conference, May 1–2, Winnipeg.

West Region Tribal Council. (June 24, 1986). *Special education funding strategy*. Dauphin, Manitoba: Author.

CHAPTER 13

What Attracts and Keeps Outstanding Black Special Education Teachers in the Profession?

Ruben Gentry
Shih-sung Wen

Generally speaking, America is facing a problem—an insufficient number of college students pursuing teacher education programs. More specifically, America is facing a crisis—a critical shortage of Black teachers. In emphasizing the need to improve and expand the pool of all future teachers, Graham (1987) states that the need to do so for Blacks is particularly acute.

Reporting in *NEA Today*, Weiss (1986) indicated that minority teachers are becoming an endangered species. The 12.5% representation they held in 1980 is expected to drop to less than 5% by the year 2000. Indeed, by 1986 the figure had dropped to 6.9% (Lytle, 1987). On the other hand, the minority student population is expected to show an increase from 27% to 33% during the years 1980 to 2000.

The concern over minority teachers is of such magnitude that two reports—*A Nation Prepared: Teachers for the 21st Century* (Carnegie Forum on Education and Economy, 1986) and *Tomorrow's Teachers* (Holmes Group, 1986)—made it a central issue. The Carnegie Forum report called for a policy to "mobilize the nation's resources to prepare minority youngsters for teaching careers" (p. 3). Points emphasized included (a) having schools provide and demand what is needed for success, (b) recruiting minorities into teaching, and (c) financially assisting predominately Black institutions of higher education to prepare students.

The Holmes Group report, in addressing the teacher shortage, noted that many of the most competent members of minorities have been attracted to careers in fields other than teaching. This is not good news for schools in view of the fact that expressive behaviors of children from minority cultures are routinely misinterpreted by incompetent, insensitive teachers. The report stated that "high-risk" children need teachers who can capitalize on the social context of the environment and use a variety of teaching strategies to enhance learning.

When viewing Blacks in particular, the magazine *JET* (Supply of Black Teachers, 1986) simply stated that the supply of Black teachers does not meet the demand. The shortage has reached such a level in Mississippi that the state superintendent of education will appoint a task force to pinpoint ways to recruit and retain Black teachers (Kanengiser, 1986). In Mississippi, Blacks constitute 35% of the public school teaching force (according to the Mississippi State Department of Education), but the percentage of Black students in public schools is 49.99%.

During the middle and late 1970s, special education witnessed tremendous enrollment growth. However, the area continued to suffer a shortage of personnel to staff classes across the nation. Lacking in particular were sufficient numbers of Blacks going into special education (and current trends reflect a steady decline). Further impeding an adequate supply of Black special education teachers (and Black teachers in general) are problems in meeting requirements for admission to teacher education programs and teacher certification. Other reasons often given for the shortage of Black teachers include (a) fewer minorities (proportionately) going to college, (b) fewer minorities choosing teaching as a career, mainly because of low salaries (Weiss, 1986), and (c) use of teacher competency tests which disqualify a disproportionate number of minority teachers.

Justifications for having sufficient Black teacher representation in the schools include (a) the need to have a staff which reflects our nation's racial and cultural heritage and (b) the need for good racial role models. Ways to overcome the shortage of Black teachers, as reported by a group of college deans of schools of education are (a) higher salaries, (b) stepped-up recruitment activities, (c) a more conducive teaching environment, and (d) public recognition of the contributions made by teachers (Kanengiser, 1986).

The importance of minority teachers in the schools is irrefutable. In achieving the goal, competence and larger numbers are major concerns. Existing literature on these concerns has often reported opinions of persons (e.g. college deans) other than Black classroom teachers. We initiated a field-based study to gather information on the concerns. An assumption was made that there are currently some *outstanding* Black special education teachers in the profession. It was believed that knowledge gained from a broad-based survey of these teachers would establish a basis for resolving the problems of competence and increased numbers.

PURPOSE

The purpose of the study was to gain information from practicing outstanding Black special education teachers on what attracted them to the special education discipline and what keeps them there. The specific objective was to survey these teachers regarding factors in the areas of status information, training program, and job satisfaction. From this information, implications were formulated for recruiting and retaining more competent Black teachers to staff special education classes.

METHOD

A comprehensive investigation by the authors of Black and nonBlack special education teachers in Mississippi is in progress. The present report is limited to the Black population.

Instruments

Two instruments provided data for the study. The Outstanding Teachers in Special Education Selection Form was designed for use by school superintendents to select teachers in their school district. Measures taken to arrive at criteria for selecting outstanding special education teachers included (a) review of related literature on effective teaching (e.g., Code of Ethics and Standards for Professional Practice, 1983), (b) survey of practicing teachers in graduate programs, and (c) interviews (two in person and three by telephone) with five special educators, including a U.S. Department of Education project officer, university departmental chair, university professor, school district administrator, and a classroom teacher.

Information obtained was considered in developing the final form, which contained five selection criteria—student achievement track record, level of training and growth, role model in district, participation in organizations, and others. Explanatory information about the criteria was prepared to accompany the form. For example, explanations for student achievement track record were "The extent to which students under the teacher's supervision (a) manage daily living skills, (b) earn good grades, (c) score well on standardized tests, (d) make good social adjustment, and/or (e) do well in further schooling or employment. The type and degree of exceptionality of the students should be considered in viewing their level of achievement."

The selection form was designed for the superintendents to enter the names and addresses of the selectees and to check the criterion/criteria used in making the selection. Other items on the form requested the name of the school district, preference for a copy of the research report, and return of the form in an enclosed self-addressed, stamped envelope. A statement of thanks for cooperation with the research effort was included on the form.

The Outstanding Teachers in Special Education Survey Form was designed for use with the teachers. It contained items about status information, family background, scholastic achievement/aptitude, training program, job performance, job satisfaction, and basic beliefs.

The present report reveals information on the areas of (a) status information—items soliciting information on personal attributes, degrees held, teaching experience, children taught, professional organization affiliations, and hobbies; (b) training program—information on factors regarding choosing special education as a career and the extent of appeal that selected training program components had for them based on a 5-level scale; and (c) job satisfaction—items reflecting various conditions of the teaching situation for respondents to indicate how true the conditions were for them based on a 5-point scale. Content of the items was based on a review of literature on teaching effectiveness (Gentry & Jefferson, 1986; Mercer & Mercer, 1985; Polloway, Payne, Patton, & Payne, 1985; Powell & Beard, 1984; Zumwalt, 1986) and other relevant materials (Code of Ethics, 1983; ARA Attitude Survey, 1966).

The items were arranged to make responding as easy as possible. A copy of the survey form was reviewed by the same group of special educators used in formulating the selection criteria form in terms of appropriateness of content and general structure of the instrument. Their input was used in finalizing the form.

Subjects

The entire official list (167; however, clarification by telephone revealed 154 central districts plus one special district, thus N = 155) of school district superintendents in the state of Mississippi were asked to complete the Outstanding Teachers in Special Education Selection Form. All teachers (the 101 Blacks were separated for this report) designated by the superintendents or their designees were the subjects for completing the survey form.

Procedures

The current list of Mississippi school district superintendents was obtained from the state superintendent's office. A letter was prepared requesting that district superintendents support research on effective teaching by designating on the selection form two to four outstanding special education teachers in their district. The letter also stated that the selectees would be congratulated for having been designated as outstanding for the purpose of the research and requested to complete and return a survey form. The letter, selection form, explanation sheet, and a self-addressed stamped envelope were mailed to each district superintendent during the period September 24 to October 1, 1986. Three follow-up letters (each time including another selection form and explanation sheet) were sent (October 31; December 9; January 21–30, 1987) to increase the number of replies. Each follow-up letter indicated the current number of respondents and further encouraged participation.

The designated outstanding teachers were congratulated in a letter and told of the researchers' desire to learn more about them to ascertain implications for recruiting and training more competent personnel to staff special education programs. They were encouraged to complete and return the enclosed survey form. A self-addressed stamped envelope was also enclosed. The first letters were mailed October 24, 1986, and the last of the three follow-up letters (each containing another survey form) was mailed May 19, 1987. Data received from the respondents were tabulated and analyzed.

RESULTS

The number of district superintendents who participated in the study of outstanding special education teachers was 108 (70% of the 155). However, two did not submit names because no special education teachers in the districts were certified in the area. The 106 districts submitting names yielded a total of 320 possible subjects, of whom 236 (74%) completed and returned the survey form. Among the respondents were 101 (43%) identified on the form as Black. They were represented in 64 (60%) of the 106 school districts. Findings regarding this Black population are reported here.

The Black teachers selected as outstanding by the superintendents most frequently met the criterion of role model in the district (85%)—"Demonstrated ability and effort of the teacher in (a) executing his/her professional responsibilities associated with the job, (b) exemplifying interpersonal skills in working with parents and school personnel, and (c) achieving established goals and objectives in the school district." Two other criteria that often distinguished them were student achievement track record (79%) and level of training and growth (71%).

Table 1 contains detailed status data on the outstanding Black special education teachers in Mississippi. It reflects a primarily female (94%) group that is relatively young (60% between 30 and 39) and most often married (65%). Most were professionally trained in Mississippi (91%), often at historically Black colleges (65%), and many (60%) held the MS degree. They averaged 11.01 years teaching experience with most of that time spent teaching exceptional children (9.69 years) in the district of present employment (8.72 years). The children whom they most often taught were educationally handicapped (69%; EdH in Mississippi includes the mentally retarded, learning disabled, and mildly emotionally handicapped). They averaged about two (1.98) professional organization memberships and engaged in an average of about three (3.13) different hobbies.

Relative to coming into the special education field, more of the outstanding Black special education teachers were attracted to it after having received the bachelor's degree (36%) than at any other level of training. Two other points at which sizable numbers decided to teach special education were college freshman (21%) and high school (19%).

The major source of motivation for the group in choosing to teach special education was internal. Forty-seven percent of the teachers were self-motivated in selecting the teaching area. Some (13%) were influenced by encounter with a special education student. The others (40%) were swayed to join the profession by a number of different persons (e.g. principal, counselor, regular education teacher, or family member).

Once a serious look was given to special education, the desire to help exceptional children (56%) became the primary factor influencing the teachers to pursue the discipline. With others it was often desire coupled with opportunity for employment (14% as a single entity) or interest in the curriculum (4% as a single entity) that accounted for their going into special education.

Thirteen (13) key factors considered basic for a sound training program in special education were contained on the survey form to ascertain their appeal to the teachers (see Table 2). It was found that content of courses in the curriculum (87%) and student teaching and practicum experiences (81%) had the highest appeal. Other training factors that had high appeal were field trips and observation experiences (78%), the way teachers taught (77%), interaction with students and professionals (74%), and materials used in teaching (71%).

Factors having low appeal in the training program were student organization activities (combined low or less rating = 60%) and the way courses were scheduled (54%). Other factors that were not favorably viewed by the teachers were library resources (low or less rating = 39%), advisement by faculty (38%), opportunities for graduate studies (38%), research activities (37%), and seminars and conferences (36%).

Now that the teachers are in the schools, just how happy are they on the job? A review of responses on 24 job satisfaction indicators (see Table 3) shed light on the question. On the 5-point scale (5 and 4 = very true, 3 = true, 2 and 1 = not true), four items were rated as very true by 90% or more of the teachers. They were: successfully complete difficult assignments

TABLE 1

Demographic Data on Outstanding Black Special Education Teachers

Item	Number of Subjects	Mean	Percent
Age–20–29	29	-	.29
30–39	59	-	.60
Other	11	-	.11
Sex–Female	95	-	.94
Male	6	-	.06
Marital Status–Married	65	-	.65
Single	29	-	.29
Other	6	-	.06
Offspring	98	1.62	-
Advanced degrees held–M.S.	58	-	.60
Ed.S.	8	-	.08
Degrees earned in MS/other states			
B.S.	88/9	-	.91/.09
M.S.	58/4	-	.94/.06
Ed.S.	6/2	-	.75/.25
Degrees from historically Black colleges			
B.S.	72	-	.75
M.S.	29	-	.49
Ed.D.	7	-	.88
Years total teaching	101	11.01	-
Years teaching exceptional children	101	9.69	-
Years teaching in school district	98	8.72	-
Type children they teach			
Educationally handicapped	69	-	.69
Learning disabled	13	-	.13
Mentally retarded	13	-	.13
Others	5	-	.05
Grade level they teach			
Elementary	35	-	.36
Combined (e.g., Jr., Sr. High)	32	-	.33
Other	30	-	.31
Professional organization affiliations	95	1.98	-
Hobbies	99	3.13	

(93%), enjoy kind of work they do (93%), like people with whom they work (91%), and job is very interesting (90%). There were three items rated by a majority as not true. They were: feel satisfied with salary (70% not true), opportunities for advancement (63%), and salary is a good one (63%). Another item relatively not true was: progress toward promotion is satisfactory (42%).

DISCUSSION

The study of outstanding Black special education teachers in Mississippi revealed some interesting findings. The criteria and number of Blacks selected was noteworthy. District

TABLE 2

Appeal of Selected Program Training Factors to Outstanding Black Special Education Teachers

		Extent of Appeal (%)			
Factors	No.	High	Low	No	Nega-tives
Content of courses in curriculum	98	.87	.12	.01	.00
Way teachers taught	100	.77	.18	.05	.00
Materials used in teaching	98	.71	.24	.04	.00
Way courses were scheduled	99	.45	.37	.14	.03
Seminars, conferences	100	.64	.29	.06	.01
Field trips, observation	100	.78	.14	.07	.01
Organization activities	96	.41	.40	.20	.00
Student teaching, practicum	96	.81	.10	.07	.01
Advisement by faculty	97	.62	.28	.09	.01
Library resources	100	.61	.32	.07	.00
Interaction with students, professionals	101	.74	.21	.04	.01
Research activities	101	.63	.28	.07	.02
Opportunities for graduate studies	100	.62	.25	.12	.01

superintendents most often selected the teachers based on their being role models for other teachers. As stated on the explanation sheet sent to superintendents, role model implies demonstrated ability and effort in executing professional responsibilities, exemplifying interpersonal skills, and achieving established goals and objectives. They were also well-recognized for student achievement track record. In the open nomination process of all special education teachers in the state, Blacks represented 43% of the respondents. Thus, the assumption that there are competent Black special education teachers in the field was confirmed by superintendents.

If the percentage of Blacks in special education approximates that of the general teaching population (35% Black), the 43% included here is a proportionately high figure. The finding speaks well for the ethnic group and the predominately Black colleges where most were trained. Support is also given to contents of the *A Nation Prepared* report (Carnegie Forum, 1986) and others calling for recruitment of minorities into teaching and for financial assistance to predominately Black institutions of higher education. The high frequency of Blacks among outstanding Black special education teachers suggests that increasing the number of Blacks in a school district may have a positive effect on quality instruction.

Another demographic feature of the Black teachers warranting attention is their tenure in the district. Though not happy with certain job conditions (salary and opportunity for advancement), they stay in the district in special education. Investment in training this caliber of teacher is considered wise.

If role model by ethnicity is important, representation by gender would also appear valuable. If so, the recruitment to special education of males capable of achieving the status of outstanding is desperately needed.

Ascertaining what attracts outstanding Black teachers to the profession began at the point of making the decision to teach special education. The fact that many made the decision after receiving the bachelor's degree suggests numerous speculations and raises many questions. For example, did lack of knowledge about special education training programs or lack of exposure to exceptional children delay the choice of field? While the knowledge and exposure

TABLE 3

Selected Job Satisfaction Indicators: The Extent to Which They Are True for Outstanding Black Special Education Teachers

Job Satisfaction Indicators	Number	How True (%)				
		5	4	3	2	1
Feeling of worthwhile accomplishment	101	.55	.31	.13	.00	.01
Complete difficult assignments	101	.54	.39	.07	.00	.00
Considerable decision making power	99	.26	.43	.19	.08	.03
Enjoy responsibility of the job	100	.58	.29	.10	.03	.00
Enjoy kind of work you do	101	.71	.22	.05	.01	.00
Job is very interesting	100	.69	.21	.09	.00	.01
Receive praise for work	101	.45	.29	.13	.08	.06
Are told you do a good job	101	.51	.32	.12	.03	.02
Opportunities for advancement	98	.05	.14	.18	.29	.34
Progress toward promotion is okay	98	.15	.16	.26	.18	.24
Like people with whom you work	99	.64	.27	.07	.00	.02
Considerable cooperation from coworkers	99	.51	.27	.17	.00	.05
Have top-notch supervisor	100	.38	.29	.24	.05	.04
Supervisor is a good one	99	.41	.29	.19	.08	.02
Supervisor listens to suggestions	99	.48	.32	.13	.03	.03
Feel supervisor and you understand each other	100	.56	.28	.07	.04	.05
Feel satisfied with salary	98	.03	.07	.19	.20	.50
Salary is a good one	99	.03	.09	.24	.22	.41
Feel secure on job	99	.36	.30	.24	.07	.02
System provides steady employment	99	.46	.29	.19	.02	.03
Personnel policies and practices are good	99	.21	.34	.25	.13	.06
Policies are well communicated	99	.22	.31	.26	.13	.07
Physical surroundings are pleasant	96	.35	.32	.18	.06	.08
Feel satisfied with working conditions	99	.33	.23	.23	.09	.11

elements are encouraged, the authors believe that the finding warrants further investigation in view of its implications for both recruitment and training.

Knowing that self-interest propelled many of the teachers toward special education is revealing, but this too is open in terms of implications for recruitment. Is there something in common about their background and character that could be profiled and used for more effective recruitment? On the other hand, we cannot help but wonder why special education school teachers (accounted for 3%) and college teachers (5%) were not perceived as influential persons. Perhaps the relatively recent development of special education as a discipline is a plausible answer for now, but if this finding persists, perhaps practicing teachers and teacher educators should be challenged to seek ways of effectively attracting persons to the field.

The overriding desire of the teachers to help exceptional children as a factor in choosing to teach special education is commendable in view of its possible benefit in enhancing learning. It may be applauded by educators. Equally as pleasing may be the finding that only a small number sought the field simply because of opportunities for employment (14%). The findings suggest that the teachers are truly committed to the education of exceptional children. Recruitment and training would benefit from an assessment of this interest or potential interest of prospective trainees in high school or as soon as possible.

There is considerable room for making special education teacher training more appealing. Even the items with the highest ratings could be improved. The factors listed on the survey form appear to be programmatically sound and could be made better with reasonable effort and resources. With knowledge of these findings it is hoped that universities will assess their status in these areas and respond accordingly.

The relative high level of job satisfaction achieved on a majority of items in the section reflects well on the status of the schools. Of the four areas (from a total of 24) where there is trouble, the two relative to salary come as no surprise. The findings on salary are in accord with what the literature has often reported (very low). The other two areas of concern dealt with opportunities for advancement. Ways to accommodate this need have reached various discussion levels but little known accomplishment has been made in this regard. We hasten to add that though the four problem areas are small in number, any one is reason for a large number of teachers to leave the profession.

In summary, this study has reflected on what attracts and keeps outstanding Black special education teachers in the profession. They were found to be attracted mainly because of self-discovered interest in the field and their desire to help exceptional children. They are kept in the field because of overall job satisfaction (tolerating low salary and limited chance for advancement) obtained from the employment setting. Major recommendations drawn from the findings for recruiting more competent Black teachers are (a) concentrate some effort at post-baccalaureate level, (b) expose prospective education majors to special education students, and (c) ascertain if prospects have a strong desire to help exceptional children. To retain competent teachers in the profession, salaries need to be raised and provisions made, perhaps through staff development and/or differentiated staffing, for teachers to experience professional advancement.

REFERENCES

A nation prepared: Teachers for the 21st Century. New York: Author.

ARA attitude survey. (1966). Chicago: Science Research Associates, Business and Industrial Division.

Carnegie Forum on Education and the Economy. (1986).

Code of ethics and standards for professional practice. (1983). *Exceptional Children, 50*(3), 205–209.

Gentry, R., & Jefferson, C. (1986). *OK, not-so-OK strategies for teaching the mildly handicapped*. Jackson, MS: Jackson State University. (ERIC Document Reproduction Service No. Ed 269 945)

Graham, P. A. (1987, April). Black teachers: A drastically scarce resource. *Phi Delta Kappan*, pp.598–603.

Holmes Group. (1986). *Tomorrow's teachers: A report of the Holmes Group*. East Lansing, MI: Author.

Kanengiser, A. (1986, August 31). Task force to study ways to recruit, retain black teachers. *The Clarion Ledger Jackson Daily News*. pp. 20A, 1C.

Lytle, V. (1987). Here's looking at you, teacher! *NEA Today, 6*(2), 3.

Mercer, C. D., & Mercer, A. R. (1985). *Teaching students with learning problems* (2nd ed.). Columbus, OH: Charles E. Merrill.

Polloway, E. A., Payne, J. S., Patton, J. R., & Payne, R. A. (1985). *Strategies for teaching retarded and special needs learners* (3rd ed.). Columbus, OH: Charles E. Merrill.

Powell, M., & Beard, J. W. (1984). *Teacher effectiveness: An annotated bibliography and guide to research*. New York: Garland.

Supply of black teachers does not meet demand. (1986). *JET, 71*(7), 23.

Weiss, S. (1986). Where have all our minority teachers gone? *NEA Today, 5*(4),6.

Zumwalt, K. K. (Ed.). (1986). *Effective teaching*. Alexandria, VA: Association for Supervision and Curriculum Development.

CHAPTER 14

American Indian Exceptional Children: Improved Practices and Policy

Bruce A. Ramirez
Marilyn J. Johnson

Enactment of the Education for All Handicapped Children Act, P.L. 94–142, heralded an era of increased educational opportunities for American Indian and Alaskan Native children in need of special education irrespective of where they are geographically or whether they attend public, federal, or tribally controlled schools. At the same time, the procedural protections embodied in the law provided a framework to address concerns related to the disproportionate representation of Indian children in certain special education programs.

Other areas of concern related to the education of American Indian exceptional children and youth include (a) training programs to prepare American Indians as special educators and related support personnel; (b) multicultural training specific to American Indians for personnel serving or preparing to work with American Indian children with handicaps; (c) involvement of parents and families of American Indian children receiving or being considered for special education (National Indian Education Association, 1977); and (d) the educational needs of American Indian gifted and talented children and their families.

This chapter reviews pertinent literature and public policy developments over the past decade related to the education of American Indian exceptional infants, children, and youth. Areas of further study and research are identified, including suggestions for improved service delivery.

CHILDREN WITH HANDICAPS

The following section contains information on the prevalence of handicapping conditions among American Indian children.

Public Schools

Between 1978 and 1986, the number of American Indian students attending public elementary and secondary schools in the United States increased from 329,430 to 355,796 students, an increase of 8% (DBS Corporation, 1987; Office for Civil Rights, no date). During the same period, the number of American Indian students enrolled in programs for the mentally retarded, speech impaired, seriously emotionally disturbed, and learning disabled rose 41.8%. Of the 36,973 American Indian students in special education programs, nearly 55% of the students were in classes for the learning disabled. The categories of speech impaired and learning disabled accounted for more than 80% of the American Indian children and youth in special education.

FIGURE 1

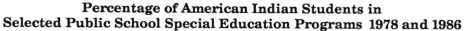

**Percentage of American Indian Students in
Selected Public School Special Education Programs 1978 and 1986**

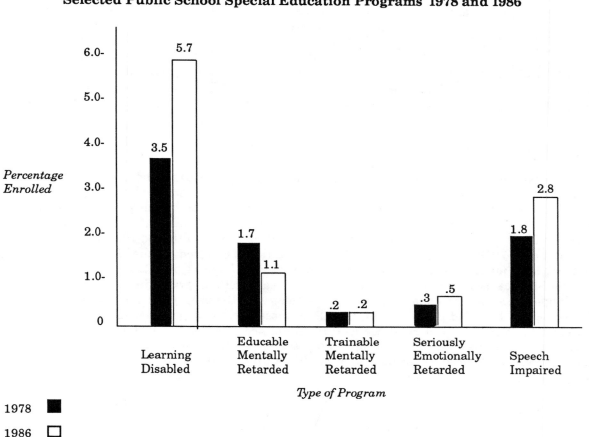

1978 ■

1986 ☐

Note: From *Elementary and Secondary School Civil Rights Survey, National Summaries* by DBS Corporation, 1987, Washington, DC: Office of Civil Rights, U.S. Department of Education and *Directory of Elementary and Secondary School Districts and Schools in Selected School Districts: School Year 1978–1979* (Vol. 1) by Office for Civil Rights, U.S. Department of Education, (no date), Washington, DC: Author.

Figure 1 depicts the proportion of American Indian public elementary and secondary school students in selected special education programs in 1978 and 1986. During this period the proportion of American Indian students identified as learning disabled and speech impaired increased more than 60% and 50% respectively. The proportion of these students enrolled in programs for the seriously emotionally disturbed and trainable mentally retarded also increased. The sole decrease occurred in the percentage of Indian students in classes for the educable mentally retarded.

Bureau of Indian Affairs

In 1986 Bureau of Indian Affairs (BIA) elementary and secondary schools served approximately 38,000 American Indian students. During the 1985–1986 school year, 5,388 students received special education and related services in accordance with the requirements of P.L. 94–142 (U.S. Department of Education, 1987). Of this number 53.9% were identified as learning disabled and 24.7% as speech/language impaired. Smaller numbers of students were classified as mentally retarded (9.2%), emotionally disturbed (4.5%), and multiply handicapped (5.4%). Less than 3% of the students were identified as other health impaired, orthopedically impaired, hearing impaired, or visually handicapped.

Since 1977–1978 the number of children receiving special education and related services in BIA-operated and -supported schools increased by 35%. During this period the number of learning disabled and speech/language impaired children and youth doubled whereas the number of mentally retarded students declined (Ramirez, 1987). In terms of age, students 6 to 17 years old accounted for 90% of the children and youth receiving special education and related services.

Head Start

The vast majority of American Indian children participating in Head Start programs reside on Indian reservations or in Alaskan Native villages and are served through programs operated by the governing bodies of an Indian tribe or Alaskan Native village. In 1984–1985 the 103 Indian Head Start grantees enrolled 16,548 children of which 1,907 (11.52%) were professionally diagnosed as handicapped (U.S. Department of Health and Human Services, 1986). Between 1979–1980 and 1984–1985, the proportion of children enrolled in Indian Head Start programs identified as handicapped increased from 8.7% to 11.5% (Ramirez, 1987).

Of the handicapped children enrolled in Indian Head Start programs in 1983–1984, 66% were diagnosed as speech impaired. This is consistent with the proportion of speech impaired children served by Head Start overall as well as those served by public schools under P.L. 94–142 (U.S. Department of Health and Human Services, 1986). The distribution of other categories of children with handicaps was 10.7% health impaired, 6.4% physically handicapped, 4.4% mentally retarded, 3.8% specific learning disabled, 3.5% hearing impaired, 2.3% seriously emotionally disturbed, 2.3% visually impaired, .2% blind, and .2% deaf.

GIFTED AND TALENTED CHILDREN

Public elementary and secondary school survey data from the U.S. Office for Civil Rights (OCR) indicates that the proportion of American Indian students in programs for the gifted and talented has increased from .8% in 1978 to 2.1% in 1986.

Even though the national proportion of Indian students in public school programs for the gifted and talented has increased, marked differences exist among the various states. In the 11 states with 10,000 or more Indian elementary and secondary students, the proportion of children and youth in classes for the gifted and talented ranged from a low of .7% to a high of 3.5% (DBS Corporation, 1986). California with an 80% urban Indian population and Oklahoma whose total Indian student population exceeds that of any other state by nearly 2 to 1 reported proportions of 2.8% and 3.1% respectively. Of the six states with a rural Indian population of at least 75%, that is, Alaska, Arizona, Montana, New Mexico, North Carolina, and South Dakota, only Arizona had more than 2.0% of its Indian students in gifted and talented classes.

DISPROPORTIONATE REPRESENTATION

Over- and underrepresentation of culturally diverse students in certain programs for the handicapped and gifted and talented classes remains a serious concern in special education. After analyzing OCR biannual survey data from 1978 through 1984, Chinn and Hughes (1987) reported that the percentage of American Indians in learning disabilities classes was consistently disproportionately high; whereas, their representation in classes for the gifted and talented was consistently low.

As can be seen in Table 1, American Indian students continue to be much more likely to be in classes for the learning disabled when compared to White students or to the entire student population. Representation in classes for the gifted and talented was less than half of that for the White and total elementary and secondary student populations.

IDENTIFICATION AND EVALUATION

The implementation of fair nondiscriminatory testing and evaluation procedures continues to be an area of much concern in light of the disproportionate representation of American Indian students in certain special education classes.

Referral

Previous research has found that children referred for special education consideration by teachers have a high probability (e.g., 75% to 90%) of being placed in such programs (Algozzine, Christenson, & Ysseldyke, 1982). In contrasting referral rates for Indian and non-Indian students, McShane (1979) reported that Indian students were referred proportionately more often than non-Indian children for poor achievement (48% and 41%), reading or math problems (21% and 4%), being quiet or a loner (13% and 7%), and excessive absences or skipping of classes (10% and 1%). On the other hand non-Indian children, as compared with Indian children, were referred more often for physical or neurological problems (20% and 8%) and bad or nonconforming behavior (14% and 7%).

TABLE 1

Participation of American Indian Public Elementary and Secondary School Students in Selected Special Education Programs: 1986

Program	Participants as Percentage of Specific Racial / Ethnic Group		
	American Indian	White	Total*
Gifted and talented	2.1	5.4	4.7
Educable mentally retarded	1.1	.9	1.1
Trainable mentally retarded	.2	.2	.2
Seriously emotionally disturbed	.5	.6	.6
Speech impaired	2.8	2.6	2.5
Specific learning disabled	5.7	4.3	4.3

*Based on enrollment in U.S. public schools, kindergarten through 12th grade.

Note: From *Elementary and Secondary School Civil Rights Survey, National Summaries* by DBS Corporation, 1987, Washington, DC: Office of Civil Rights, U.S. Department of Education.

Assessment

Interest in the assessment process as it relates to American Indians has centered on test instruments, procedures, and practices.

Scores on various achievement tests administered to American Indian children indicate that Indian children performed close to the national norm on tests of performance, but considerably below the national norm on the verbal tests (MacArthur, 1969; McShane, 1980). When disparity in scores occurs, the verbal score often carries greater weight in the interpretation of test scores (Browne, 1984). Interpretation, therefore, reflects primarily the problem areas for many American Indian children rather than the strengths they show on other parts of the test.

McShane's (1979) study of the assessment procedures and practices in use with American Indian students indicated that:

- Only 8% of the evaluation reports contained any indication that the culture or race of the student was an important factor in the evaluation process.
- In the administration and scoring of the Wechsler, 70% of the test was administered to Indian children in a nonstandard manner compared with 25% of test administrations for non-Indian children. Circumstances of nonstandard procedures included omission of subtests (e.g., vocabulary), administration of a partial test (e.g., performance portion), and/or scoring anomalies.
- Involvement of Indian parents in the evaluative process is lower than for non-Indian parents, 22% and 37% respectively.

Several alteratives have been suggested to reduce the bias associated with the use of standardized tests. The language barrier remains, however. Difficulties associated with the translation of tests into a native language such as Navajo include:

1. Different level of syntactic difficulty . . . which could not be overcome by paraphrase;
2. Differences in the way English and Navajo languages organize experience into concept units;
3. Accidental similarity of concept words in Navajo that have no such similarity in English;
4. Different range of meaning in concept words in Navajo leading to duplication of Navajo test words in items that are not similar in English. (Rosenbluth, 1976, p. 33)

The development of tests specific to a tribe or cultural group is costly and would require combined efforts of linguists and native speakers.

Culture, English proficiency, test-taking attitudes, test anxiety, and unfamiliarity with test items outside of the child's cultural and/or linguistic milieu have all been found to influence test performance (McShane, 1980; Seyfort, Spreen, & Lahmer, 1980). Since changing the administration of a test will alter its reliability, the interpretation and use of test results are promising areas for improving present assessment practices. The recommendations of the psychologist and other members of the assessment team can address language and culture issues and how these may have influenced the assessment results.

In light of the key role that assessment personnel can play in interpreting test results, the need for such personnel to be knowledgeable about the student's culture and language is evident. An individual familiar with language or culture of the students will be more likely to recognize nuances which might not otherwise be identified or might be misinterpreted.

PARENT INVOLVEMENT

Special education has long recognized and supported active parental involvement in the education process. Public Law 94–142 and its implementing regulations embody this principle in terms of parental involvement in the development of the individual education program

(IEP), parental consent for initial placement in special education, parental notice, and procedural protections with regard to resolving disagreements. Communication with parents, moreover, is to be in their native language.

After passage of the Act, parents of handicapped children received information on their rights and the educational responsibilities of public and Bureau of Indian Affairs schools. Recent research, however, indicates that Indian parents are significantly less informed about their rights under P.L. 94–142 than White parents. Connery (1987) found that less than 25% of the Navajo parents surveyed were aware of the law's existence as compared with over 75% of the White parents. In both groups, however, 68% indicated that they did not understand their rights under federal special education policy.

To enhance communication and interaction between Indian parents, school, and social and health agencies in rural areas, states such as Minnesota utilize trained Indian liaisons (Stuecher, 1985). The liaisons, or "Indian advocates" as they are known, interpret and communicate the concerns of Indian parents to school personnel, explain aspects of special education and rehabilitation, and facilitate interagency contacts.

PERSONNEL

Federal Indian self-determination policies, high staff turnover, and low student achievement and expectations have fueled efforts to increase the number of Indian teachers across all education disciplines. Ramirez and Tippeconnic (1979) urged that efforts be undertaken to increase the number of American Indian special education and related services personnel and that Indian education course work be an integral component of all training for personnel involved in the education of American Indian children with handicaps.

Gajar (1985) reviewed components of a graduate program for American Indians in special education that combines elements of special education and Indian education training. Other training programs have been field-based and have focused on infusing bilingual special education into existing special education course work (Baca & Miramontes, 1985). Such training permits students to gain valuable experience within the context of local Indian communities while at the same time fostering greater tribal and community involvement.

In 1985 there were at least 10 federally funded training programs located in various sections of the country preparing American Indian special education teachers, diagnosticians, speech pathologists, administrators, and paraprofessionals (Gajar, 1985). Unique features of some of these programs include intensive summer sessions with optional course work during the academic year; inclusion of bilingual education courses; seminars focusing on issues related to the education of Indians with handicaps; tutorials to reinforce course content; and guest lecturers.

POLICY ADVANCES

Existing federal policy pertaining to American Indians with disabilities can be traced to the inclusion of the Secretary of the Interior and Indian tribes within broad legislative enactments for special education and rehabilitation. Funding for the Secretary of Interior under the Education of the Handicapped Act (EHA) and Indian tribes under the Rehabilitation Act is in the form of a set-aside of the total amount available to the states.

Special Education

The set-aside for the Secretary of the Interior under the EHA state grant program has had a significant effect on BIA elementary and secondary education funding and policy (Figure 2). Subsequent to the participation of the Secretary of the Interior under Part B of EHA, identifiable on-going fiscal support for special education was established within Department

FIGURE 2

Evolution of Education Policy for Children with Handicaps Served by the Bureau of Indian Affairs (BIA)

1974

Secretary of Interior eligible to receive not more than 1% of the funds available for state grants under Part B of the Education of the Handicapped Act (EHA). (P.L. 93–380)

1975

Secretary of Interior to comply with rights, procedural protections, and administrative requirements under Part B of EHA (P.L. 94–142).

1977

$2.0 million earmark for special education within the BIA school operations budget; report on unmet special education needs. (appropriations legislation)

1978

$5.0 million added to the special education earmark within the BIA school operations budget. (appropriations legislation)

Special education administrative unit established within the BIA Office of Indian Education Programs.[1]

1979

$7.0 million special education earmark maintained within the BIA school operations budget. (appropriations legislation)

Line item funding established within the BIA school operations budget for handicapped children in residential facilities.

Weighted student units for handicapped children included within the final regulations for the BIA Indian School Equalization Formula.

1985

BIA Special Education Standards issued as final regulations.[2]

1986

EHA state grant set-aside for the Secretary of Interior increased to 1.25%; mandated services for handicapped children age 3–5; expanded public participation requirements. (P.L. 99–457)

Secretary of Interior eligible to receive 1.25% of the funds available for state grants under the handicapped infants and toddlers program. (P.L. 99–457)

[1]Prior to this time projects for the education of children with handicaps were planned and coordinated through a field office—the Indian Education Resources Center, located in Albuquerque, New Mexico.

[2]Proposed regulations issued in 1980.

of Interior funding processes, and detailed special education policies to govern the provision of special education and related services were adopted.

Special education program planning and development was further buttressed by the enactment of Title XI of the Education Amendments of 1978, P.L. 95–561. This legislation aimed to improve the overall effectiveness and responsiveness of Bureau-operated and -funded schools through the adoption and implementation of a funding formula, academic and dormitory standards, Indian education policies, and other standards. In establishing these policies and procedures, specific provisions were included for the education of children with handicaps. The funding formula, for example, includes weighted student units for children in part-time and full-time special education programs and incorporates fiscal support for the handicapped within BIA elementary and secondary funding procedures.

The Education of the Handicapped Act Amendments of 1986, P.L. 99–457, reaffirmed the institutionalization of special education programs and services within BIA education and enlarged the Bureau's role with respect to young children and infants with handicaps.

Strengthened State Grant Participation. In terms of BIA's participation under the EHA state grant program, the 1986 EHA amendments

- Ensured that the Secretary of Interior will receive payments under the Act (previous legislation left this to the discretion of the Secretary of Education).
- Increased the set-aside percentage reserved for use by the Secretary of the Interior from 1.0 to 1.25%.
- Required the Secretary of the Interior to ensure that there are public hearings, adequate notice of such hearings, and an opportunity for comment by members of Indian tribes, tribal governing bodies, and designated local school boards before adoption of special education policies, programs, and procedures.

Preschool. Section 404 of the Act further requires the Secretary of the Interior to ensure that Indian handicapped children aged 3 through 5, on reservations served by the Bureau of Indian Affairs schools, receive special education and related services by or before the 1987–1988 school year.

Early Intervention. In authorizing funding to assist states in developing comprehensive early intervention services for handicapped infants and toddlers (birth to age 2) and their families, P.L. 99–457 specifies that the Secretary of the Interior is to receive 1.25% of the funds available to the states. Such funds are to be used for the development of a comprehensive, coordinated, multidisciplinary, interagency program on reservations served by BIA schools. To receive funds, the Secretary of the Interior is required to submit an application to the Secretary of Education specifying such things as (a) the lead agency that will be responsible for the supervision, administration, and monitoring of early intervention programs and activities; and (b) the establishment of an interagency coordinating council. The accompanying legislative history indicates that the Department of Interior is expected to enter into interagency agreements with agencies such as the Indian Health Service and the Department of Health and Human Services to carry out the purposes of this program (U.S. House of Representatives, 1986).

Discretionary Programs. Other P.L. 99–457 amendments include provisions to ensure that Indian tribes and Indian community colleges are eligible to participate in EHA discretionary programs concerned with personnel training, parent training and information, and early education.

Rehabilitation

In response to service delivery difficulties relating to multiple state and federal jurisdiction, socioeconomic conditions, and cultural and linguistic diversity on Indian reservations (Navajo Nation, 1977), the 1978 amendments to the Rehabilitation Act authorized tribal vocational rehabilitation projects. While any tribe on a federal or state Indian reservation is eligible to participate in the program, limited funding and other administrative and procedural problems precluded other tribes from seeking funds under this program (Ramirez, 1986). Until recently the Navajo Nation was the sole tribe to receive funds to plan and develop a tribal vocational rehabilitation program (Morgan, Guy, Lee, & Cellini, 1986).

The 1986 Amendments to the Rehabilitation Act, P.L. 99–506, made several important changes to the federal rehabilitation program in terms of increased attention to the needs of Indians with handicaps and broader involvement of Indian tribes and federal health and social service agencies with responsibilities for American Indians. In addition to the provisions discussed in the following sections, the Act called for a national study on the special needs and problems of Indians with disabilities as well as afforded Indian tribes an opportunity to participate in many of the programs and activities authorized under the Act.

State Vocational Rehabilitation. Section 202 of P.L. 99–507 requires states to actively consult with Indian tribes and tribal organizations in the development of their state plan for vocational rehabilitation. The accompanying legislative report (U.S. House of Representatives, 1986) specifies that the consultation process should involve "the governing bodies of Indian tribes, intertribal organizations, and tribal organizations particularly concerned with problems of the handicapped" (p. 21).

American Indian Vocational Rehabilitation Services. In an effort to expand and improve this program and make it more responsive to the needs of Indians with disabilities on reservations, the 1986 amendments made the following legislative changes: (a) guaranteed the program a minimum level of funding of at least 1.25% of the total amount available to the states; (b) authorized consortia of Indian tribal governing bodies as eligible recipients; (c) reaffirmed traditional American Indian healing practices as part of the rehabilitation process; (d) clarified that grants could be awarded for as many as 3 years; and (e) made other procedural improvements so that the program is administered similar to other rehabilitation grant programs.

SERVICE DELIVERY AND RESEARCH NEEDS

This section details future directions based upon the reported number of handicapped and gifted students, the literature, and recent policy advances.

Children Served

Children with Handicaps. In most respects the number of American Indian children receiving special education and related services is reflective of national trends. There are, however, some paradoxes that require further study. Among American Indians, handicapping conditions such as fetal alcohol syndrome and hemophilus influenza meningitis have been reported to occur at higher rates than the general population, yet the number of Indian children with mental retardation has decreased since the late 1970s. The prevalence of otitis media among young American Indian children has also been reported to be extemely high (McShane, 1982; Scaldwell and Frame, 1985). With respect to otitis media, McShane indicates there is a need to clarify the connection between this middle ear disease and language and psychoeducational disabilities.

The consistently high percentage of Indian children identified as learning disabled is an area that needs further inquiry. It is not clear whether some of these students are receiving special education because other instructional alternatives are not available, learning disabilities is a more socially acceptable label, or differences in the cognitive style of American Indians exist. In terms of assessment practices, information is needed on the indices and criteria used to categorize children as learning disabled, the weight afforded culture and language as well as other social influences and the role of teachers and other professionals in the assessment process. Such study also needs to consider the effectiveness of these programs.

Gifted and Talented. Increased educational opportunities for gifted and talented students have generally been hampered by the absence of state policy requiring the identification and provision of services to these children. The BIA, for example, lacks policies requiring the identification and instruction of gifted and talented students. Other than 3 or 4 experimental projects, gifted and talented students do not receive specialized instruction in BIA schools.

Narrow definitions of giftedness, for example, intellectual levels or academic performance, have also contributed to the underrepresentation of American Indian, Black, and Hispanic students in gifted and talented programs (Masten, 1985). Tonemah (1987) proposed that American Indian gifted and talented students can be identified using four categories of criteria: aesthetic abilities, acquired skills, tribal/cultural knowledge, and personal/human qualities. Increasing the number of Indian students in programs for the gifted and talented will necessitate continued attention to traditional as well as nontraditional assessment practices.

Identification, Assessment, and Placement

Prereferral is receiving increased attention in terms of the identification and provision of effective instructional services prior to referring culturally diverse students to special education. How this practice relates to American Indian students needs to be examined in view of their overrepresentation in learning disabilities classes and the existence of other federally supported programs such as Chapter 1 and Indian Education in many schools serving American Indian children.

Research previously cited indicated that the evaluation reports for American Indian students generally did not contain any information regarding the culture or race of the student. The influence of culture, language, and other pertinent social charactersitics need to be reflected in the psychological evaluation reports of such children, youth, and adults.

Parental Involvement

Tafoya (1986) has emphasized the need to understand the family structure, child-rearing practices, social norms, and institutions of Indian families in developing parent involvement and training activities. Cunningham, Cunningham, and O'Connell (no date) examined the differing cultural perceptions of American Indians on special education to understand child development, family relationships, and authority relationships. They have developed a process for understanding cultural perceptions among various Indian groups.

Tribal traditions and ceremonies and family relationships and responsibilities are important aspects of American Indian life that can affect parent participation. This area needs to receive greater attention in the literature as does the training and support of American Indian parents as advocates. Traditional models for advocacy may require modification and/or elaboration prior to their application in American Indian settings.

Personnel

American Indian professionals in special education, gifted education, related services fields, and rehabilitation are very much needed in all levels of endeavor (i.e., direct services, personnel preparation, research, administration). This will necessitate continued support for existing projects, the development of training programs in other disciplines, and specific efforts to recruit American Indian students into various other types of training programs. Others involved in the preparation of American Indian special education teachers, administrators, and related services personnel need to have access to the unique features of existing American Indian training programs, such as, course content related to learning styles, culture, language, and parent involvement; practica; and recruitment and retention strategies.

In particular the training of individuals as psychologists and diagnosticians needs to include course work and practica which increases sensitivity toward cultural and language differences and how these considerations can influence the identification, evaluation, and placement process.

Early Education

In addition to providing needed services to American Indian infants and toddlers, the newly enacted federal early education legislation provides an opportunity to develop and refine service delivery to Indian families and communities. As BIA and the states begin to plan and develop early intervention programs and services, careful consideration needs to be given to areas such as the following:

* Cooperation with Indian Head Start programs to provide additional opportunities for children with various types of handicaps. While an extensive network of these Head Start programs already exists, additional resources and support will be needed to provide a full range of services as well as to increase their capacity to serve young children with more severe handicaps.

* Involvement of Indian tribes in the planning and development of state and BIA early intervention delivery systems. States need to include Indian representation on the interagency coordinating council and/or establish procedures for ongoing consultation with tribes and Indian organizations. Likewise, both BIA and the states need to establish cooperative relationships with the Indian Health Service at national, regional, state, and local levels.

* Development of model or innovative service delivery systems at the community level. Earlier demonstration projects in Indian communities for young children with handicaps and their families have fostered community understanding and support (Johnson, Ramirez, Trohanis, & Walker, 1980). O'Connell (1985) described a family systems approach which takes into consideration characteristics related to variations in family membership and relationships, cultural style, and ideological style to ensure that service providers function effectively within American Indian communities. Such projects should also encompass the design and implementation of local collaborative interagency activities.

Rehabilitation

The underutilization of vocational rehabilitation services by American Indians with disabilities was a major consideration in the establishment and strengthening of the provisions authorizing Indian tribes to administer vocational rehabilitation programs. This option combined with the assurance that states must consult with Indian tribes and organizations in the development of the state vocational rehabilitation plan should provide increased opportunities for American Indians with disabilities. As a part of consultation, it will be important for states to develop formal, ongoing relationships with tribes. Given that some tribes may be unfamiliar with vocational rehabilitation, it will be encumbent upon state vocational rehabilitation offices to solicit and sustain tribal involvement and participation.

Rehabilitation, employment, and community services needs to be a priority for American Indian tribes and communities. For many individuals with handicaps, leaving the school system means an exit from services. American Indians are significantly less likely to be rehabilitated than clients from the general population (Morgan & O'Connell, 1987). Transition needs to be understood in relation to schools, agencies, and businesses in reservation and urban settings and factors identified by Morgan and O'Connell (1987) contributing to the poor rehabilitation of American Indians such as lower socioeconomic status, disabilities related to alcohol and drug abuse, and the inability of counselors to locate clients and complete the rehabilitation plan.

Because of the high unemployment rates on most reservations, labor market anaylses can facilitate the identification of existing and future employment opportunities for persons with disabilities. With such data tribes and other agencies can include individuals with disabilities in their vocational education training programs and economic forecasting.

SUMMARY

There has been substantial progress in the availability of services to American Indian children and youth with handicaps. Recent federal policy advances will extend this momentum to early education and vocational rehabilitation. The growing attention to the needs of American Indian gifted and talented students is also encouraging and long overdue. These efforts need to continue in view of disparaties across states, tribes, and programs.

The provision of services needs to be bolstered by training, research and demonstration, and the development of a knowledge base specific to American Indians with exceptionalities. Several areas of future inquiry have been suggested. Each area of service delivery is in need of greater scrutiny in terms of various exceptionalities, geographic and community settings, school type, and American Indian tribes and groups. Other important topics such as advocacy, curriculum and instruction, and transition, although beyond the scope of this chapter, also need to be explored.

REFERENCES

Algozzine, B., Christenson, S., & Ysseldyke, J. (1982). Probabilities associated with the referral to placement process. *Teacher Education and Special Education, 5*, 19–23.

Baca, L., & Miramontes, O. (1985). Bilingual special education teacher training for American Indians. *Journal of American Indian Education, 24*(2), 38–47.

Browne, D. B. (1984). WISC-R scoring patterns among Native Americans of the Northern Plains. *White Cloud Journal, 3*(2), 3–16.

Chinn, P. C., & Hughes, S. (1987). Representation of minority students in special education classes. *Remedial and Special Education, 8*, 41–46.

Connery, A. R. (1987). *A description and comparison of Native American and Anglo parents' knowledge of their handicapped children's educational rights.* Unpublished doctoral dissertation, Northern Arizona University, Flagstaff.

Cunningham, K., Cunningham, K., & O'Connell, J. (no date). Impact of differing cultural perceptions on special education service delivery. *Rural Special Education Quarterly, 8*(1), 2–8.

DBS Corporation. (1987, December). *1986 Elementary and Secondary School Civil Rights Survey, National Summaries* (Contract Number 300–86–0062). Washington, DC: Office of Civil Rights, U.S. Department of Education.

Gajar, A. (1985). American Indian personnel preparation in special education: Needs, program components, programs. *Journal of American Indian Education, 24*(2), 7–15.

Johnson, M. J., Ramirez, B. A., Trohanis, P. L., & Walker, J. L. (Eds.). (1980). *Planning services for young handicapped American Indian and Alaska Native children.* Chapel Hill: Technical Assistance Development System, University of North Carolina.

MacArthur, R. S. (1969). Some cognitive abilities of Eskimo, White and Indian Metis pupils aged 9 to 12 years. *Canadian Journal of Behavioral Science, 1*(1), 50–59.

Masten, W. G. (1985). Identification of gifted minority students: Past research, future directions. *Roeper Review, 8*(2), 83–85.

McShane, D. (1979, October). Differences in assessment procedures used with American Indian and non-Indian children. *Listening Post, 1*(4).

McShane, D. (1980). A review of scores of American Indian children on the Wechlser intelligence scales. *White Cloud Journal, 1*(4), 3–10.

McShane, D. (1982). Otitis media and American Indians: Prevalence, etiology, psychoeducational consequences, prevention and intervention. In S. P. Manson (Ed.), *New Directions in Prevention Among American Indian and Alaskan Native Communities* (pp. 265–297). Portland: Oregon Health Sciences University.

Morgan, C. O., Guy, E., Lee, B., & Cellini, H. R. (1986, April-May-June). Rehabilitation services for American Indians: The Navajo experience. *Journal of Rehabilitation*, 25–31.

Morgan, J., & O'Connell, J. C. (1987). The rehabilitation of disabled Native Americans. *International Journal of Rehabilitative Research, 10*(2), 139–149.

National Indian Education Association. (1977). *Position paper on the classification of handicapped children as it affects Indian children.* Minneapolis, MN: Author.

Navajo Nation. (1977, June 20). *Statement on the Rehabilitation Act of 1973: Services to Native Americans*. Presented before the Subcommittee on the Handicapped, Committee on Human Resources, U.S. Senate.

O'Connell, J. C. (1985). A family systems approach for serving rural, reservation, Native American communities. *Journal of American Indian Education, 24*(2), 1–6.

Office for Civil Rights, U.S. Department of Education. (no date). *Directory of elementary and secondary school districts, and schools in selected school districts: School year 1978–1979* (Vol. 1). Washington, DC: Author.

Public Law 94–142, Education for All Handicapped Children Act of 1975, November 29, 1975.

Public Law 95–561, Education Amendments of 1978, November 1, 1978.

Public Law 95–602, Rehabilitation, Comprehensive Services, and Developmental Disabilities Amendments of 1978, November 6, 1978.

Public Law 99–457, Education of the Handicapped Act Amendments of 1986, October 8, 1986.

Public Law 99–506, Rehabilitation Act Amendments of 1986, October, 1986.

Ramirez, B. A. (1986, September). *Federal special education, vocational education and rehabilitation policy and American Indian handicapped children, youth, and adults*. Paper presented at the Native American Research Symposium, Scottsdale, AZ.

Ramirez, B. A. (1987). Federal policy and the education of American Indian exceptional children and youth: Current status and future directions. In M. J. Johnson and B. A. Ramirez (Eds.), *American Indian Exceptional Children and Youth* (pp. 37–54). Reston, VA: The Council for Exceptional Children.

Ramirez, B. A., & Tippeconnic, J. W., III. (1979). Preparing teachers of American Indian handicapped children. *Teacher Education and Special Education, 2*(4), 27–33.

Rosenbluth, A. R. (1976). The feasibility of test translation between unrelated languages English to Navajo. *TESOL Quarterly, 10*(1), 33–43.

Scaldwell, W. A., & Frame, J. E. (1985). Prevalence of otitis media in Cree and Ojibway school-children in six Ontario communities. *Journal of American Indian Education, 25*(1), 1–5.

Seyfort, B., Spreen, O., & Lahmer, V. (1980). A critical look at the WISC-R with Native Indian children. *The Alberta Journal of Educational Research, 26*(1), 14–24.

Stuecher, U. (1985). Problems facing the Indian handicapped child in rural settings: A case for Indian advocacy. *Rural Special Education Quarterly, 6*(2), 22–23.

Tafoya, T. (1986). Native American families. *Reaching out: Proceedings from a special education symposium on cultural differences and parent programs*. Eugene, OR: Western Regional Resource Center.

Tonemah, S. (1987). Assessing American Indian gifted and talented students' abilities. *Journal for the Education of the Gifted, 10*(3), 181–194.

U.S. Department of Education. (1987). *To assure the free appropriate public education for all handicapped children* (Ninth annual report to Congress on the implementation of the Education of the Handicapped Act). Washington, DC: Author.

U.S. Department of Health and Human Services, Head Start Bureau. (1986). *The status of handicapped children in Head Start programs* (Thirteenth annual report to Congress). Washington, DC: Author.

U.S. House of Representatives, Committee on Education and Labor. Rehabilitation Act Amendments of 1986, H.R. 4021. 99th Congress, 2d Session, May 5, 1986, Report No. 99–571.

U.S. House of Representatives, Committee on Education and Labor. Education of the Handicapped Act Amendments of 1986, H.R. 5520. 99th Congress, 2d Session, September 22, 1986, Report No. 99–860.

Contributors

Alejandro Benavides is the special education administrator responsible for bilingual and transitional special education in the Chicago Public Schools. He is also a lecturer for Southern Illinois University's Bilingual Special Education Master's Program. He has teaching and administrative experience in bilingual and special education and has served as consultant to local and state education agencies.

Arlene W. Blaylock is a Research Analyst in the Planning and Institutional Research Department of Montgomery College, Rockville, Maryland. Prior to this she served as an Evaluation Specialist for both the Program of Assessment, Diagnosis, and Instruction (PADI) and the Gifted Program in the Montgomery County School System.

Ford R. Cranwell was formerly the Special Education Consultant for West Region Tribal Council in Dauphin, Manitoba, and is currently employed as a school psychologist for the Manitoba Department of Education.

Jana Echevarria-Ratleff is Educational Specialist in Bilingual Special Education with the joint grant program between Loyola Marymount University and California State Department of Education, Division of Special Education. She holds credentials and has teaching experience in elementary and secondary education, bilingual education, special education, and English as a second language. Echevarria-Ratleff serves as consultant to school districts.

Shernaz B. Garcia is Lecturer, Department of Special Education, The University of Texas at Austin. She also coordinates the Bilingual Special Education Training Program and is a Research Associate with the Handicapped Minority Research Institute.

Ruben Gentry is Professor and Chairman of the Department of Special Education, Jackson State University, Mississippi, and a staunch believer in quality public education. He attended the public schools in Mississippi and earned degrees from Jackson State University, Atlanta University, and the University of Florida. His 3 rewarding years of teaching the handicapped served as a basis for lifelong commitment to teacher education.

Victoria L. Graf is Associate Professor of Education and Director of Special Education at Loyola Marymount University, Los Angeles, California. As coauthor of the Bilingual Special Education grant, she directs the program. She has had teaching experience in hospitals and clinics of severely and learning handicapped children and is a consultant to public schools.

Donnelly A. Gregory is Coordinator of the Program of Assessment, Diagnosis, and Instruction (PADI) for Montgomery County Public Schools, Rockville, Maryland. After teaching graduate and undergraduate courses in special education and supervising student teachers in the College of Education at the University of Maryland, he joined the school system, first as Coordinator of Identification for the gifted program, then assuming leadership of the PADI project as it was initiated.

Vicki A. Jax is currently completing requirements for the Ph.D. in special education at both the University of California, Los Angeles, and California State University, Los Angeles. Her dissertation research explored narrative construction by Hispanic children learning English as a second language and reading comprehension performance. Ms. Jax is a lecturer in the

Department of Communicative Disorders at California State University, Long Beach, and is a Speech/Language Pathologist in private practice in Los Angeles County. Prior professional work has included research at the National Center for Bilingual Research and the Handicapped-Minority Research Institute in California.

Marilyn J. Johnson is Director of the Native American Research and Training Center at Northern Arizona University, Flagstaff. She has directed American Indian early education demonstration and special education teacher training programs and was most recently a contributor to a Congressionally mandated study on the special problems and needs of American Indians with handicaps.

Esther K. Leung is Professor of Special Education in the area of Learning and Behavioral Disorders, Eastern Kentucky University, Richmond. She was awarded a foundation professorship (1988–1990) for outstanding teaching, scholarship, and service. She is a consultant for the national Child-Adolescent-Service-System-Program (CASSP) for emotionally disturbed minority children and their families. Currently, she is chairman for CEC's Asian-American/Pacific Islander Caucus and has been active in lecturing and consulting on matters of ethnic and multicultural concerns.

LaDelle Olion is Professor of Special Education and Assistant Dean in the School of Education at Fayetteville State University, North Carolina. He has teaching experience in mental retardation, learning disabilities, and emotional disturbance and has spent over 20 years working with parents of handicapped children.

Alba A. Ortiz is Associate Professor, Department of Special Education, The University of Texas at Austin, and Director of Bilingual Special Education Training. She also directs the Handicapped Minority Research Institute on Language Proficiency.

Ron S. Phillips was formerly Special Education Advisor with the Manitoba Indian Education Association (M.I.E.A.). Currently employed by Winnipeg School Division #1, he also acts as a special education consultant to several Indian bands and a tribal council in Canada.

Eleoussa Polyzoi was formerly Research Associate in the Handicapped Minority Research Institute in the Department of Special Education at the University of Texas at Austin and Coordinator of the longitudinal study investigating the language assessment of Hispanic learning disabled and speech and language handicapped students. Currently she is Assistant Professor in Developmental Studies and Education at the University of Winnipeg, Manitoba.

Bruce A. Ramirez is Special Assistant for Ethnic and Multicultural Concerns at The Council for Exceptional Children. He has had experience in public policy activities nationally, conducted policy research, and taught elementary school on the Navajo Nation. He is the author of several publications on the education of American Indian exceptional children and youth.

George Sugai is an Assistant Professor in Special Education at the University of Oregon. He currently directs graduate teacher training programs in behavior disorders in the College of Education. He has been a special education teacher for students with behavior disorders and a treatment director of a program for youth with severe behavior problems.

Waveline T. Starnes is Coordinator of Gifted Programs for Montgomery County Public Schools, Rockville, Maryland. She has provided leadership in staff development as Coordinator of a Learning Center jointly administered by Montgomery County and the University of Maryland and as a Staff Development Specialist developing and coordinating Teacher Competency courses for a master's equivalence program. She wrote the grant that initiated the Program of Assessment, Diagnosis, and Instruction (PADI) and has directed comprehensive curriculum development activities to support gifted instruction.

Shih-Sung Wen is Professor and Chairman of the Department of Psychology at Jackson State University, Mississippi. A native of Taiwan, China, he earned the bachelor degree in that country and higher degrees from the University of Oregon and the University of Florida. He cherishes his years of grade school teaching as invaluable professional experience.

James R. Yates is Professor and Chairman of the Department of Educational Administration at The University of Texas at Austin. He holds academic appointments in the Special Education Department, as well as in the Department of Educational Administration, and relates his training activities to the preparation of special education administrators. His research interests have centered upon educational futures and technological forecasting methodologies. These research interests have produced more than 60 publications.